# a

# HOUSE

# without

# WALLS

DAN CRABTREE

a

# HOUSE

## without

# WALLS

HOW CHRIST UNITES HIS
ETHNICALLY DIVIDED CHURCH

AMBASSADOR INTERNATIONAL
GREENVILLE, SOUTH CAROLINA & BELFAST, NORTHERN IRELAND
www.ambassador-international.com

# A House Without Walls

How Christ Unites His Ethnically Divided Church
©2021 by Dan Crabtree

Hardcover ISBN: 978-1-64960-393-7
Paperback ISBN: 978-1-64960-121-6
eISBN: 978-1-64960-171-1

Cover Design by Joshua Frederick
Interior Design by Dentelle Design
Edited by Katie Cruice Smith

Scripture taken from The Holy Bible, English Standard Version. ESV® Text Edition: 2016. Copyright © 2001 by Crossway Bibles, a publishing ministry of Good News Publishers.

AMBASSADOR INTERNATIONAL
Emerald House
411 University Ridge, Suite B14
Greenville, SC 29601
United States
www.ambassador-international.com

AMBASSADOR BOOKS
The Mount
2 Woodstock Link
Belfast, BT6 8DD
Northern Ireland, United Kingdom
www.ambassadormedia.co.uk

The colophon is a trademark of Ambassador, a Christian publishing company.

Para mi Amor, quien me ha mostrado un amor sin paredes.

# CONTENTS

# PREFACE

"AM I ENCOURAGING DISUNITY AND/OR segregation? I don't know yet."

A Christian writer asks this question in his article titled "Why Black Christians Should Leave White Evangelicalism."[1] His growing frustration with mostly pale-skinned congregations had reached the limit, so he suggests that Christians racially part ways. According to this author, "White Christian America" and the "Black identity" are simply irreconcilable. And so, he says, the time has come to divide.

He's not alone in his call for division. Another Christian author and historian likewise told CNN regarding African American Christians in mostly European American churches, "We are telling them to get out."[2] And many have. A handful of pastors led their churches in the last few years to leave the Southern Baptist Convention over issues of race, racism, and critical race theory.[3] *The New York Times* noted that in 2018 a "quiet exodus" of African American worshippers from European American congregations was already underway. A researcher and spiritual leader in the multiethnic church movement recently lamented, "It's about to completely break apart."[4]

So, that's it then? The Church just needs to divide? Is racial division too big for Christ to solve? Or is His finished work on the cross sufficient even for a time like this?

As I write, ethnic division not only marks Christianity but also dominates the headlines. In May 2020, the death of George Floyd, an African American man, under the knee of Derek Chauvin, a European American cop, lit the powder keg of mounting racial pain and exploded into nationwide protests, riots, and desperate cries for justice. The country groans; the streets erupt; and many in the church call for change.

As a shepherd in a local church, my heart is heavy for my brothers and sisters in Christ who suffer from racism and her sour fruits. Especially in a cultural moment like this, many in the Church tremble with fear and seethe with anger when faced with gut-wrenching questions. "Will I keep getting pulled over by the cops because I'm not white?" "Does my skin color not just *inform* but *define* how others see me?" "Will my black, teenage son make it home tonight?" Regardless of politics, these questions are real, and pastors feel the heavy hearts of their people.

What also makes me sad as a pastor is to see *conversations* about race dividing the Church. For some, the mere mention of racism sparks assumptions of Cultural Marxism, critical race theory, and woke theology. For others, any sign of hesitance to radically reorient the Christian life around racial reconciliation, corporate repentance, and financial reparations is the reincarnation of Jim Crow ethics. Others are unfamiliar with the terminology and feel paralyzed to speak up at all. The fallout of this kind of grenade-lobbing Christianity is a spiritual wasteland of division, hurt feelings, fear of engagement, and, ultimately, dishonor to Christ. The Church is dividing because of race.

Surely, there must be a better way to talk about race in the Church! Shouldn't we be able to find a path forward that doesn't lead to fracturing parties and mass migrations from the Bride of Christ? Recent, divisive conversations about race have revealed a deep ideological fault line underneath the Evangelical surface. Where did that chasm come from, and how can it be bridged? Shouldn't the one household of faith, the pillar and buttress of the truth, the Church of the Living God, be able to maintain some semblance of unity even in a dark and divisive world? How might God bring His diverse people together as one?

The Bible's answer to ethnic division in the Church is surprisingly simple and not at all what the world would tell us. Here it is: *The church is united by Jesus.*

I assure you, "simple" in this case does not mean "simplistic." The outflow of Jesus' Lordship in His Church means thoughtful discernment and diligent study for His people. Jesus mediates His authority to His Church through His Word, so ethnic harmony in the Church will take some serious Bible study. But that's what the church has always done; it's what we still do; and it's what will bring us together when absolutely nothing else can.

To be clear, what I'm proposing in this book is *nothing but* the work of Jesus. I'm not advocating for a new methodology, ideology, or theology. If Church history has taught us anything, it's that we should be leery of new ideas. No, what I propose as the salve to heal the wounds of the Church is a remedy older than the Church itself. I contend that unity in the Church will always depend, fully and finally, on the Lord Jesus Christ and His Word. As we agree with Christ in His Word, we will have unity. As we contradict Christ and His Word, we will have division. We must come together by coming under the Lordship of Jesus Christ through His Word.

So, the way I intend to approach united submission to Jesus through this book is to study the Bible. We need to see how Jesus defines the Gospel that creates, animates, and sustains His Church so that we won't fall victim to false fixes. We need to know the authority of Scripture to use it rightly as our guide in navigating conversations about race and ethnicity. We need to know what the Bible says about the origins of ethnicity so that we understand God's purposes in our differences. We need to esteem our Lord and His Word if we would find ethnic unity in the Church, and that's what I hope to do with you in these pages.

Let me be clear, however, about what this book won't do. This book won't retread the now well-worn ground of the various arguments about race from a sociological or political perspective. Others have already done that far better than I could. This book is squarely focused on the Church, on people who care about what the Bible says, and so appeals to Scriptural arguments rather than census data or historical anecdotes as the final authority.

The goal in this material is not a Tweetable slam dunk on critical race theory but the lived-out unity of the Church. If you're hoping to find more ammo here for your online squabble, you'll be disappointed. The truth has two-edges—both razor-sharp. Expect the Bible to challenge your political commitments, not as a "third way" but as *the* way. That's where this book is headed, anyway.

More than anything, I want Jesus to be worshipped. Don't you? There just isn't anything more important in all of creation than Jesus' glory. "For from him and through him and to him are all things. To him be glory forever" (Rom. 11:36).

Though we will get into the weeds in this conversation, dealing with all kinds of particular points of doctrine and historical details, don't ever take your eyes off of Jesus. He is the One Who can unite His Church; He is the reason for the Church; and He is the great joy of the Church. Without Him, every letter you read is utter vanity. So, if you do nothing else as a result of reading this book, please worship Jesus. Let's exalt Jesus in our hearts through this study and watch the walls of ethnic division in the Church crumble as we lift up one voice to the glory of our great God and Savior.

# AN OLD CHURCH, AN OLDER PROBLEM, AND THE OLDEST ANSWER

A BLACK AND WHITE BANNER on the weather-beaten red brick walls of Bruton Parish Church read, "Black lives matter." The Episcopal congregation had gathered outside on June 19, 2020, masks covering their mostly white faces, to celebrate Juneteenth, a holiday commemorating the delayed emancipation of African American slaves 155 years prior. Plywood covered the large, portal windows surrounding the historic church building, while a virus spread through the town of Williamsburg, Virginia, and across the globe, prohibiting the congregation from its weekly gatherings.

Small groupings of churchgoers stood distanced from each other, scattered across Duke of Gloucester Street in front of the old church building. They listened while a priest voiced her lament over America's long history of oppression and racism.

Inside the empty, cruciform church building, white-painted wood walls separated the boxed pews, where famous Americans once sat. George Washington had his own assigned pew toward the center of the cross. So did Thomas Jefferson, Patrick Henry, George Mason, and other founding fathers. On any given Sunday during the era of the American Revolution, the Bruton Parish rector would ascend the high-walled, elevated pulpit to lead psalm-singing and to preach from the Bible.

The doctrines of liberty and justice (for all) would echo through Bruton Parish, past the politicians to the back wall and up into the balcony. A few mismatched chairs held a congregation of its own on the separate landing. The balcony was reserved for slaves.

Ethnic prejudice, partiality, and hatred have indelibly marked America's story, and the professing church has not been exempt. Many Protestant churches in American history reinforced the racism that they should have condemned. The evil motives behind American chattel slavery, Jim Crow laws, and "separate but equal" have poisoned our country's churches from their earliest days. Today, the rise of divisive ideologies combined with our haunting, painful past have produced streets and hearts filled with violence and suspicion. It seems like our country is being torn apart at its ethnic seams—and many churches right along with it.

That service outside of the worn walls of Bruton Parish Church captures in an image the central reason why ethnic division has prevailed so long in American churches: the Church has often settled for merely secular solutions. As long as our answer to ethnic division *in* the Church comes from *outside* the Church, dependent on extra-biblical powers, man-made coalitions, and earthly sources of influence, we'll remain distant and divided by walls we've erected and can't destroy. To our shame, we're good at building walls, but not at taking them down. Our hands and hearts are too futile and too frail.

Of course, that's not to say that social and political efforts to combat racism can't help. Where unjust laws exist, they call for just law-making. But if we aim for *just* law-making, our remedy is incomplete. The cut may be sealed up, but it's still infected. The suffering of our fellow image-bearers under the burdens of discrimination and false ideological frameworks can and should be stemmed, silenced, and stopped by many and various means. Protests, petitions, and policies may be sorely needed, but they can't heal the hurting heart. Left to our own devices, we can't bring lasting unity to an ethnically splintered Church.

There is simply no force on earth that can dismantle the ethnic dividing walls we've constructed. Our barriers stand immovable—racist indifference, corrupted justice, sociological blame-shifting, counterfeit authorities, bankrupt worldviews, superficial salvation, and political posturing. Our human tools can fix symptoms but not hearts. Outside of the Church, there is no hope for ethnic unity, and we shouldn't hope to find it there.

Brothers and Sisters, what we want to discover together in God's Word is that in His Church, Jesus Christ has the unparalleled power to tear down every last brick in our ethnic dividing walls and build from the rubble a new, diverse, and united people from every tribe and tongue and nation for His eternal worship.

His death, resurrection, and reign construct a multiethnic canopy for all colors, shapes, and sizes of sinners. Here in the Church, Christians with every kind of skin tone and with all manner of sinful baggage find a welcoming family under the shelter of the cross. Here, the halls echo with the harmonies of redeemed sinners as we join our broken voices to declare together, "Amazing grace, how sweet the sound that saved a wretch like me!" Here, Christ assembles a spiritual temple out of former slaves and out of former slave-owners.

The world can't understand this kind of blueprint. Only Christ can reconcile all things on earth and in heaven. Only Jesus can bring unity to an ethnically divided Church. Only the Carpenter from Nazareth can build a house without walls because only He uses nails.

## WE NEED TO TALK

Even to broach the subject of ethnic division in the Church may seem problematic to some. The pushback I've heard has sounded like this:

- "Isn't it too negative to harp on our divisions?"
- "Aren't we trying to deal with far bigger structural issues right now?"

- "Why are we talking about quarrels between Christians when we should be talking about mass incarceration, police brutality, and economic disparity plaguing the black community?"
- "Doesn't talking about race just lead to more anger and division?"
- "Why can't we just focus on the Gospel and not worry so much about the amount of melanin in our skin?"
- "Aren't you white, Dan? Shouldn't we be hearing from a person of color about race?"

These are all understandable questions, and I hope to answer them, but you'll have to stick with me. For now, let me offer three brief answers from God's Word to address why we absolutely do need to talk about ethnic dividing walls in the Church.

First, our love for our fellow believers compels this conversation. Paul writes to the Corinthian church that "if one member suffers, all suffer together; if one member is honored, all rejoice together" (1 Cor. 12:26). African American, Latin American, Asian American, and Native American believers have suffered unjustly, but they must not suffer alone. European American Christians reel from feelings of guilt, uncertainty, and fear. If we love God and neighbor, then the author of Hebrews would exhort us to "remember . . . those who are mistreated, since you also are in the body" (Heb. 13:3). We can't ignore the pain in our own body, so we need to talk.

Second, it's the example we're given in Scripture. You may search in vain for an explicit biblical command to engage in cross-cultural conversations about race in the body of Christ, but the apostle Paul consistently models for us the importance of addressing this topic. He taught the Galatians the theology behind diverse Christian unity when he wrote, "There is neither Jew nor Greek, there is neither slave nor free, there is no male and female, for you are all one in Christ Jesus" (Gal. 3:28). He confronted the apostle Peter's ethnically-charged fears when they threatened to divide the Church (Gal. 2:11-14). To the fractured factions of the Corinthian church, Paul wrote,

"I appeal to you, brothers, by the name of our Lord Jesus Christ, that all of you agree, and that there be no divisions among you, but that you be united in the same mind and the same judgment" (1 Cor. 1:10). Paul's faithful legacy charts an unmistakable course into the waters of ethnic conflict in the Church, and we're commanded to follow him there (1 Cor. 11:1).

Third, Jesus is committed to the unity of the Church. It is no overstatement to say that the reason Jesus came to earth was to unite the Church to Himself. That was his prayer to the Father the night before His death: "The glory that you have given me I have given to them, that they may be one even as we are one" (John 17:22). He came to give His glory through the Gospel to unite the Church. But Jesus goes even further than *praying* for the Church's unity. He *dies* for the Church's unity. Paul writes:

> For he himself is our peace, who has made us [Jews and Gentiles] both one and has broken down in his flesh the dividing wall of hostility by abolishing the law of commandments expressed in ordinances, that he might create in himself one new man in place of the two, so making peace, and might reconcile us both to God in one body through the cross, thereby killing the hostility" (Eph. 2:14-16).

Jesus' aim in the cross is reconciliation between God and man and between ethnically divided man. This is but one of the multifaceted goals in the Gospel, and it's absolutely critical to how we live as a Church. Jesus hung on the tree to turn racists into peacemakers, to transform prejudice into empathy, and to build a house of worship not separated by balconies, buildings, or walls but united in the bonds of love. If He would suffer the wrath of the Father for our unity, then surely that unity is worth protecting, and we can't protect what we won't frankly address.

So, we need to talk. These will be hard conversations, no doubt, and we won't say everything we should the way we should. I know I won't. But I ask for your grace as I try to start the conversation, in weakness and in trembling. If we can't stumble through uncomfortable conversations about race and division toward greater harmony and love for Jesus, then the world will assume we're just as hopelessly divided as they are. May it never be.

## UNITY IS GLORIOUS

Some might ask, though, what's so great about multi-ethnic unity in a church, anyway? What's all the fuss about? The answer is God's glory.

The Bible tells us why God ultimately wants to make one family out of many ethnicities; it's for "the praise of his glorious grace" (Eph. 1:6). There is no higher motive than the glory of God. It's what motivates God Himself to save people from different ethnic backgrounds and unite them in the Church. Through ethnically diverse, harmonious worship, God demonstrates that the cross of Jesus overcomes the strong forces of ethnic hatred, partiality, and pride to make one beautiful, new people in His image. He makes much of His power and His Son by tearing down the dividing walls and bringing the nations together in univocal, multilingual worship. Psalm 67:1-3 establishes this glorious truth: "May God be gracious to us and bless us and make his face to shine upon us, *Selah* that your way may be known on earth, your saving power among all nations. Let the peoples praise you, O God; let all the peoples praise you!"

God glorifies Himself by superseding human dividing lines and creating a united body out of diverse peoples to worship Him. Why does ethnic unity in the Church matter so much? Because the glory of God is at stake.

## ROADS DIVERGED

If the unity of an ethnically diverse body of believers has such massive, eternal importance, then naturally, the question is, "How does Christ empower us to live out this glorious reality in the Church?" Answering that question from the Bible is the burden of this book.

In our day, there's been no shortage of proposed strategies to accomplish ethnic harmony. Outside of the Church, people of all ethnicities have been summoned to participate in nationwide protests against the police; to show solidarity with minority advocacy groups like Black Lives Matter; and to demonstrate ongoing allyship by renouncing all affiliations with people, organizations, and products that have been touched by racism.

My goal right now is not to biblically critique all of these proposals, only to acknowledge the dominant methods that are being proposed today. Many of these proposals are unbiblical. Some harm more than they hurt. None of them can do what Christ alone can do. That being said, ethnic division in the Church is a complex issue. Simplistic, broad-brush responses in any direction will only reveal that we lack the love necessary to work hard at empathizing, understanding, and searching God's Word for light to illumine the path ahead.

At least one thing is clear: unity does not grow through more division. In the turbulent waters of conversations about ethnicity, we can be tempted to look for simplistic responses that lump our fellow believers into camps rather than treating them as individual image-bearers. We may alienate those who should be closest to us because they disagree in part, and that only further fractures the body of Christ. So, if you find yourself already responding by trying to neatly fit your brothers and sisters into "sides" (the ones you agree with and the ones who are wrong), look to the humility of Christ. Does your attitude reflect the gracious, lowly heart of your Savior? In Christ, truth and unity go hand in hand, and so do believers who disagree.

Tribalism opposes the unity of the Gospel, so we should be opposed to tribalism. We dare not approach the stubborn walls of ethnic division in the Church *primarily* as Republicans or Democrats; as social justice advocates or discernment guardians; as black, white, brown, or anything else that is secondary to our identity. The Church must approach ethnic discord with one all-consuming identity in mind: we are a family of blood-bought believers in the Lord Jesus Christ under the authority of His Word for the sake of His glory.

We are Christians before we are anything else. Our Gospel-grounded self-recognition needs to come first in absolutely everything we think and do on the hard road toward ethnic harmony in the Church. The cross of Christ is not just a rhetorical flourish in the conversation about ethnic division; it is the only hope. That doesn't mean we ignore political engagement or difficult conversations. But if we are to work for true ethnic unity in the Church, all of our efforts must start and end with Jesus. And Paul helps us understand why.

## WHEN THE WALL CAME DOWN

The apostle Paul shows us how ethnic dividing walls are destroyed in the body of Christ. The pattern he describes has universal application and will be our pattern going forward. To see Paul's plan for a unified Church, we need to return to a passage we already mentioned and see it in context. In Ephesians 2:11-22, Paul writes:

> Therefore remember that at one time you Gentiles in the flesh, called "the uncircumcision" by what is called the circumcision, which is made in the flesh by hands—remember that you were at that time separated from Christ, alienated from the commonwealth of Israel and strangers to the covenants of promise, having no hope and without God in the world. But now in Christ Jesus you who once were far off have been brought near by the blood of Christ. For he himself is our peace, who has made us both one and has broken down in his flesh the dividing wall of hostility by abolishing the law of commandments expressed in ordinances, that he might create in himself one new man in place of the two, so making peace, and might reconcile us both to God in one body through the cross, thereby killing the hostility. And he came and preached peace to you who were far off and peace to those who were near. For through him we both have access in one Spirit to the Father. So then you are no longer strangers and aliens, but you are fellow citizens with the saints and members of the household of God, built on the foundation of the apostles and prophets, Christ Jesus himself being the cornerstone, in whom the whole

structure, being joined together, grows into a holy temple in the Lord. In him you also are being built together into a dwelling place for God by the Spirit.

If we would have eyes to see and ears to hear it, this passage could become a sledgehammer to break through the walls of our ethnic divisions. In writing to the Ephesians, Paul sketches for us the work of Christ to make one out of two, to bring the far near, to unite the divided and bring peace out of hostility. In fact, he lays out the logic that becomes the basis for how we approach all division in the Church, ethnic or otherwise.

Paul brackets this Gospel reminder with two radically different situations. He begins with the alienation and separation of the Gentiles (to include the Ephesians) from the Jews and from God (v. 11-12). Then he concludes with one holy temple made up of united Jews and Gentiles (v. 19-22). Ethnic division to ethnic unity in eleven verses.

So, what happened in those eleven verses to bring this unity out of division? How did these distinct ethnic groups, separated by religion, culture, politics, and just about every imaginable social dimension, become "fellow citizens" and "members of the household of God?" To put it in our setting, how could the Church in the suburbs have one mind, one spirit, and one purpose with the Church in the inner city? How can African Americans and European Americans call each other "brother" and "sister" today when some of their grandparents killed and were killed by each other because of their ethnicity? What bond could possibly hold together those who are still so distanced by race, injustice, and centuries of festering hostility?

If we're going to see ethnic division erased in the Church, we would be wise to hear how it happened in Ephesus. It takes something stronger than resolve, more all-encompassing than an apology, and deeper than social reform. It takes the blood of Jesus Christ. As Paul says, "But now in Christ Jesus you who once were far off have been brought near *by the blood of Christ*" (v. 13).

## A MOUNTAIN BETWEEN

Some have argued that the division Paul speaks about in Ephesians 2 is almost entirely unrelated to the kinds of division we see in the Church today. Others have written off this passage as irrelevant to the current conversation about ethnic strife in our country and in our churches. But a closer look at the context reveals that the truth Paul sets before us is an ancient mirror of the struggle we're engaged in right now.

Paul begins by reminding the mostly-Gentile, Ephesian believers that they used to be *persona non grata* in the Jewish world. They were called "the uncircumcision," which was a derogatory slur used by the Jews to emphasize the unholy otherness of their Gentile neighbors. Those Persians and Greeks and Bythinians didn't have the sign of the covenant like the Jews, whom Paul calls "the circumcision, which is made in the flesh by hands" (v. 11). Paul not-so-subtly points out that this mark of ethnic superiority that the Jews so valued was, in fact, something *they did to themselves*. It was fleshly, external, and man-made. And in their pride, it had become yet another reason to distance themselves from the dirty, unclean, unworthy Gentile rabble.

But the division between Jew and Gentile went even deeper than circumcision. Paul reminds the Gentile believers in Ephesus that at one time, they were also cut off from the Messiah—"separated from Christ" (v. 12). They had a completely different religion with different gods and different styles of worship and different festivals and even different languages. It was similar to the distinction that comes through "Christianese" words and phrases that we use today: "I'm so blessed." "We had a great time of fellowship." "Man, I feel like I was so fed today." The Jews had their own kind of religious insider talk. The Ephesians were "strangers" from all of that, including the promises of salvation to Abraham's descendants. They were, as Paul puts it, "without God in the world" (v. 12).

Paul doesn't stop there but continues to heap up existing divisions between Jew and Gentile. They were "far off," meaning they were so spiritually estranged from God and His people that it was like being in a totally different zip code, across the ocean, in the opposite hemisphere. The Jews were intentionally separate from the Gentiles by the establishment of "the law of commandments expressed in ordinances" (v. 15), that is, the Mosaic Law which had as its primary aim the holiness, the set-apartness, of the people of God. In the minds of the Jewish people, they were the clean-cut church folks; and the Gentiles were the debauched, riotous worldlings. They could never cohabit a hall of worship; they were too different.

Paul also pictures the entrenched barriers between Jew and Gentile as "the dividing wall of hostility" (v. 14). This is the metaphor I'm picking up on to describe ethnic division, in part because the picture Paul uses is so palpable. But what did Paul mean by it?

In first-century Jerusalem, Herod's temple was the largest religious structure of its day. The massive complex had several entrances, gates, chambers, and courtyards, including a space specifically set apart for women and an inner sanctum for the priests.[5] One of the largest dividers on the dusty temple grounds was a thick, foreboding wall separating the Court of Israel from the infamous "Court of the Gentiles."[6] The Court of the Gentiles housed Solomon's Portico and hosted the temple's moneylenders and sheep-sellers. Non-Jewish sojourners were allowed, by Jewish law, to come into the Court of the Gentiles but no further. No Old Testament command required this ethnic separation at the temple; the Jews invented this barrier. The next court in the temple, fourteen steps up and surrounded by a stone wall, was only accessible to those with top secret clearance—namely, being born to Jewish parents. The Gentile converts, on the other side of the wall, would have to worship from afar.[7]

Can you picture it? One place of worship for one ethnicity, and another for a different ethnicity. No mixing, no mingling. Stark divisions, marked by an imposing, unambiguous, towering wall of separation. And for any Gentiles who didn't immediately get the picture, the ancient historian Josephus tells us that there was a placard on this dividing wall[8] with the following inscription: "No alien may enter within the balustrade around the sanctuary and the enclosure. Whoever is caught, on himself shall he put blame for the death which will ensue."[9]

This ethnic division ran so deep in Judaism that the death penalty was enforced to maintain it. Jew and Gentile remained separate, physically divided by an unassailable stone wall. But that wall only reinforced the spiritual, cultural, and relational division that constructed it. Jewish and Gentile lives were defined by walls.

Think back to the Civil Rights era. Separate drinking fountains. Divided schools. Segregated churches. African American men and women killed for trying to cross ethnic lines. These barriers may have been physical in some sense; but the spiritual, cultural, and relational divisions represented by those walls defined the American experience in far more powerful, painful ways. And in our country, some of those walls never really came down. They just got a fresh coat of paint.

The Ephesians also faced a world profoundly divided by race. How could a foreign people group so far, so unwelcome, so different in so many ways become even closer than biological brothers? I mean, even if you removed the wall separating the temple courts, the long-held bitterness and racial pride that built the wall would still remain. In the minds of the Jewish people, Mount Sinai itself stood between them and the unwashed Gentile masses below.

And you can't just move a mountain.

## HOW CHRIST WORKS

Well, we can't, but *God can*. And in the death of Christ, God moved more than mountains. He brought together Jew and Gentile at last. Paul says the "far-off have been brought near" (v. 13); the hostile now are at peace, and the two are now "one new man" (v. 15). All have been "reconcile[d] . . . to God"

(v. 16), accomplished "by the blood of Christ" (v. 13) "in his flesh" (v. 14) and "through the cross" (v. 16).

Jesus moved Mount Sinai with His bare, bloody hands. When Jesus, the sinless Son of God died in the place of sinners on Golgotha, He bore on His shoulders for three interminable hours the eternal Hell that His people deserved. God poured out His wrath on His Son in order to give his multi-ethnic Bride the clothing of Christ's righteousness. And in Jesus' resurrection and ascension, He crushed the head of Satan, removed the sting of death, and gave the gift of his Spirit to make one spiritual family out of individual people from every different ethnicity. In the Gospel, Jesus tore down the wall of sin that separated God and man, and He "abolished the law of commandments" (v. 15) that separated Jew and Gentile. The stone wall with its death threats and racist motives crumbled at the cry, "It is finished" (John 19:30).

I want you to see, though, that Jesus didn't stop at removing the obstacles to fellowship between believers from different ethnic groups. In fact, removing the dividing wall was a means to an end. Paul says in verses fourteen and fifteen that Jesus "has broken down in his flesh the dividing wall of hostility [that's obstacle removal] by abolishing the law of commandments expressed in ordinances [that's how he removed the obstacle], that he might create in himself one new man in place of the two, so making peace" [that's the purpose]. The word "that" in Paul's sentence indicates a goal, a desired end state. God had an intent in the cross beyond demolition. As the miner removes dirt for the purpose of unearthing a diamond, so Jesus destroys the dividing wall of hostility for the purpose of creating something far more precious: the multi-ethnic unity of His reconciled people.

Notice also the sphere of reconciliation—He creates one new man "in himself." The kind of unity the Church receives in Christ is different from the superficial exhibitions of the world. What Christ accomplishes in His death and resurrection far surpasses the semblance of ethnic civility that man can muster. He takes people with all their differences and distinctions, spiritually unites them to each other in Himself, and thereby makes them into one new entity that does not divide itself from its members. Paul says, "he himself is our peace" (v. 14). Think of this unity like a wagon wheel with Jesus as the spoke at the center and all His people of Jewish, Gentile, African, European, Latino, Chinese, Pacific Islander, Dutch, Iranian, and Russian descents connected to each other through that spoke. They maintain their ethnic distinctiveness, their cultures, and their different physical appearances; but they are spiritually one in Christ. That spiritual union changes everything.

Jesus takes people broken, cursed, and fractured by sin and division, draws them to Himself, and makes beauty out of the rubble. Paul tells us that having crafted one new man out of ethnically diverse believers, Jesus sets about the work of growing those redeemed sinners "into a holy temple in the Lord" (v. 21). We are "joined together" like bricks in a building. The bricks in the wall that used to divide are now the bricks in the Church that worships as one. Our solid basis for unity comes through "the foundation of the apostles and the prophets" (v. 20); that is, for us today, the Old and New Testaments. And the pivotal connecting point for every brick in the building is "Christ Jesus himself being the cornerstone" (v. 20). He tears down the wall to unite disparate people in Himself to be like a stained-glass window of multi-hued worship, reflecting the light of the Son to all who see the Church.

This is how Jesus always works. Our ethnic dividing walls may not stem from a misappropriation of Mosaic cleanliness laws, but they can create a separation just as bitter and far-reaching. African Americans can feel miles apart from their European American next-door neighbors while seated in the same pew and vice versa. But the cross of Christ breaks down exactly those kinds of ethnic walls and unites those who, in their racism and indifference, were once far-off. And in that act of union, Jesus builds for Himself a Church where Christians of every skin tone and culture gratefully receive and gladly share His cross-ethnic love. The kaleidoscopic worship of Christ in His multiethnic Church helps us to see that what was once a reason to divide has now become a cause for celebration. Oh, may we look at the multi-ethnic Church that Christ has built and glory in His unmatched power to unite the hopelessly divided!

That's how Jesus will continue to work in His Church today. This work of Jesus to unite divided ethnicities in His Church is the focus of our study. We won't settle for imposters who would try to hot-glue us together around causes and ideologies. Too much is at stake to settle for superficial solutions and an impermanent union. We want Jesus to bring us together as one forever.

## DEFINITIONS MATTER

Now, there's one more topic we need to address before we can get to the meat of the matter. We need to understand what we mean by the words we use if we're going to work out ethnic unity.

Today, so much of the confusion in conversations about ethnic division in the Church arises from divergent definitions. For example, "reconciliation" for one person means finding peace between two hostile parties. For another, reconciliation means dealing with the sins of people of the same race from the past. In this understanding of reconciliation, the historical, white enslavement of kidnapped Africans must be removed as a barrier between white and black people in the Church in order for reconciliation to occur. For others still, reconciliation focuses more on social programs and political discourse. Others would emphasize the personal, spiritual aspect of reconciliation. And that's just one word!

So, let's take a moment to define our terms to make sure we're using biblical definitions and biblical logic when it comes to ethnic division and unity. Note that I'll explain each of these critical words in greater detail later, but it may be helpful to know at the outset what I mean when I'm using these words so we can get the conversation going. These brief definitions will also serve as an outline for where we're headed.

- **Ethnicity:** Ethnicity, coming from the Greek word *ethnos*, differs from race in that it describes from what people group a person actually comes. The word for "ethnicity" appears in the Bible and describes a person's cultural, geographic, social, familial, and linguistic heritage.[10] It's inherently fluid and, to some degree, subjective, though tied to real differences between people groups. While ethnicity highlights a person's familial and cultural background, race has historically and incorrectly been tied to biological differences between people groups. That's why throughout our study, I will more frequently use terms like European American than I will the term "white" and African American instead of the term "black." No single group term can precisely account for all the nuances of each individual person's background, but ethnic terminology seems to be the most appropriate way to talk about groups of people with a similar cultural heritage. From that standpoint, I'll note several ways in which ethnic differences have been construed as racial differences and used to justify oppression in a brief historical prelude.

- **Gospel:** The Gospel is the Good News that Jesus Christ, the Son of God, has died to save sinners from the wrath of God for himself. While that may seem like an uncontroversial statement to most believers, the word "gospel" has taken on a number of connotations in conversations about ethnicity. I'll assert that the Gospel is Good News to people from every tribe and tongue because it is a free offer to all people of escape from God's just judgment and reconciliation to God in Christ. The implications of the Gospel in the lives of Christians are many and yet not infinite. I'll talk more about the walls being called "gospel" and the true Gospel that tears them down in chapter one.

- **Truth:** Of all people, Christians should be able to agree on the meaning of truth. But in the world of ethnic division, truth becomes as malleable as the purposes of the author, even inside the Church. Philosophically, truth is whatever corresponds with reality. But the Bible often uses the word "truth" to refer to the facts of the Gospel or even the whole of biblical revelation. If we conflate biblical truth with personal experience, we build more walls than we remove. Unity can only happen in the Church under the banner of biblical truth, though not ignorant of the Christian's experience. I'll cover this topic more in chapter two.

- **Race:** Race is a social construct that had been used almost exclusively in the history of the world for the purpose of oppression and division. Race has no grounding in biological fact (despite a long history of efforts to prove as much) but is merely a conceit that has been developed and morphed over time to suit different agendas and purposes. That being said, though race is not real biologically, it is real sociologically (that is, in people's minds), so we shouldn't ignore the language or implications of race in our day. I'll explore this topic more in chapter three.

- **Racism:** Two definitions for racism are common today—one personal, one structural. While I broken-heartedly agree that individual people with racist thoughts and desires build societal systems that propagate their racist motives (see: Jim Crow laws, segregated schools, societies promoting racial superiority), a structural definition of racism tends to conflate the problem of unjust policies with sinful motives. In other words, racism ends up meaning two things rather than one. For the sake of clarity, I will only use the term "racism" in its personal sense to refer to what the Bible calls "partiality" on the basis of ethnicity. That's not to deny the existence of structural racism, only to be clear in my terminology. Personal racism sees one race as more or less valuable or preferable than another.[11] It is a sin and condemned by God and His Word, so we must condemn it as such. I'll deal with the topic of racism in more detail in chapter four.

- **Reconciliation:** As we'll discuss in an upcoming chapter, reconciliation (biblically defined) deals with the peace and restoration accomplished in an interpersonal relationship, either between estranged people or between people and God. Though I understand that there are ways in which groups of people can individually reconcile with each other en-masse in such a way that it takes on a corporate dimension, I will stick to talking about reconciliation individually rather than, for instance, calling on white people as a group to reconcile with black people as a group. I'll talk about guilt, repentance, and reconciliation more fully in chapter five.

- **Justice:** Justice is fundamentally an attribute of God. Our own sense of justice is derived from God's justice. Justice is God being, knowing, and maintaining what's intrinsically right, giving what is due. God is not just or righteous because He conforms to a standard outside of Himself, but because He upholds His own inherent character of righteousness—that's what I mean by "intrinsically right." Therefore, our definition of justice has to flow from the intrinsic justice of God, which we see in starkest relief on the cross of Christ. Calls for justice in our world must be made in light of God's justice in the Gospel, which I'll deal with more in chapter six.

- **Unity:** Multiethnic unity can be talked about in two ways. There is a positional unity that the Church receives from Christ that we do not ourselves accomplish because it refers to the spiritual union that we have through the work of the Spirit in regeneration. But unity can and often is used to refer to degrees of relational harmony, peace, and agreement between people in the Church. For example, Peter writes in 1 Peter 3:8, "Finally, all of you, have unity of mind, sympathy, brotherly love, a tender heart, and a humble mind." According to Peter, that kind of unity requires effort on our part just like love and humility require effort. Relational unity is a working out of our positional, real, spiritual unity that we have in Christ; but it can wax, wane, and grow in application. I will talk about both kinds of unity, and I'll do my best to distinguish between which type I'm addressing. For the most part, though, I'll be referring to the relational unity that can grow or diminish in the Church because that's the work set before us by our Lord. In the conclusion, we will try to capture a biblical vision for that unity in the church.

## CHRIST AND OUR WALLS

I said that relational unity flows from positional unity, that our peace in the Church depends entirely on the peace accomplished for us by Christ in the cross. That is, in a nutshell, the main idea of this book.

I'm compelled to write at length about Christ at the crux of ethnic unity because it seems like often the Cornerstone is being left out of the building plans. In the struggle for ethnic unity in the Church, some would have us focus on political engagement, which is important and valuable. Others would have us spend our time and money on church programs, which can also be helpful. The problem with both of those approaches, however, is that they can easily be built on sand instead of the Rock.

We've had too many conversations in the Church that assume the Gospel without obeying the Gospel. Oceans of ink have been spilled on Christless manifestos while the black-and-white pages of Scripture remain unread. The red letters get twisted into the message of a million authors who aren't the Author of life. Jesus must have Lordship in and through the ethnic unity of His Church. When we stand on His firm foundation, we can stand for justice and love in the Church and in the world.

In case you're not convinced that Jesus and His glorious Gospel need to ground every inch of our efforts at ethnic unity, look back to the book of Ephesians. After unloading a theological deluge of Gospel truth in chapters one through three, Paul turns his attention to the application of that truth. In Ephesians 4:1-3, Paul writes, "I therefore, a prisoner for the Lord, urge you to walk in a manner worthy of the calling to which you have been called, with all humility and gentleness, with patience, bearing with one another in love, eager to maintain the unity of the Spirit in the bond of peace."

The word "therefore" tells us that a drivetrain of Gospel power is behind these exhortations. And the culminating summary of those applications, driven by the reconciliation purchased by Christ at the cross, is: "walk . . . eager to maintain the unity of the Spirit in the bond of peace."

Paul didn't create the unity between Jew and Gentile in the Church at Ephesus. Neither did the Jews or the Gentiles. Christ did. But they are called to maintain it. And so are we. In the Church, our aim is the glory of God; our way is peace; and our ground is the Lord Jesus Christ.

I don't doubt that the following pages will be challenging for you—they've cut open and exposed my heart. But the precious unity of the Church hangs in the balance. Will we maintain what Christ has bought by His blood, or will we allow it to succumb to the bitterness and division in the world around us? Where will we look for the unity that brings eternal praise to the

Creator? Will we persevere in love and in one mind until we're ushered into the doors of that eternal Church, the multi-ethnic saints extolling our Savior around His throne? Or will we be divided by walls of ethnic hostility like so many before us?

As important as this topic is for the Church, ethnic unity is also intensely personal for me. I didn't realize how many dividing walls I'd allowed to stand in my own heart until I married my beautiful, godly wife, Darlene, who is Mexican American. Through those wedding vows, I was added to a wider family tree with my precious Mexican, Filipino, and Kenyan relatives. I've watched Christ work in my own heart and in my extended family to tear down ethnic barriers, to bring harmony out of hostility, and to magnify his awesome power to save and to sanctify people from every kind of background. So, a book about ethnic unity isn't an academic conversation to me—it's family business.

That's why I love visiting my mother-in-law's church. She may be the only Mexican in the predominantly Filipino congregation, but the parade of hugs she receives just inside the door says that these are her people. Add to that a warm smile from her faithful Chinese American pastor; a rich, multi-ethnic potluck feast for lunch; and the sounds of voices young and old singing hymns written by dead, white Englishmen. That congregation, like ours, reminds me of how powerfully Christ has brought multi-ethnic unity into my own life. And I praise Jesus for it.

## DISCUSSION QUESTIONS

1. How does ethnic division manifest in the world? What have you heard people say about racism in our country? How does that affect you?

2. How can ethnic division manifest in the Church? What does ethnic partiality in the body of Christ communicate to the world? What about to other Christians?

3.  Why is multi-ethnic unity in the Church worth talking about? Are there wrong ways to have conversations about ethnic division? Are there wise ways to have those same conversations?

4.  In Ephesians 2:11-21 (it may be helpful to reread it as a group), how are Jews and Gentiles united as "one new man?" Why is Jesus at the center of all true multi-ethnic unity? What do you see in this passage that's applicable to ethnic division in the church today?

5.  Do you have any questions about the terms that have been defined and used in this study so far (like ethnicity, racism, reconciliation)? What do you hope to learn through this study? How do you hope to grow through this study?

HISTORICAL PRELUDE

# THE CHURCH'S CHECKERED PAST

## ON A HILL DOWN THE ROAD

In July 2019, just eight miles down the road from the church building where I pastor, a flash flood washed away the remnants of a segregation wall.[12]

The Hall's Hill Wall was built in the 1930s to physically separate the historically African American neighborhood of Hall's Hill from the then-burgeoning suburban community of Woodlawn. At the time of its construction, Jim Crow laws still prohibited the black neighbors from shopping at the nearby white stores, eating at the white restaurants, calling the white firefighters, or even using the white hospital (now Virginia Hospital Center). The cement sidewalks themselves were segregated. The wall stood not only as a physical barrier, but also as a reminder to the African American neighborhood of the deep, pervasive social division enshrined in America's segregation laws,[13] a monument to a long history of humiliation.

But the Hall's Hill Wall represented an even deeper fissure between the adjacent neighbors than their separate sidewalks and malls—it divided them spiritually. To this day, Mount Salvation Baptist Church sits on North Culpeper Street just a few blocks north of the wall,[14] and Mount Olivet United Methodist Church occupies a plot a few blocks south of the wall on the same street.[15] One is a historically black church, the other a historically white church, and both were planted at least fifty years before the wall was constructed.[16] When the barrier was erected, it cruelly put in brick and mortar what had already been engraved into the hearts of the people who had lived there for decades: There could be no union between African and European Americans, not even in Christ.

Today, near the corner of North Culpeper and Seventeenth Street, you can see a crumbling portion of the Hall's Hill Wall still standing next to a plaque lamenting its racist origins. While a deluge of rain may have been able to carry away the bricks between the two communities, the divided demographics of the two neighborhood churches remain largely unchanged.

The sharp ethnic divide on Hall's Hill doesn't stop in Arlington but cleaves churches all across our country. According to a 2015 study, four out of five Americans attend a church where eighty percent of the congregation is from a single ethnic group.[17] While there are innumerable factors influencing those kinds of statistics, the reality on the ground is that the American church has stayed staunchly separated by ethnicity. There are mostly African American churches, and there are mostly European American churches.

So, it shouldn't come as a surprise to the American Church that our ethnicity can be a profound source of division, even between born-again believers in the body of Christ. To respond to these ethnic divisions only with "color-blindness"—as in, "I just don't see people according to ethnicity"—ignores the walls all around us. Though I will argue forcefully that our identity in Christ is primary, our cultural identities aren't erased by grace through faith. I'm not a light-skinned, European American Christian, so to speak, but I am a Christian who is both light-skinned and European American. And though my spiritual union with my brothers and sisters from all nations far outweighs my ethnic background, my skin tone, or my cultural experiences, those things are still a part of my life as a Christian. We shouldn't ignore the lasting impact of ethnic differences in our church today or the long, segregated road that brought us where we are.

Before we see how Christ tears down ethnic dividing walls, we need to look back at how those walls were built and maintained. To that end, I think it's valuable to spend a few pages considering the vile history of racism in America and particularly in the Church.

My goal is not to make anyone feel personally guilty about the crimes of the past (I'll explain the concept of corporate guilt more fully in chapter five), or to stir up animosity and anger about a painful past that we can't change. More than anything, I don't want to diminish the glory of Christ by simply bemoaning the heinous sins of our country without any reference to His sovereignty over it. May it never be.

But the Church today has been meaningfully shaped by her forebearers, the attitudes they had toward each other, and the blood on their hands. Even today, the sins of chattel slavery and segregation laws are visited upon us, the children and the children's children. From my home, Hall's Hill Wall is still standing only miles down the road! If we would care well for all our fellow believers of all ethnicities, we would do well to know a little about the stories that have divided us.

## A PAINFUL LOOK BACK

By the time that privateers had sunk their anchor into the Jamestown coast in 1619 with "20. and odd Negroes"[18] for sale, five hundred thousand Africans had already been forced in chains across the Atlantic.[19] By the late 1700s, over ten million Africans had been captured, sold to Europeans, carted to the Americas, and subjugated as slaves. Two million precious image-bearers died in the Middle Passage in the hulls of slave ships.[20] Countless more were beaten, treated with inhumane cruelty, and worked literally to the exposed tissue and bone. European slave traders frequently justified their barbaric treatment of African slaves by calling it "evangelization."[21][a]

---

a   It should be noted, however, that some European colonials initially opposed the Christianization of the African slaves because they assumed it would lead to their freedom. Eventually, states passed laws clarifying that baptizing a slave did not free them from slavery, and the evangelization continued.

But Olaudah Equiano, a West African sold into slavery in the Caribbean, saw through the hypocrisy. He wrote concerning the barbaric slave trade and mistreatment, "O, ye nominal Christians! Might not an African ask you— Learned you this from your God, who says unto you, Do unto all men as you would men should do unto you?"[22] So began our country's wicked history of racism, even in the Church.

During the 1700s, Baptist and Methodist churches began to include more African slaves and freedmen in their mostly European American congregations, albeit alongside their racist convictions.[23] In many churches, the best seats were reserved for the rich, European landowners, and the back and balconies were reserved for slaves. But one African American, Methodist preacher rejected racist segregation within the Church. Under the threat of being forcibly removed for sitting with Europeans in a church service, Richard Allen walked out and started his own church. He would go on to establish the oldest predominantly African American denomination, the African Methodist Episcopal Church.[24] African American Christians flocked to these churches as safe havens in an unwelcoming land.

Frederick Douglass, a statesman and escaped slave, excoriated the hypocrisy of European American Christianity in his autobiography *Narrative of the Life of Frederick Douglass, An American Slave:*

> I therefore hate the corrupt, slaveholding, women-whipping, cradle-plundering, partial and hypocritical Christianity of the land . . . I look upon it as the climax of all misnomers, the boldest of all frauds, and the grossest of all libels. Never was there a clearer case of "stealing the livery of the court of heaven to serve the devil in." I am filled with unutterable loathing when I contemplate the religious pomp and show, together with the horrible inconsistencies, which every where surround me. We have men-stealers for ministers, women-whippers for missionaries, and cradle-plunderers for church members. The man who wields the blood-clotted cowskin during the week fills

the pulpit on Sunday, and claims to be a minister of the meek and lowly Jesus . . .  The slave auctioneer's bell and the church-going bell chime in with each other, and the bitter cries of the heart-broken slave are drowned in the religious shouts of his pious master. Revivals of religion and revivals in the slave-trade go hand in hand together. The slave prison and the church stand near each other. The clanking of fetters and the rattling of chains in the prison, and the pious psalm and solemn prayer in the church, may be heard at the same time. The dealers in the bodies of men erect their stand in the presence of the pulpit, and they mutually help each other. The dealer gives his blood-stained gold to support the pulpit, and the pulpit, in return, covers his infernal business with the garb of Christianity. Here we have religion and robbery the allies of each other—devils dressed in angels' robes, and hell presenting the semblance of paradise.

The abolition of American slavery in 1863 (followed by its full application in 1865, which we now call "Juneteenth") did not abolish racism. States in the North and the South used the excuse of a depressed economy to pass Jim Crow laws segregating, humiliating, and denigrating the now-freed African American population. These racist laws were codified in the case *Plessy v. Ferguson* with the now-infamous phrase "separate but equal."[25] Nobody during the Reconstruction era or the Jim Crow era was confused about America's radical inequalities. From voter registration to job discrimination to underfunded facilities to pig laws[26] to convict leasing to legalized lynching, European Americans continued to perpetrate all manner of cruelty on their African American neighbors.[27]

The racism of the Jim Crow era infected the Church like every other institution. Under the leadership of Reverend Dr. Basil Manly, Sr., scores of Baptist churches in the South separated from their denomination to found the Southern Baptist Convention and protect their unjust claims to own African American slaves.[28] Just after the Civil War, Nathan Bedford Forrest convened the first meetings of what would become the Ku Klux Klan, which tied itself to Protestant churches throughout the country, even while perpetrating despicable, violent hate crimes against African Americans.[29] In one horrific account of this violence, a European American mob lynched African American Georgia farmhand Samuel Thomas Wilkes by parading him through town, stripping him naked, torturing him for half an hour (the details of which are too gruesome for me to repeat), and eventually burning him alive. It was a Sunday. The thousands in the lynch-mob came directly from worshipping at church. One man, as he watched the brutal execution, called out, "Glory be to God!"[30]

The turn of the twentieth century brought massive revolutions in industry, but the same partiality and hatred continued to mark the ethnic landscape of America. A race riot targeting African Americans in St. Louis ushered in what would become known as the Red Summer of 1919, which included ethnic violence and murder across twenty-five American cities.[31] The Tulsa Massacre in June 1921 saw a white mob torch an affluent black neighborhood, prompting the National Guard to respond and imprison six thousand African American Tulsans.[32] The danger to African Americans all across the South was felt palpably and eventually prompted the Great Migration, the movement of six million African Americans from Southern to Northern cities in search of safety from ethnic violence.[33] According to the Smithsonian, "Between 1880 and 1950, an African American was lynched more than once a week for some perceived breach of the racial hierarchy."[34]

Through the Civil Rights era, while many decried these widespread racist atrocities and fought for equal rights across ethnic lines, others fought back. In August of 1955, Emmett Till's almost unrecognizable body was found floating in the Tallahatchie River after he had been beaten, shot, and tied to a metal fan for allegedly whistling at a lighter-skinned woman, and his killers walked free.[35] Till's murder stoked the civil rights movement into a flame, but racism persisted. Following the protests of school integration and *Brown v. Board of Education,* church schools began to form all over the country as

European American Protestants sought to keep their children separate from African American children.[36] Pastors instructed their European American congregations to not allow African Americans into their neighborhoods, publishing messages like, "Please help us 'Keep Kirkwood White' and preserve our Churches and homes."[37]

From the 1980s into the 2000s, racism continued to shape America's political and social landscape. Lee Atwater, a presidential campaign consultant, admitted to championing policies he knew would disproportionately affect African Americans, which continues to affect public policies to this day.[38] On June 17, 2015, Dylan Roof, a young, white supremacist, brutally shot and killed nine churchgoers at Emmanuel African Methodist Episcopal Church after attending their Bible study.[39] According to the FBI, the number of hate crimes in America peaked in 2018, reaching levels not seen for sixteen years.[40] America continues to reel with ethnic division.

## WARNING TO WEEP

Oh, is your heart broken by such a legacy of wickedness and suffering? And this brief survey of racism in America's past doesn't even begin to deal with Japanese internment camps, Chinese exclusion laws, the virtual genocide of whole Native American tribes, the mass slaughter of Mexican populations in the West, and hundreds of other acts of discrimination and violence that have characterized American history. Countless other stories could be told, but just these few overwhelm me. In a way, I hope they're overwhelming for you, too.

But be careful how you respond to a historical survey of America's skeleton-filled closet. Your first reaction to hearing (maybe all over again) about the evil partiality woven into the fabric of our country may be to defend the country you love. The Lord has certainly blessed the United States in a number of ways, and we can be thankful for his kindness to preserve a country and protect it through years of war and depression. I'm personally grateful for my own parents, who served in the United States Army to defend our country and the prospect of my own free future. But God has not commanded us to overlook sin in the history of a nation any more than He's called us to uncritically celebrate its virtues. You can love your country and hate her sins.

Second, if you respond to a historical survey of racism in America by trying to explain away its severity or importance, hold that thought. It's absolutely true that racism doesn't occur in a vacuum, and accounts of perceived bigotry and bias can be overblown. And it's also true that there are many other pressing concerns in the history of our nation, as in our present day. Statistically, it may even be true that other issues of injustice in our country have caused greater death or harm than racism. But be careful to not too-quickly politicize a discussion that has powerful relational implications.

Christians from all ethnic groups are suffering today because of the treatment of different ethnicities throughout American history. For many, the names Eric Garner, Tamir Rice, and Breonna Taylor sound just like Samuel Thomas Wilkes and Emmett Till. Of course, these are each complex instances with many diverging influences, but Christlike love should motivate us on this point to prioritize empathy over investigation. We ought to weep with those who weep before demanding an explanation for their sadness. While I'm strongly opposed to many of the cultural lies of our day that unjustly victimize people to reorganize power structures, I am even more strongly disposed to place my head in my hands and cry for my hurting fellow Christians.

So, let's be discerning, but embracing. Careful, but full of care. Thoughtful, but also sorrowful. Our country is racked by its racist roots even today. Let's not be so quick to correct that we forsake our command to be quick to listen (James 1:19). Let's love one another well and so prove to be Jesus' disciples (John 13:35).

## A REASON TO REJOICE

If we've felt each other's pain from our racist past, then it's also appropriate that we go on to rejoice. In spite of the horrors of American slavery, Jim Crow laws, and continuing racism, Christ continues to call His elect to Himself from every ethnic group. He is building His Church. Pastor Anthony Carter writes:

> The African American church is an enigma. It is an institution whose existence is unlikely and unpredictable. How could African American men and women embrace the same Christ that their oppressors professed? Despite the worst intentions of many and because of the best intentions of others, the African American church, as an institution, is arguably the most indomitable in American history. God literally raises his church up from chains.[41]

Just marvel at the radiant grace of God against the evil backdrop of America's racist history. That He would rescue any of us from our sins is a remarkable mercy, but that He would sovereignly use wicked slave masters to get the Gospel to their slaves and continue to preserve His Church through hundreds of years of despicable violence and hatred demonstrates His unstoppable power in the Gospel. "As for you, you meant evil against me, but God meant it for good" (Gen. 50:20). Christ will redeem His people, even through the most heart-breaking circumstances, even our racist past.

Our Lord will unite His people. He will tear down the dividing wall between Jew and Gentile, and He'll tear down Hall's Hill Segregation Wall as well. So, it was with the beginning of the church at Pentecost; so it has been throughout Church history; and so it is with the Church in America today. And that gives us a reason to rejoice.

# CHAPTER 1
# ETHNICITY AND THE GOSPEL

## A SERVANT, A SLAVER, AND A SAVIOR

Lemuel never knew his parents. They had abandoned him after five months, leaving him to the Rose family, who raised him as a beloved servant. At twenty-one years old, Lemuel volunteered to fight with the Minutemen and two years later made his way into the Continental Army. After only two months, he contracted typhus and left military employment for religious pursuits. He studied Greek, Latin, and the writings of Great Awakening preachers like Jonathan Edwards and George Whitefield. Soon, Lemuel received a license to preach. In 1785, he became "the first African American ordained by any religious body in America," and in 1788 took his post as the pastor of a church in Rutland, Vermont. He served the all-European congregation as their pastor for thirty years.[42]

In one of his most well-known sermons, Lemuel Haynes described the fixed focus of a pastor's heart in a world divided by slavery:

> The work of a gospel minister is not with the temporal but with the spiritual concerns of men: they watch for souls. Their conversation is not to be about worldly affairs but about things that relate to Christ's kingdom, which involves the everlasting concerns of men's souls. When a minister's affections are upon this world, his visits among his people will be barren. He will inquire about the outward circumstances of his flock

and perhaps, from pecuniary motives, rejoice at prosperity, as though that was of greatest concern. But he will have nothing to say with respect to the health and prosperity of their souls, having no joys or sorrows to express on account of the fruitful or lifeless state of the inward man.[43]

While Lemuel Haynes was still preparing to enter the pastorate in the fall of 1780, John Newton had begun serving the congregation at St. Mary Woolnoth in London. A former debauched slave trader, Newton had been radically converted after facing certain death on the stormy seas. Years later, he entered the Christian ministry and composed one of the best-loved English hymns, "Amazing Grace."

Newton partnered with William Wilberforce in his later years to oppose the British slave trade he had once served, which stirred up opposition in Parliament and in his church. In one of his letters, Newton describes his politically divided London congregation and his strategy in ministering to them:

> My congregation is made up from various and discordant parties, who, in the midst of differences can agree in one point—to hear patiently a man who is of no party. I say little to my hearers of the things wherein they differ, but aim to lead them all to a growing and more experimental [experiential] knowledge of the Son of God and a life of faith in Him.[44]

Both Lemuel Haynes and John Newton teach us the same truth about how Christ unites a divided Church, even though they came from remarkably different backgrounds. Haynes was separated from his congregation by ethnicity and Newton from his by politics. But did you notice their shared strategy for long-term, effective pastoral care?

They preached Christ.

They preached the primacy of the soul and its need for new life. They preached sin and repentance. They preached growth in godliness and joy in the Lord. Both of them also passionately decried the racist abomination of slavery on their shores, but neither regarded racial justice as their first focus. The redeemed servant and the redeemed slaver relentlessly preached their precious Savior and the salvation of souls in Him.

Two men. Two worlds. Two stories. Two churches. United by one passion—the Gospel of Jesus Christ.

## A LONG LINE OF PREACHERS AND PREACHING

Haynes and Newton are just two of the long litany of Christian pastors who have faithfully heralded the Good News of Jesus Christ. Christ had rescued both of them from their depravity in sin, so they were compelled to share about this precious freedom with others. Their ethnicities did not change the message, and neither did the racism that engulfed the world around them. They prioritized the preaching of the Gospel, following the patterns and commands laid out for them in Scripture. Haynes and Newton carried a Gospel torch that has been blazing since the first century AD, beginning with Jesus Himself and stretching into pulpits today. They preached the Gospel.

Jesus' own ministry was overwhelmingly concerned with Gospel preaching. At the outset of His public ministry, Matthew tells us that "Jesus began to preach, saying, 'Repent, for the kingdom of heaven is at hand'" (Matt 4:17). Mark's account also focuses on this priority in Jesus' ministry: "Now after John was arrested, Jesus came into Galilee, proclaiming the gospel of God, and saying, 'The time is fulfilled, and the kingdom of God is at hand; repent and believe in the gospel'" (Mark 1:14-15). Our Lord even went so far as to say to his disciples, "'Let us go on to the next towns, that I may preach there also, for that is why I came out'" (Mark 1:38). Jesus came to proclaim the Gospel.

In his last words on earth, Jesus commanded His disciples to be "witnesses in Jerusalem and in all Judea and Samaria, and to the end of the earth" (Acts 1:8). So, what did that apostolic witness look like? "Now when they had testified [lit. witnessed] and spoken the word of the Lord, they returned to Jerusalem, preaching the gospel to many villages of the Samaritans" (Acts 8:25). When

Paul and Barnabas went on the first missionary journey, they were chased out of Iconium and went to Lycaonia "and there they continued to preach the gospel" (Acts 14:7).

Paul himself described his ministry as centered on Gospel preaching when he told the Ephesian elders, "I do not account my life of any value nor as precious to myself, if only I may finish my course and the ministry that I received from the Lord Jesus, to testify [witness] to the gospel of the grace of God" (Acts 20:24). And in commenting on this ministry to the Corinthians, Paul writes, "Necessity is laid upon me. Woe to me if I do not preach the gospel!" (1 Cor. 9:16). The witness of Gospel preaching made up the mandatory ministry priority for the apostolic Church.

And Gospel preaching didn't stop with the apostles. This God-given ecclesiastical priority continued through two millennia of Church history. When he was burned at the stake for claiming Christ as Lord, the early church father Polycarp preached the Gospel. Amidst doctrinal controversy in the Roman church, the North African bishop Augustine preached the Gospel. Threatened by some of the most powerful men in the medieval world, the rogue German monk Martin Luther preached the Gospel. To desperate, unbelieving masses in India, the British missionary pioneer William Carey preached the Gospel. The faithful legacy of Church leaders throughout the millennia has primarily and consistently been Gospel-preaching.

## WHY GOSPEL-PREACHING?

While nuance is needed, we can confidently assert from Scripture that the Church must always preach the Gospel before and above everything else. Gospel preaching is the exclusive mission of the church. Christ has given His church orders, and we don't change them to preach another message. To make known the Gospel of Jesus isn't the only work the Church is involved in, but it's chief among them. Only the Church can preach the Gospel, so the Church must preach the Gospel, first and foremost. To preach another cause as primary would erect dividing walls in the body of Christ that can only be removed through the power of the Gospel.

It's worth asking, then, why Gospel preaching? Of all the activities that the Church could be involved in, why did Jesus and the apostles make such a big deal out of this one? Shouldn't the Church focus on meeting practical needs? Is it necessary to exclusively herald Christ and His salvation story, such that all other pursuits are, at best, secondary? Particularly in light of ethnic tensions, violent racism, and hateful oppression, which were rampant in Jesus' own day, is the Gospel enough? What does Gospel-preaching even sound like in an ethnically divided world?

Before we answer those questions, allow me to clarify what I mean and don't mean when I contend for the priority of Gospel-preaching.

First, I need to emphatically state that the Church never turns a blind eye to suffering, racism, and injustice. Our Lord is the perfect Model of compassion for the hurting—He preached, and He healed—and we always follow His lead. But the Church never substitutes her Christ-given priorities for other ambitions. Jesus charged His disciples with disciple-making (Matt. 28:18-20), so we make disciples before we do anything else. Christ himself prioritized Gospel preaching, so Gospel preaching must be the Christlike priority of His Church. And though our communities would press in on a thousand sides with worthwhile, desperate needs, they are not the Head of the Church. Jesus is the Head of the Church, and He commands us through His word to preach the Gospel.

Second, please understand that when I say Gospel-preaching is the Church's priority, I don't mean to limit church activity to evangelism only. I'm emphatically not advocating that we "just preach the Gospel" or even adhere to the "miracle motif" method for societal change.[45] Of course, churches should minister to their communities in tangible, compassionate, explicitly Christian ways. In fact, I would even advocate for Christians to participate in the political process (where appropriate) to advocate for righteous governance in our land. But my burden is to make clear the distinction between the cross and social action. For Christians, they are related, to be sure, but they are not the same. And the proclamation of the Gospel must remain the Church's top priority, regardless of the changing winds in our country. Thabiti Anyabwile puts it this way:

> The church finds herself pursuing many noble and necessary pursuits while leaving aside the one thing that only the church can do—proclaim the gospel of our salvation to a perishing world. Other agencies will assist the poor or battle injustice, but no other agency will preach the gospel. Though the church must do her part to alleviate poverty and oppression, such efforts should never become the main function of the church. If they do, the church will indeed die a terrible death.[46]

Pastor Anyabwile reminds us why the Gospel has been passed down with such great care and vigilance to the Church today, such that she might continue to preach it. He calls it "the gospel of our *salvation* to a perishing world" [emphasis mine]. Why Gospel-preaching? Because the Gospel is Good News about our salvation.

Paul affirms that the heartbeat of the Gospel is salvation. "The gospel . . . is the power of God for *salvation* to everyone who believes, to the Jew first and also to the Greek" (Rom. 1:16—emphasis mine). He even calls this message "the word of truth, the gospel of your *salvation*" (Eph. 1:13—emphasis mine). Gospel-preaching is so central to the mission of the Church because what's at stake is nothing less than the salvation of God's rebellious image-bearers.

Eternal, cross-bought salvation for people from every ethnicity is God's offer in the Gospel.[b] The Church must preach this Gospel to the world above all other pursuits because salvation is the greatest need of every human being. Paul contends that if the nations would be saved by hearing this Gospel

---

b   It should be noted that the Gospel is a many-faceted diamond with all kinds of different implications. My hope in this study is to address those implications of the Gospel that are most pertinent to the discussion of ethnic division in the Church.

message, then someone has to preach it (Rom. 10:14). We need to preach the Gospel! The Church is consumed with Gospel-preaching because all people need to hear the Gospel to be saved.

## SAVED FROM

But what does it even mean for someone to be "saved"? The word "salvation" has become so ubiquitous both inside and outside of the Church that it's almost lost the distinctly Christian meaning found in the Gospel. And some pastors and preachers today have radically redefined the Gospel to offer a salvation that Jesus never preached. We need to clarify the biblical meaning of the word "salvation" and its various implications; otherwise, we risk putting words in God's mouth. If we're prioritizing a message about salvation, what kind of salvation are we preaching?

To grasp the biblical concept of salvation in the Gospel and, ultimately, why it's so critical for the unity of the body of Christ, I'll explore this rich truth from two angles. First, I want to answer the question, "What are we saved from?" Then, I want to answer, "What are we saved to?" The first deals with the negative aspect of salvation, and the second looks at the positive aspect of salvation. It's to the first aspect ("What are we saved from?") that we now turn our attention.

The verb most often translated "save"[47] in the New Testament carries a number of connotations, but the overwhelming sense of Gospel salvation is this: to be saved is to be rescued from the eternal wrath of God.

That definition may at first sound simplistic, particularly because of the way we tend to use the word "saved" in the American church. But first, note that the basic meaning of the word in Greek [48][c] (and its Hebrew[49] counterparts)[50] is to cause someone to escape danger, to deliver a person from harm. Of course, this word was first used in the Greek-speaking world to talk about temporal, earthly, material, tangible deliverance (like being physically healed or spared

---

c   "To save means to deliver when there is a particularly perilous situation, a mortal danger."

from dying in a storm), and the New Testament authors sometimes use it the same way.[51] But far more often, they use "save" and "salvation" to talk about spiritual, supernatural, eschatological, God-wrought rescue.[d] Significantly, in the entirety of the New Testament, the whole-person salvation made available in the Gospel is spoken about only as relating to deliverance from God's punishment for our sin. The salvation offered in the Gospel is not from immediate, natural suffering but from eternal, transcendent wrath.[52]

According to Jesus and His disciples, the primary focus of the salvation event described in the Gospel is not a new heart, godly living, or even incorporation into the Church (as precious as those realities are to us). Salvation comes when Christ rescues His people from the impending judgment of God.

It may also be helpful to distinguish between the promises of salvation made to national, ethnic Israel and the promises of salvation made to the Church. They are not the same, though they draw on the same theological concept and come from the same God. God often promised to deliver Israel from natural and political dangers and did so through judges, kings, prophets, miracles, and armies. Old Testament salvation promises were made to Old Covenant Israel, a theocratic, geopolitical entity whose role in God's redemptive plan was intrinsically tied to their governance and political freedoms. The Church, however, is not a geopolitical entity but a spiritual one, belonging to a King Whose kingdom is "not of this world." So, it shouldn't surprise us to find the Old Testament replete with promises regarding temporal salvation because the nature of the kingdom at that time

---

d   One hundred thirty-six (out of 192) references in the New Testament, where the root "sozo" is used, refer to salvation from a transcendent danger (rather than a natural one). This includes the words translated "Savior," "save," and "salvation" (Matt. 1:21, 10:22, 16:25, 19:25, 24:13, 24:22; Mark 8:35 (x2), 10:26, 13:13, 13:20; Luke 1:47, 1:69, 2:11, 2:30, 3:6, 7:50, 8:12, 9:24 (x2), 13:23, 18:26, 19:9, 19:10; John 3:17, 4:22, 4:42, 5:34, 10:9, 12:47; Acts 2:21, 2:40, 2:47, 4:12 (x2), 5:31, 11:14, 13:23, 13:26, 13:47, 15:1, 15:11, 16:17, 16:30, 16:31, 28:28; Rom. 1:16, 5:9, 5:10, 8:24, 9:27, 10:1, 10:9, 10:10, 10:13, 11:11, 11:14, 11:26, 13:11; 1 Cor. 1:18, 1:21, 3:15, 5:5, 7:16 (x2), 9:22, 10:33, 15:2; 2 Cor. 1:6, 2:15, 6:2 (x2), 7:10; Eph. 1:13, 2:5, 2:8, 5:23, 6:17; Phil. 1:28, 2:12, 3:20; 1 Thess. 2:16, 5:8, 5:9; 2 Thess. 2:10, 2:13; 1 Tim. 1:1, 1:15, 2:3, 2:4, 2:15, 4:10, 4:16; 2 Tim. 1:9, 1:10, 2:10, 3:15; Titus 1:3, 1:4, 2:10, 2:11, 2:13, 3:4, 3:5, 3:6; Heb. 1:14, 2:3, 2:10, 5:9, 6:9, 7:25, 9:28; James 1:21, 2:14, 4:12, 5:20; 1 Peter 1:5, 1:9, 1:10, 2:2, 3:21, 4:18; 2 Peter 1:1, 1:11, 2:20, 3:2, 3:15, 3:18; 1 John 4:14, Jude 3, 23, 25; Rev. 7:10, 12:10, 19:1).

was temporal, tied to the nation of Israel, its laws, its land, and its citizens. Likewise, it also shouldn't surprise us to find that New Testament promises of salvation, while holistic, deal more with transcendent, eternal realities than with nation-states and their policies.

A handful of New Testament verses addressing Gospel salvation will demonstrate that the biblical focus of this word translated "saved" or "salvation" takes on at least three unique, transcendent dimensions. These aspects of salvation in the Gospel stand over and against immediate, temporal, political dimensions that many attribute to the Gospel today.

The first dimension of deliverance in the Gospel is that it rescues us from God's righteous anger and judgment. To use the biblical term, Gospel salvation "propitiates," or satisfies, the justice of our Holy God against our condemnatory sin (Rom. 3:25; Heb 2:17; 1 John 2:2; 1 John 4:10). Note the connection between the concepts of salvation and wrath in the following verses:

- **"For God has not destined us for wrath, but to obtain salvation through our Lord Jesus Christ" (1 Thess. 5:9).** Paul contrasts the obtaining of salvation with the reception of wrath. Instead of facing wrath, Christians receive salvation from that wrath, and it comes through Christ. And in the context, Paul is addressing the future Day of the Lord when God will pour out His wrath on the earth, leading to eternal judgment.

- **"Since, therefore, we have now been justified by his blood, much more shall we be saved by him from the wrath of God" (Rom. 5:9).** In the present, those who believe in Christ have declared righteous in the court of Heaven because of the substitutionary death of Christ. But the word rendered "shall we be saved" is a future passive verb. Not right now but in the future, the living Christ will cause us to be spared from God's just anger and punishment for our sin on the basis of the justification accomplished at the cross and declared at the moment of conversion.

- **"For God so loved the world, that he gave his only Son, that whoever believes in him should not perish but have eternal life. For God did not send his Son into the world to condemn the world, but in order that the world might be saved through him" (John 3:16-17).** According to Jesus, He was sent into the world to save people from perishing (that is, death) which is a kind of condemnation from God. This, of course, assumes that those who make up "the world" are heading for a penalty of eternal death from the Almighty, and Jesus explains in the following verses that this everlasting judgment is a direct response to their sin. When He saves people in the world, He delivers them from the wrathful condemnation of God found in the second death, which John calls "the lake of fire" (Rev. 20:14).

The second transcendent aspect of Gospel salvation is that it's forward-looking, yet-to-come, or in the future:

- **"Besides this you know the time, that the hour has come for you to wake from sleep. For salvation is nearer to us now than when we first believed" (Rom. 13:11).** Note the chronology in Paul's mind. First, they believed. Then, salvation comes at some time in the future, such that it draws nearer with the passage of time. For the Christian, salvation, in this sense, is not a reality right now but is yet to come.

- **"Who by God's power are being guarded through faith for a salvation ready to be revealed in the last time" (1 Peter 1:5).** As with Paul, Peter affirms that those who have been born again will, at some later time, see a salvation that has not yet come. That is, when God pours out His wrath in the final days, they will be rescued from it at that time.

- **"You are to deliver this man to Satan for the destruction of the flesh, so that his spirit may be saved in the day of the Lord"**

**(1 Cor. 5:5).** Though there's plenty of debate about the specifics of Paul's injunction in this verse, the timing of salvation is clear: "in the day of the Lord." Here, Paul picks up on the Old Testament concept of the Day of the Lord, a future, eschatological season when God will pour out His wrath on mankind. If this Corinthian's spirit is going to be saved, it's going to happen at the time of the coming Day of the Lord.

Third, and finally, the New Testament authors relentlessly point to a singular, Divine agent as the transcendent Worker of Gospel salvation:

- **"There is only one lawgiver and judge, he who is able to save and to destroy" (James 4:12).** James wants to warn us about being judgmental, and his argument is that there's only one Judge. According to James, Jesus' exclusive claim as Judge also means that he has an exclusive claim to save.

- **"'This Jesus is the stone that was rejected by you, the builders, which has become the cornerstone. And there is salvation in no one else, for there is no other name under heaven given among men by which we must be saved'" (Acts 4:11-12).** If ever there were a slam-dunk statement about the unique, unimpeachable power of Christ to save sinners, it's this. Peter leaves the Sanhedrin no room for misunderstanding—Jesus, and Jesus alone, saves His people from the coming wrath of God that they deserve.

- **"'Salvation belongs to our God who sits on the throne, and to the Lamb'" (Rev. 7:10).** What does the every-nation, tribe, and tongue choir declare around the throne of God? God alone saves because salvation belongs to Him!

Unless they are rescued, all unbelievers will one day face the full fury of the wrath of God. The second death. Eternal Hell. A torturous lake of unextinguishable fire. Every person on this planet is born facing unimaginable, infinite suffering because of their own sin against the holy, righteous Judge. All people need to be saved from God's anger against their sin. The Good News of the Gospel message is that the God-man Jesus Christ has taken the punishment for that sin on the cross. He drank the cup of God's wrath in unimaginable, infinite suffering. He has been raised from the dead, never to die again. Whoever repents and believes in Him will be spared from eternal perishing because God will have poured out their deserved punishment on Christ. Those who come to Christ are offered eternal life with Him instead of eternal death for their sin.

Even now, hope in that coming salvation is what binds the Church together. Former slaves and former slave-traders rejoiced together on opposite sides of the Atlantic because Jesus had absorbed their punishment on the cross. Our salvation in Jesus from God's wrath creates for us a shared future, a corporate expectation, and a common confidence that transcends the divisions brought about by ethnic differences. We're pilgrims marching together toward the Celestial City, no matter our cultural background. We're sojourners longing to finally go home together, regardless of our country of origin. And we're fellow kingdom ambassadors with a message of salvation for any who would hear and join us from any people group on the planet.

This is the greatest news we could ever hear, no matter what's going on around us. The Gospel message that brings us together centers on our salvation—not from our painful, present circumstances but from the righteous anger of Almighty God and a fate more deadly than systemic racism. In the Gospel, Jesus Christ saves sinners from something far worse than injustice—He saves us from justice.

## SUBSTITUTE SALVATION

Even so, as in every age, counterfeit alternatives have crept into the Church and undermined the Good News of Jesus Christ. Cries for temporal justice have drowned out the clarion call of the Gospel and have been called "gospel" just the same. While we must rejoice in the goodness and purity of salvation from the wrath of God, we can't afford to be naive about the voices that would sideline the work of God in His Church. So, we turn our attention to the ethnic dividing wall of man-made gospels.

It's possible to preach *a* gospel of salvation without preaching *the* Gospel of salvation, and only *the* gospel will unite Christ's church. Anything less than the exclusive Gospel of Jesus Christ is powerless to tear down our ethnic dividing walls. Self-styled, substitute salvation can't create compassionate harmony between a former slave and slave-trader. The biblical Gospel alone can knit together those most divided by ethnicity; and by God's grace, He does. A false gospel only sows more seeds of division and offers a kind of salvation that Christ did not die to secure in this life. Despite the manifold glories of the biblical Gospel, we also need to be clear about counterfeit gospels for the sake of the Church's unity.

One of these splintered, twisted, substitute messages that subtly dominates many evangelical churches today is the gospel of liberation theology. This false gospel and similar social gospel lookalikes usually try to hide inside the language of love and justice (who could disagree with those thoroughly biblical words?) but smuggle into the message of Jesus a social, political, and ultimately racist agenda. Liberation theology seeks to reverse the New Testament teaching on salvation, putting natural, political deliverance over rescue from God's holy wrath. Like any theological system, its proponents cover a wide spectrum of beliefs but are united in their conviction that Christ's work is to save the poor and oppressed from their present poverty and oppression.

Liberation theology emerged first in the early 1970s when Gustavo Gutierrez in Peru and James Cone in America began to articulate their frustration with the "white, evangelical gospel." The development of a new gospel called black liberation theology gained traction in the United States as a framework for responding to racism and injustice.

Today, the language associated with this theological position is akin to the tenets of critical race theory and intersectionality (CRT/I), a secular ideology grounded in Marxism and postmodernity.[53] The guiding concepts of CRT/I have often come into the evangelical world through liberation theologians and their writings. In fact, evangelical proponents of CRT/I ideas will sometimes distance themselves from some of the foundations of that secular framework but will openly acknowledge their dependence on the work of liberation theologians.

Let me be unmistakably clear—the salvation of liberation theology is no salvation at all. It opposes the Gospel and opposes Christ, even though it claims His name and invades His Church. This social gospel is incompatible with Jesus' message to repent and believe *the* Gospel of salvation from the wrath of God.

In his seminal, 1970 work *A Black Theology of Liberation*, the father of black liberation theology, James Cone, repeatedly asserted that the salvation of the Gospel is seen in political upheaval by the oppressed against the oppressor.[54] Namely, God saves in America when black people start a revolution to reverse positions of power with white people.[55] According to Cone, the work of God in Christ is the work of the black community in dismantling the institutions of white supremacy.[56] Cone explicitly argued for violent action to overthrow all institutions of white power, even if it meant murdering white people to do it.[57] And all of it, said Cone, was the Gospel of God's salvation.

The summary purpose of liberation theology, according to Cone, was "to put into ordered speech the meaning of God's activity in the world, so that the community of the oppressed will recognize that its inner thrust for liberation is not only *consistent with* the gospel but *is* the gospel of Jesus Christ" (emphasis mine).[58] That is, Christ's message of salvation is temporal, political, and only for the black community. More recently, Cone wrote, "Salvation is broken spirits being healed, voiceless people

ETHNICITY AND THE GOSPEL  59

speaking out, and black people empowered to love their own blackness."[59] Cone hoped to merge the contextual application of Malcolm X in the black power movement with the religious overtones of Martin Luther King, Jr. in the civil rights movement. And to get there, Cone did not mince words:

> To participate in God's salvation is to cooperate with the black Christ as he liberates his people from bondage. Salvation, then, primarily has to do with earthly reality and the injustice inflicted on those who are helpless and poor. To see the salvation of God is to see this people rise up against its oppressors, demanding that justice become a reality right now, not tomorrow. It is the oppressed serving warning that they 'ain't gonna take no more of this [expletive], but a new day is coming and it ain't goin to be like today.' The new day is the presence of the black Christ as expressed in the liberation of the black community.[60]

Cone explicitly rejects the concept of a future salvation, of a salvation solely by the work of Christ, and of a salvation from the wrath of God. All of the essential components of salvation that we have already seen in Scripture Cone directly opposes and supplants with political revolution. One of his liberation theology colleagues, J. Deotis Roberts, put it baldly when he said, "Our understanding of the gospel is political."[e] [61]

The message of liberation theology is a false gospel that condemns its adherents to eternal suffering by solely concerning itself with temporal suffering. This warped worldview only serves to deepen divides in the church and offers no healing or hope for unity. And worse, liberation theology's errors weren't limited to the 1970s but have been carried into our time, repackaged and reproduced.

---

e    While Roberts did explicitly critique Cone's violent appeals and absence of calls for reconciliation, his explanation of the Gospel shared the political dimension of Cone's. He may have pushed back against some of Cone's radicalism, but his critique was incomplete.

## LEGACIES OF LIBERATION

The divisive worldview of liberation theology didn't stop with James Cone, J. Deotis Roberts, and their contemporaries. The blight of this false gospel has reemerged in evangelicalism today in a number of different forms. Though I don't want any Christian to be overly consumed with the study of false teaching, I think it's important to know what this novel gospel sounds like to guard the Good News against it.

One current form of liberation theology remains largely unchanged from its twentieth century roots. Some continue to boldly, openly herald the dictates of this false gospel of liberation theology without apology. For example, Dr. Samuel Cruz, professor of religion and society at Union Theological Seminary, teaches courses explicitly promoting liberation theology and its attendant worldview. Cruz writes:

> If you miss the reality of why Jesus was killed, you miss the whole story. Jesus was assassinated because he condemned injustice. In Jesus' day, those who could afford good health care and medicine were not happy when the marginalized received good health care and medicine from Jesus . . . He died because there were evil individuals in society who wanted to maintain their power and found it necessary to kill him.[62]

Cruz reinterprets the cross of Christ as a political murder (which is *partially* true—John 18:12-14) in order to prop up his wholly untrue argument that Christ's chief purpose in the resurrection is to assert political dominance over His oppressors. When anyone replaces God's wrath with man's schemes in the Gospel narrative, the offer of genuine salvation is gone.

Other pastors and authors will distance themselves from liberation theology's architects while still living in the house. Without attributing their ideas to liberation theologians like Cone or Gutierrez, they use the same language and distortions of the Gospel, albeit with gentler words. For example, in his book *Reconstructing the Gospel*, Jonathan Wilson Hartgrove completely rejects the Gospel of salvation from wrath as a "slaveholder religion [that] has infected every corner of the church in America."[63] He goes on to describe the Gospel as a "political call"[64] to "[proclaim] that the unjust systems of this world must give way to the reign of a new King."[65] He even argues that the organization Black Lives Matter, which claims for itself opposition to biblical Christianity,[66] can "illuminate the gospel for young black men."[67] Wilson-Hartgrove continues the legacy of liberation theologians by promoting the same false gospel of political revolution in place of salvation from God's wrath.

Still other authors have tried to blend liberation theology with biblical theology. Daniel Hill, the senior pastor at River City Community Church, writes about his own experience of discovering racial justice as a kind of conversion:

> To be theologically awake is to take these words of Jesus seriously: "No one can see the kingdom of God unless they are born again" (John 3:3). It is also to embrace the fact that a spiritual rebirth ushers in both the salvation of our souls and our participation in the redemption of this world. It is also to hold together activism and evangelism; protest and prayer; personal piety and social justice; intimacy with Jesus and proximity to the poor.[68]

Like many others, Hill attempts to blend a biblical understanding of the Gospel with some of the ideas in liberation theology. Notice his affirmation of the transcendent "salvation of our souls" immediately followed by an inclusion of human effort—"participation"—in the redemption of the Gospel. Where liberation theology blurs the lines between evangelism and activism (eventually to the exclusion of evangelism altogether), the Bible maintains a crystal-clear distinction. The biblical Gospel can't be blended with any other gospel (Gal. 1:6-9).

But in its most covert forms, those who have been influenced by liberation theology will use the biblical Gospel merely as a springboard to talk about racism in America. Rather than outright deny the content of the

Gospel, some proponents will turn Christ's glorious message of salvation into a folded napkin under the wobbly table of a social platform. In churches that discretely promote liberation theology, you'll likely hear a commendable statement or two explaining substitutionary atonement, individual guilt for sin, and maybe even the existence of Hell. But the overwhelming emphasis of many who secretly promote liberation theology will be societal change, legal reform, racial repentance, and political activism.[f] They assume the Gospel in order to move quickly onto another agenda. Or, even worse, they redefine the Gospel to necessarily include social and political forms of "racial reconciliation."[69] Dr. Jarvis Williams, for example, is a professor at Southern Baptist Theological Seminary who included the following statement in his class notes: "According to Paul, racial reconciliation is NOT an implication of the Gospel and certainly not a social issue instead of a gospel issue. But it is a GOSPEL ISSUE!!!!!!!!!!!"

At a certain point, emphasis becomes exclusion, and salvation from wrath has been substituted for salvation from racism.

My point is not that talking about any topic except the Gospel denies the Gospel—of course not. My point is that when social action is trumpeted as the Gospel, the Good News has been subtly replaced.

In contrast to pastors who promote liberation theology's ideas, Pastor Anthony Carter brings succinct, sorrowful clarity to this lamentable legacy when he writes:

> What was once the treasure chest of the church—namely, the person of Christ and the message of the gospel—has been exchanged for social expedience and financial gain. What has been lost, indeed forfeited, is an uncompromised, orthodox, biblical view of Jesus and the message of the gospel that saves sinners from the death that is due to all of us because of our sin. What has been lost is the unique message and calling of the church.[70]

---

f   For example, Jemar Tisby's *The Color of Compromise*, Latasha Morrison's *Be the Bridge*, and Robert P. Jones' *White Too Long*.

Samuel Sey, a Ghanaian-Canadian writer, concurs with Carter on the dangers of liberation theology for the Church and suggests the only alternative:

> Black Liberation Theology is one of the most destructive heresies in Black American churches today. It's shaped the way many Black people think about God and government. It's shaped the way many people in Black American churches perceive themselves and others . . . instead of capitulating to its heresies by adopting a form of their social justice theology to win their approval, we need to challenge Black Liberation Theology with the true gospel of Jesus Christ, who lived, died, and was resurrected for White, Black, and all sinners.[71]

Thabiti Anyabwile encapsulates the priority of the Gospel over and against Conian theology when he writes that "the salvation of souls far outranks liberation and prosperity in this life."[72]

The gospel of liberation theology peddles a cheap, substitute salvation in place of the wonderful, Good News of salvation in Jesus Christ. Of course, we should want to be charitable and understanding with those who disagree with us. We don't want to alienate our spiritual family in Christ and unintentionally create new walls by trying to rip others down. But when the content of the Gospel of salvation is undermined, we want to be as razor sharp as the Scriptures as we rightly divide the Word of Truth from error. So, for the sake of clarity, let me summarize.

- In the Gospel, God saves us from justice, not injustice.
- In the Gospel, God saves us from Himself, not each other.
- In the Gospel, God saves us through Jesus, not through other men.
- In the Gospel, God saves us later, not right now.
- In the Gospel, God saves us from the consequences of our own sin, not the sin of others.

## SAVED TO

While it's absolutely critical that we define what the Gospel saves us *from*, we must be equally clear about what the Gospel saves us *to*.

Every Sunday of my childhood, as far as I can remember, I heard about the Gospel of salvation without being changed by it. I would have told you that Jesus' death rescues me from the future, fair penalty for my sins. I would have nodded along with sermons on atonement, propitiation, and Jesus' wrath-absorbing, righteousness-imputing cross. But I thought simple agreement to the facts of this Good News equaled faith. I thought that repentance from sin and righteous living were, of course, preferable but saw them as an optional add-on to the Christian life. And I was dead wrong.

To separate a changed life from a changed mind decapitates the Gospel. There is no such thing as a believer who doesn't repent from sin or a Christian who hates good works. That's why James says, "So also faith by itself, if it does not have works, is dead" (James 2:17). John concurs when he writes, "Whoever says, 'I know him' but does not keep his commandments is a liar, and the truth is not in him" (1 John 2:4). Jesus Himself affirms the transformational character of the Gospel when He so powerfully and simply says, "If you love me, you will keep my commandments" (John 14:15).

While we ought to carefully distinguish between the salvation offered in the Gospel and the transformative effects of the Gospel, it is impossible to divide them from one another. If you have faith, you have works. If you know Him, you keep His Word. If you love Him, you obey Him.

We are saved by grace alone through faith alone in Christ alone. My tears of repentance and my works of compassion do not contribute one iota to my righteous standing before my Judge. Jesus' perfect life has been substituted for my filthy one in order that I might stand before God justified, declared holy by His mercy alone (Rom. 3:26; 2 Cor. 5:21; Titus 3:4-5). I am not saved *by* works. But I am saved *to* them.

One of the clearest passages explaining the relationship between faith and works is Ephesians 2:1-10. In describing our glorious spiritual resurrection from deadness to sin, Paul says, "For by grace you have been saved through faith. And this is not your own doing; it is the gift of God, not a result of works, so that no one may boast" (Eph. 2:8-9). Paul bends over backwards to help us see that we are emphatically not saved by our works. If we were, he argues, then we'd have something to boast about, and God is too jealous for His glory to allow humble bragging in the courts of Heaven. We are saved only by faith, which is no work but is itself a precious gift from God.

Though we are saved apart from works, Paul tells us that we are saved *to* good works. "For we are his workmanship, created in Christ Jesus *for* good works, which God prepared beforehand, that we should walk in them" (Eph. 2:10, emphasis mine). The word "for" after "Christ Jesus" and before "good works" is extraordinarily significant. This little preposition indicates purpose and intent. Why did God cause a dead sinner to receive new spiritual life, creating a new nature in them that's united to Jesus? What was God's aim in raising us spiritually together with Christ before we're raised physically with Christ? If He's going to save us from His wrath later, why bother making us new now? Paul answers, "for good works."

If God intends for our present spiritual transformation to manifest itself immediately in good works, then we would be foolish to separate the root from the fruit. We are "saved from," and we are "saved to." It's not one or the other but always both. In the Gospel, God offers escape from the condemnation we deserve and freedom to obey our new Heavenly Father rather than persist in sin. Ours is a message of deliverance from the penalty *and* the power of sin. We are rescued "for good works," and God Himself prepared those works beforehand so they will surely be done! Gospel believers will produce good works. We dare not undermine the integrity of the Gospel by omitting its necessary effect on our lives today.

## GOSPEL EFFECTS

But as dangerous as it may be to try to separate the future salvation of the Gospel from the present application of the Gospel, it's just as dangerous to blend them together. I'll quote D. A. Carson at length on this point for his powerful precision and insight:

> The first two greatest commands—to love God with heart and soul and mind and strength, and our neighbor as ourselves—do not constitute the gospel, or any part of it. We may well argue that when the gospel is faithfully declared and rightly received, it will result in human beings more closely aligned to these two commands. But they are not the gospel. Similarly, the gospel is not receiving Christ or believing in him, or being converted, or joining a church; it is not the practice of discipleship. Once again, the gospel faithfully declared and rightly received will result in people receiving Christ, believing in Christ, being converted, and joining a local church; but such steps are not the gospel. The Bible can exhort those who trust the living God to be concerned with issues of social justice; it can tell new covenant believers to do good to all human beings, especially to those of the household of faith; it exhorts us to remember the poor and to ask, not "Who is my neighbor?" but "Whom am I serving as neighbor?" We may even argue that some such list of moral commitments is a *necessary* consequence of the gospel. But it is not the gospel. We may preach through the list, reminding people that the Bible is concerned to tell us not only what to believe but how to live. But we may not preach through that list and claim it encapsulates the gospel. The gospel is what God has done, supremely in Christ, and especially focused on his cross and resurrection. Failure to distinguish between the gospel and all the effects of the gospel tends, on the long haul, to replace the good news as to what *God* has done with a moralism that is finally without the power and the glory of Christ crucified, resurrected, ascended, and reigning.[73]

Carson's observation has proved sadly prophetic. In many cases, the Good News has been subverted in pulpits across America because of this confusion of the Gospel and its effects. For example, one author writes, "I cannot read the Gospels without seeing social justice as an essential concept and undertaking of Jesus' message and ministry. Social justice was at the heart of His Gospel. He came to save the whole person—mind, body and soul."[74]

It's absolutely true that Jesus came to save the whole person, but not through you and not just yet. He Himself will do it when He returns. To say that social justice, or the pursuit of racial harmony, or feeding the needy, or helping the hurting, or any other specific good work is "the heart of His Gospel" is to substitute the saving news of God's accomplishment with man's achievements.

Of course, Christ's followers should be the most empathetic, caring, upright, godly people on the planet because we're emulating our Lord. "Whoever practices righteousness is righteous, as [Jesus] is righteous" (1 John 3:7). Where there is suffering, there you'll find the disciples of Jesus ministering, weeping, and praying. We don't ignore injustice; we don't explain away racism; and we don't dismiss the plight of the poor. Our transformed hearts beat in sync with our Savior, leading us to lives of good works, love for our neighbor, and deep, heartfelt compassion. Paul writes in Galatians 6:10, "So then, as we have opportunity, let us do good to everyone, and especially to those who are of the household of faith." We prioritize the needs of our spiritual family in Christ, and we also do good works for those outside of the church (more on this in chapter six).

But our transformed lives are the *working out* of the Gospel, not the Gospel itself. Love for our neighbor is what Paul calls keeping "in step with the truth of the gospel" (Gal. 2:14), not the content of the Gospel. God has done all that is required, and we add nothing to it. Rather, we are changed by the Good News through the power of the Spirit unto good works.

## NOT JUST HAMMERS

But there's another danger in talking about how we work out the Gospel in our lives: We can wrongly go beyond God's Word to define what those good works must be for every Christian. Several passages certainly do go into specific detail about how Christians must provide for the needs of our brothers and sisters in Christ,[g] but we're not given such direct orders about serving the world outside the Church. In fact, it may surprise you to hear what Jesus *doesn't* command.

- Nowhere in the New Testament are all Christians commanded to fight for political justice.[h]

- Nowhere in the New Testament are all Christians commanded to lament for economic inequality.

- Nowhere in the New Testament are all Christians commanded to feed the world's hungry.[i]

- Nowhere in the New Testament are all Christians commanded to unite divided neighborhoods.

- Nowhere in the New Testament are all Christians commanded to dethrone corrupt governors.[j]

- Nowhere in the New Testament are all Christians even commanded to end slavery (though Paul sows the seeds of abolition in Philemon).

---

g   For example, Matthew 25:34-46; 1 Timothy 5:1-20; 1 John 3:17.

h   Note that I used the words "New Testament" and "Christians." There were plenty of calls for corrections of injustice to Israel in the Old Testament because the Mosaic Law called for precisely that kind of work. The New Covenant community is not a nation-state, and those commands are not given directly to us, though they do reveal to us the character of God and His desire for justice in this world. More on this in chapter six.

i   Every passage in the New Testament that does command feeding someone else (Matt. 25:31-46; James 2:14-18; 1 John 3:17-18) is explicitly referring to feeding fellow believers, not the world's poor. While there are several proverbs lauding the generosity of feeding the poor without qualification (Prov. 14:31, 19:17, 22:9, 31:20), those do not constitute a binding command. Giving generously to all certainly reflects the heart of God, but it cannot be included as a necessary effect of the Gospel for all Christians without going beyond the bounds of Scripture.

j   Actually, the Bible commands the opposite: that Christians submit to all governing authorities (even evil ones) until they command what God forbids or forbid what God commands (Dan. 3:16-18; Matt. 22:15-22; Acts 5:27-32; Rom. 13:1-7; Titus 3:1; 1 Peter 2:13-17).

Now, understand what I'm saying. It breaks a believer's heart to see fellow image-bearers gunned down unarmed in the streets or locked up with a life sentence while innocent. Unfair suffering makes us long for justice to be done, and that will compel some to speak up and even protest in defense of hurting victims. When motivated by Christlike wisdom and compassion, working for proximate, political justice is a wonderful and righteous outflow of the Gospel.

But while these efforts may be exactly how Christians should help people in their communities, that application isn't commanded in the Bible, so we dare not make it an essential component of the Gospel. There are countless, godly ways for believers to produce "good works" as the fruit of our belief, all of which are significant and worthy of exhortation. To one is given the gift of mercy, and to another giving, and to another teaching (1 Cor. 12:8-11). So it is with our spiritual gifts, and so it is with our works. The Church isn't a wall of hammers but a workshop with every different kind of tool for a variety of tasks. If we assume that all Christians were gifted by the Spirit for the same exact work, then everything will start to look like a nail—even the screws—and we'll leave a lot of important work undone. Paul tells us that God has given Christians different burdens for different kinds of work all moving toward the same goal of building up the body (1 Cor. 12:18-19). Christians aren't just hammers.

So, to say that one particular work is a necessary component of the Gospel, thereby mandating that action for all Christians, is unhelpfully myopic and potentially legalistic. We wouldn't demand that all Christians must protest the injustice of abortion in order to genuinely believe the Gospel, so why would we demand the same for racial injustice? Compassion ought to compel Christians to alleviate suffering in the world around us in a variety of ways, including the suffering that comes through the condemnation of God in Hell. But woe to us if we replace the varied effects of the Gospel with the Gospel itself. John Piper writes, "The gospel was meant to explode with saving power in the lives of politicians and social activists, not help them decorate their social agendas."[75]

Consider for a moment just how astonishingly silent Jesus was about the cultural sin and suffering that surrounded him. On one occasion, Jesus was given the perfect opportunity to decry racism and majority-culture oppression. Pilate had just slaughtered a group of Galileans and mingled their blood with that of their sacrifices. This was a barbaric, outrageous, ethnically charged injustice. Surely, this senseless act demanded a passionate protest from this Galilean Rabbi! But what was Jesus' response when He was asked to comment on this atrocity? "Do you think that these Galileans were worse sinners than all the other Galileans, because they suffered in this way? No, I tell you; but unless you repent, you will all likewise perish" (Luke 13:2-3). He turned the focus away from injustice toward justice! Jesus used a horrific story of Roman oppression not to fire up His crowd to demand restitution but instead to plead with them to flee from the wrath they deserve.

Does the Gospel "save to" good works? Yes and amen! We should be careful, though, to distinguish between the good works that God has prepared for each Christian to walk in and the good works that others demand. Let me put it this way: if someone defines what Paul calls "good works" as "fighting for racial justice," they are really defining "good works" as "the particular good work I want everyone to do." Don't buy it. You're called to holiness, compassion, and active love for believers and those around you. That will manifest in thousands of different ways—and praise God for it because that's how He grows His united Church.

## SAVED WITH

False gospels can divide the Church, but the Gospel of Jesus Christ will unite her. Lemuel Haynes and John Newton both grasped the vital importance of Gospel-preaching as the central pillar that holds up the roof of God's spiritual house. With Christ as the Cornerstone, this building will continue to be knit together in love and built up evermore into the image of Christ. Jesus' Gospel is the only solid foundation for ethnic unity in the Church because only His Gospel offers salvation to every person on earth, regardless of differences in heritage, class, or pedigree. Christ, through His Good News, brings together those who were a world apart, offers them a future free from condemnation, and transforms them into hard-working, compassionate kingdom citizens who are passionate for His glory above all.

If we want to start tearing down the ethnic divides in the Church, we must first be clear about the Gospel that unites us. If we preach two different gospels, we'll have two different bodies. But in the Gospel of Jesus, there is only one body with many diverse parts.

To give us clarity and hope, Pastor H. B. Charles writes:

> Racism is a spiritual battle that can be overcome. But you cannot win spiritual battles with worldly weapons. This is why the hope of overcoming racism cannot truly be found in human effort, worldly philosophies, or even civil rights. The gospel, which reconciles God to sinners, must also reconcile sinners to one another.[76]

It was the Gospel that united Lemuel Haynes, a former slave, and his European American congregation. And it was the Gospel that united him with a former slave trader, John Newton, whose own divided congregation eventually found harmony in the Gospel. The Gospel transcended their ethnic differences and brought together those who were far off.

Jesus unites His Church through His Gospel. Though Haynes and Newton have since joined their voices to the heavenly choir, the universal Church they served is still bringing people together today by the preaching of God's Word. Here, in the Church, the Gospel is reconciling Democrats and Republicans to God and to each other. Here, Black Panthers, Neo-nazis, Islamic terrorists, and religious suburbanites all find the tender compassion of Christ in His Church. Here one day, when the Church is raised, the Klansman who repents will worship alongside the black pastor he lynched. This is the uniting power of the Gospel of Jesus Christ.

## DISCUSSION QUESTIONS

1.  What is the Gospel of Jesus Christ?

2.  Why has Gospel preaching been the primary task of the Church throughout Church history? What does our God-given primacy of Gospel preaching tell us about God's heart?

3.  From what does the Gospel save us? From what does the Gospel *not* save us? Why is it important to be clear about those distinctions?

4.  Have you ever heard a false, substitute gospel being preached? How could you tell that it was different from the biblical Gospel? How should we respond when we hear a false gospel being communicated?

5.  Can we be "saved from" without being "saved to?" Why or why not? How is distinguishing between the Gospel and its effects different from dividing them? To what work has the Lord saved you?

6.  How can clarifying the Gospel help us "maintain the unity of the Spirit in the bonds of peace?"

CHAPTER 2

# ETHNICITY AND THE WORD

## THAT'S JUST YOUR INTERPRETATION

Eyeing the half-eaten, cardboard pizza on the kiosk next to me, he said, "That's just your interpretation." Jake (not his real name) was a regular at our evangelism table in the student center of George Mason University. Every week, I would lead a small group of mostly young adult church members to the student center, where we would set up a station with Bibles, tracts, flyers, and, of course, pizza in hopes that we could strike up conversations with students leading to the Gospel. And many nights, my outreach efforts would lead me to Jake, the vice president of the Secular Student Alliance, the atheist club on campus.

Jake liked to start up interesting conversations, especially because he's brilliant. I often felt dwarfed by his astounding knowledge of astrophysics, geo-political history, and abstract philosophy but appreciated his gregarious, playful, and sometimes abrasive attitude. Mostly, I was just glad that he was willing to talk. So, week after week, slice after slice, Jake would hover over our little kiosk; and we would chat, eventually about the Bible, Jesus, and the Gospel.

On more than one occasion, as I would start unfolding the story of redemption to Jake, Bible in hand, he would stop me mid-sentence. "Well, I mean, that's just your interpretation, but sure." "According to you, I guess."

"Says you and your holy book, but what about the others?" "Of course, that's what *you* believe."

His questions would seem more daunting if they weren't so familiar. Probably more than any other rebuttal to biblical truth, that's the sentence I hear most echoed on college campuses: "That's just your interpretation." And honestly, they have a point—I am interpreting the Bible to get at the truth it contains. But I have beef with one word in that sentence: "just."

When I explain the Gospel from God's Word, is that really "just" my interpretation? As in, the sole value of my words resides in their ability to reflect my personal biases? As in, there's zero connection between what I'm saying and what the Author of the text tried to communicate? As in, the Bible is a parrot that repeats to me only what I taught it to say?

If you've engaged in evangelistic conversations today, you've probably heard this same line. And if you're anything like me, you've probably wondered at the denial of such a basic concept. "I know that I'm reading the Bible and not just my own mind. I can honestly say that I'm doing my best to 'rightly [divide] the word of truth' (2 Tim. 2:15). I don't claim to have omniscience about the interpretation of God's Word but I certainly have an adequate understanding, right? I mean, how else would we hear the Gospel but through interpreting the Bible? And we need to know Scripture to be reconciled to God, so it can't *just* be my interpretation, or else our whole church is doomed!"

Rest assured that the Church is not doomed. Jake has not discovered an epistemological loophole that breaks all human understanding, but like many, he simply privileges his own perspective over all others as authoritative. Despite his protests, he isn't actually asserting that my interpretation is flawed because all interpretation is flawed. What he's really saying is that so long as my interpretation isn't his, it's wrong. He's elevated his own voice (or whoever's voice he chooses) as the arbiter of truth and thereby rejected the voice of God in His Word. Like so many others, Jake tries to define his own truth by privileging his perspective.

# COLOR-CODING AUTHORITY

This hot potato game of interpretative authority isn't confined to evangelistic encounters. The same question is being rephrased and repackaged in conversations about ethnic division across the U.S. today. You may not talk to an atheist college student who rejects biblical epistemology, but you're inevitably going to hear the same fundamental objection applied to various voices in dialogues about racism, the State, and the Church. Here's how it can sound today:

- It is particularly important for white Americans to approach this subject matter [race] with the right goals in mind. Our goal must be sight. Our goal must be transformation. Our goal must be a renewed consciousness.[77]

- Stopping our [European Americans'] racist patterns must be more important than working to convince others that we don't have them. We do have them, and people of color already know we have them.[78]

- There is only one way forward if we [European Americans] truly want to throw off the chains of white supremacy that have bound the white American church for 400 years. There is only one path to choose to finally move to the right side of history. This path includes the submission of ourselves to POC [people of color] Christian leadership. We must begin to heed their voices, listen to their stories, and learn their theologies.[79]

The philosophy undergirding these statements may seem innocuous at first, even humble and godly. I mean, isn't it a good thing to listen? Shouldn't we want to hear from different perspectives? Wouldn't it help me grow to acknowledge my own blind spots? And I say yes to all three.

Appreciate, however, that what's being demanded by the authors of the quoted statements is not the empathetic, meek compassion of Christian virtue but a wholesale restructuring of authority. Did it strike you as odd, for example, that in each of the statements, it was European Americans who needed to be cured of their blindness and "people of color" who could grant new sight? That's because there is an entire worldview with a racist agenda driving these authors to their conclusions. It's not meaningless that predominantly European American churches are being summoned to "self-assessment by Black and other leaders of color . . . to listen and be led."[80] There's a bigger picture behind these statements, and we can't be blind to it.

The worldview informing these efforts springs from a common source and leads to a common end. That source is an idea called "standpoint theory."

## ARE ALL VOICES CREATED EQUAL?

Standpoint Theory emerged in the 1970s as a framework for feminist ideas relating to power, perspective, and privilege. It traces its roots back to the philosophy of Karl Marx, drawing for itself parallels "between the claims Marx makes for a knowledge based in the class whose labour produces the conditions of existence for the ruling class, on the one hand, and the claims that can be made for a knowledge of society from the standpoint of women, on the other."[81] That's a way of saying, in summary, that the exploited know things that others don't. *Britannica* summarizes standpoint theory this way: "The theory emerged from the Marxist argument that people from an oppressed class have special access to knowledge that is not available to those from a privileged class."[82] Standpoint theory divides the world into the haves and the have-nots, then assigns experiential authority to the have-nots.

For our purposes, we can call the ideas of standpoint theory "perspective privilege." Dr. Voddie Baucham calls it "ethnic gnosticism."[83] Authority is tacitly and explicitly granted to certain perspectives, giving those voices not only informational dominion in the conversation but also the moral high ground. At its core, it's the same as Jake's argument against the Gospel because he chose to assign privilege to his perspective rather than the Bible's. Regardless of where the authority lands, it's still an arbitrary, manmade designation about whose voice really counts. It begins with a premise that rejects absolute truth and moves quickly to replace it with unchallengeable opinions. Perspective privilege calls feeling fact and fact fiction. Depending on who you ask, of course.

Perspective privileging matters to us because it has absolutely permeated the discussion about ethnic division. In fact, its widespread adoption is so ubiquitous, it often flies under the radar. But this relativistic worldview is profoundly shaping conversation about race and racism every day.

Think about it for a second. When you picked up this book, did you think, "Dan is white. Why is he writing about race?" If you're European American, have you ever been tempted to give the "but I have a black friend" qualification to a statement you made on race? Why did a book titled *White Fragility: Why It's So Hard for White People to Talk About Racism* become the best-selling book in America in June of 2020?[84] And why would the Black Lives Matter Philadelphia chapter hold a "black only space" meeting, explicitly refusing to grant access to white and Hispanic members?[85] In different ways, each of these is a small illustration of the massive impact of perspective privileging. And it's an impact we can't afford to ignore for the sake of the unity of the Church.

## PERSPECTIVE PRIVILEGE IS NOT

First, we need to be clear about what perspective privilege is *not*. We don't want to throw the baby out with the Marxist bathwater, so we need to be careful and nuanced in this discussion. What does perspective privilege *not* explicitly entail?

Elevating certain voices in authority over others on the basis of race is not the same as desiring to hear from a group of people that are hurting in order to sympathize with them. Mark Vroegop addresses this issue with his European American readers when he writes:

> It is important to step outside our cultural sphere and listen
> to the experiences and lessons from believers from different

backgrounds . . . [in so doing] we are better able to empathize
with the present hurts our minority brothers and sisters face.[86]

We need to hear from each other to care for each other. For Christians,
Jesus is our Model for tenderly sharing in one another's pain (Heb. 4:15). So,
too, were the Jewish believers who "had compassion on those in prison"
(Heb. 10:34), even at great cost to themselves. We eagerly obey Paul's command
to "bear one another's burdens, and so fulfill the law of Christ" (Gal. 6:2),
and we recognize that involves first listening to those who are in pain. The
source of that pain may be personal, social, or even ethnic. It may be entirely
imagined or grounded in reality. The point is, Christians should be the first
people to have an open ear for our suffering brothers and sisters.

Perspective privilege is also *not* the right and humble acknowledgement
that we all have much to learn. The book of Proverbs, in particular, reminds
us how feeble our own reasoning can be and how often we should seek
counsel from others.

- "There is a way that seems right to a man, but its end is the way to death" (Prov. 14:12).
- "Every way of a man is right in his own eyes, but the LORD weighs the heart" (Prov. 21:2).
- "The one who states his case first seems right, until the other comes and examines him" (Prov. 18:17).
- "The way of a fool is right in his own eyes, but a wise man listens to advice" (Prov. 12:15).
- "Listen to advice and accept instruction, that you may gain wisdom in the future" (Prov. 19:20).

If we would be wise, we would hear the wisdom and counsel from our
brothers and sisters in Christ. It can be helpful and eye-opening to hear from
those who have experienced race-based hatred and suspicion to learn how
godly people respond to that kind of sin, especially if your life has been
relatively free from racism and active discrimination.

We don't accept any counsel uncritically, to be sure, and we don't accept anyone's word *authoritatively*. That's what perspective privilege does, but not for Christians. In fact, let me apply this to myself: you should critically evaluate the words you're reading right now. Use biblical truth as your plumbline, not some author. I'm not the authority on anything! God's Word is the sole authority. So, be quick to listen, thoughtful to biblically analyze, and humble to learn.

## THE PROBLEM WITH PERSPECTIVE PRIVILEGE

But perspective privilege is part of a worldview that, despite its potentially beneficial byproducts, undermines the nature of Scripture, the Gospel, and the character of God. It's as old as the Fall itself and as destructive as the serpent's deception: "Did God [really] say?" (Gen. 3:1). If Christ would tear down the dividing walls of ethnic hostility in the Church today, perspective privilege should be one of the first to come down.

The danger posed by perspective privilege is captured in a quote from George Orwell's classic allegorical novel, *Animal Farm*:

> No one believes more firmly than Comrade Napoleon that all animals are equal. He would be only too happy to let you make your decisions for yourselves. But sometimes you might make the wrong decisions, comrades, and then where should we be?[87]

You don't need to know anything about the plot of the book to get the idea. Napoleon, a Marxist hog, believes that only his perspective can determine which decisions are right or wrong. He assumes on the basis of a certain class categorization that some have climbed the moral hierarchy higher than others. He privileges his perspective.

Put that in a modern context. Perspective privilege today makes use of a complex web of interconnected, oppressed identity groups to determine which perspective to privilege. In other words, the one who suffers most knows most. According to perspective privilege, skin color determines truthfulness, or as is posited in *Critical Race Theory: An Introduction,* "Minority status . . . brings with it a presumed competence to speak about race and racism."[88]

Do you see the problem? Despite statements to the contrary, authority does not and cannot come from someone's race.

But perspective privilege isn't just a logical nightmare; it's also an opponent of biblical truth. Proverbs 30:5 reads, "Every word of God proves true." Psalm 119:160 extols, "The sum of your word is truth." Jesus prayed, "Sanctify them in the truth; your word is truth" (John 17:17). Because "all Scripture is breathed out by God" (2 Tim. 3:16) and because God alone is true (Rom. 3:4), His inspired words in Scripture are our only authoritative source of truth. To imply, insinuate, or indicate that God's Word has rival truths with which to contend or that we need another person or group of people to explain morality to us apart from the Bible is to undermine the very character of God. Perspective privilege and biblical authority cannot coexist in the Church or in our hearts.

You may object, then, that my atheist friend Jake has a point. Even if the Bible is your ultimate authority for truth, you still have to interpret it. Doesn't the act of interpretation itself turn God's truth into *your* truth? Aren't you just privileging your own interpretation of God's Word over others?

While I'd like to spend several chapters addressing this important question about biblical interpretation, the summary version is this: God is the Author of language, reading, and interpretation itself; He has revealed Himself clearly and adequately in the Bible, and we can have high degrees of confidence in the accuracy of our interpretations, based on careful, contextual study, because God has given us everything we need in His Word to adequately understand it. So, using our biblically provided lens for Bible-reading (the literal-grammatical-historical hermeneutic), we can find objective truth in God's Word, know it, and live it.

Though authors who promote perspective privilege may argue that objective truth is just an inaccessible "Western ideology" because of the radicalized forces of "socialization,"[89] we know better because we trust God, not man. And God's Word is clear: "It is better to take refuge in the LORD than to trust in man" (Psalm 118:8).

## THE OMNISCIENT MIND OF CHRIST

Having established the Bible as our authoritative source of truth over any other sources, I want to briefly address two more aspects of Scripture that will affect our conversations about ethnicity: illumination and sufficiency. I'll start with illumination.

If it's true that the Bible doesn't privilege certain human perspectives over another, then what is Paul getting at in 1 Corinthians 2:14-16? Paul writes:

> The natural person does not accept the things of the Spirit of God, for they are folly to him, and he is not able to understand them because they are spiritually discerned. The spiritual person judges all things, but is himself to be judged by no one. "For who has understood the mind of the Lord so as to instruct him?" But we have the mind of Christ.

On the surface, it sounds like Paul is breaking up humanity into the *haves* ("spiritual") and the *have-nots* ("natural") and then asserting that the *haves* are the sources of authoritative truth. But read that passage again carefully because that's not exactly what Paul is saying. The truth resides in "the things of the Spirit of God" in "the mind of Christ," which is to say, God's revealed Word. And in quoting Isaiah 40:13, Paul affirms that God's comprehensive knowledge is beyond any of us, despite the revelation He has given. Nobody can pretend to know everything like God does and so claim omniscient objectivity like God can.

But Paul also labors in this passage to make it clear that not everyone has the same kind of response to God's revelation. The "natural person" responds with a rejection of God's Word; he "does not accept" the truths of Scripture. The word in Greek for "does not accept" has to do with welcoming in, like you would a guest to your house.[90] And the natural man won't do that because God's Word is "spiritually discerned"—that is, it requires the indwelling Holy Spirit to be accepted.

What is it about God's Word that non-believers always, without exception, refuse to accept? It's not necessarily mental assent to the facts contained in the words. Plenty of non-believers agree that Abraham existed, that David was king in Israel, and even that Jesus was a real Rabbi in ancient Palestine. So, what won't they accept? The unbelieving, natural heart will always reject the intended application of the Word of God because by their nature, they won't obey God (Rom. 3:10-11; Titus 3:3). As Paul puts it, "For the mind that is set on the flesh is hostile to God, for it does not submit to God's law; indeed, it cannot" (Rom. 8:7).

So, if we put that all together, what we hear Paul saying is that non-believers who do not have the Spirit of God dwelling in them are unable to accept the truths of Scripture, meaning that they will not respond with a right application of Scripture. On the other hand, believers can and will appropriately read and apply Scripture, though to varying degrees. We "judge all things" in light of the truth of God's Word, illumined by the Spirit, and so we have the ability to see truth rightly. Nobody can understand anything rightly unless they see its relationship to the ultimate Reality—God—and only believers have the spiritual enablement to do just that. And we live in light of that understanding given to us by God.

So, in a way, the Bible does create a group of *haves* and a group of *have-nots*. There are those who bow their knee to Jesus, rightly discerning and obeying His Word; and there are those who refuse to obey and, in so doing, completely miss the purpose of God's Word. It's not that unbelievers can't do accurate exegetical work, rightly arriving at the intended meaning of the authors of Scripture. The problem for anyone outside of Christ is that they can't respond to that meaning rightly, and they can't respond rightly because in their sinful, rebellious hearts, they won't. It's a problem of the will, not the mind.

It's worth taking the time to walk through the theological dynamic of the illumination of Scripture because it has huge implications for how we talk about ethnicity in the Church. Many voices in the conversation about ethnic division in the Church would have us lean on not just the Word of God but also on the wisdom of minority groups as a whole, regardless of their spiritual condition. And while I heartily agree with my own need for wisdom from different perspectives, I disagree that "the non-dominant perspective should be given heavier consideration due to the nature of the understanding necessary and provided by minoritized status."[91] Being part of a minority group doesn't supply the applicational insight to Scripture that the Church needs—the illumination of the Spirit does! Likewise, European American Christians are no more privileged in their interpretation and application of Scripture than African American Christians. We all share the same Spirit, Who gives the same life and light to all regardless of our ethnicity.

Too often, non-believers and even the enemies of Christ have been lauded within the Church as wise guides on the topic of ethnic division.[92] But "what partnership has righteousness with lawlessness? Or what fellowship has light with darkness? What accord has Christ with Belial? Or what portion does a believer share with an unbeliever?" (2 Cor. 6:14-15). I'm not saying that I can't learn anything from the non-believing world—most of my formal education as an adult has come from secular sources, for which I am extremely thankful. But we would be foolish to think that the world will give us answers for spiritual problems or that ethnic tension in the Church can be resolved by solutions from outside the Church, like critical race theory and intersectionality. If non-believers can't apply Scripture by the power of the Spirit, then how are they supposed to help us "maintain the unity of the Spirit in the bond of peace" (Eph. 4:3)?

Our solutions to ethnic division in the Church need to come from the Lord of the Church Himself, Jesus Christ. We've been given the mind of Christ through His Word and the Spirit of Christ in our hearts. We should be careful when seeking unity in submission to Christ not to heed the clarion calls of those who refuse to submit to Christ. Instead, we look to His Word for truth and to those who know and apply it well for wisdom, clarity, and help.

## SUFFICIENCY AND SILENCE

My second and related concern is the sufficiency of Scripture. Richard Caldwell dramatically argues for the sufficiency of Scripture this way:

> To state it simply, we believe in the sufficiency of Scripture. It doesn't matter what the problem is. It doesn't matter what controversy you want to discuss. It doesn't matter what issue we want to organize around, and meet around, and think about. The Word of God is sufficient to address the issue.[93]

Now, while I agree with his sentiment, Caldwell's statement requires some nuance. The Westminster Confession of Faith provides a clarifying word on sufficiency:

> The whole counsel of God concerning all things necessary for His own glory, man's salvation, faith and life, is either expressly set down in Scripture, or by good and necessary consequence may be deduced from Scripture: unto which nothing at any time is to be added, whether by new revelations of the Spirit, or traditions of men.[94]

So, when I say that the Bible is sufficient, I don't mean it's an effective manual for replacing the head gaskets on your Chevy Silverado. What I do mean is that every spiritual truth that you need to know in order to glorify God with your life can be found in the sixty-six books of the Old and New Testaments. The Bible contains the Gospel, by which we're redeemed to God's glory, and it holds every precious truth we could need to order our spiritual lives for the glory of God. The Bible is sufficient to help us respond in a godly way to every challenge we can face.

Paul argues for the sufficiency of Scripture to his protegé Timothy when he writes, "All Scripture is breathed out by God and profitable for teaching, for reproof, for correction, and for training in righteousness, that the man of God may be complete, equipped for every good work" (2 Tim. 3:16-17). Complete. Every good work. That's a comprehensive statement because we're dealing with a comprehensive book. The sufficiency of Scripture means that if our souls need it, God said it. Period.

One destructive effect of perspective privilege in the Church is the fear of insufficiency that it can conjure. European American believers who might otherwise engage their African American, Mexican American, or Japanese American brothers and sisters in conversations about ethnicity are silenced by the gnawing fear that they just don't know enough. "I can't ask about that," they might think. "I haven't experienced what my friends have, so how could I possibly understand?" Add to that confusion the pressure from authoritative voices prescribing lengthy reading lists for those uninitiated in ethnic dialogues.[95] Christians who should be speaking words of comfort, seeking genuine understanding, and taking the initiative to care for their fellow believers have shut their mouths in fearful uncertainty.

Add to that dynamic the differing worldviews at play in conversations about race and ethnicity. One group looks back in American history with nostalgia, wishing we could go back to a simpler time, afraid of a future marked by same-sex marriage, on-demand abortion, and wealth redistribution. Another group looks back in American history with horror, longing for a new age to dawn where the stain of American racism has been washed away and replaced with a utopian paradise of progress. If you put those two worldviews in the same conversation, it's easy to see how we can talk past each other, frustrate each other, and eventually silence each other because of our pride in our own perspective. This is not the time for the Church to be silent!

If you have the Bible, you have everything you need to minister to souls. You don't need to become an expert in African American history, critical race theory, or the American criminal justice system to talk about ethnicity today, though there are obviously ways in which extra-biblical study can be helpful. If the Bible is sufficient, then the Bible is what you need. Your required reading list is sixty-six books long—no more, no less.

In case you're skeptical, let me summarize some of the essential truths that God's Word holds for those who want to talk about ethnicity and racism. Most fundamentally, the Bible explains where different people groups came from (Adam, then Noah, then Babel; more on this in chapter three), why they exist (to glorify God through diverse, unified worship—Rom. 15:5-6), and where they're all headed (the throne room of God or the lake of fire—Rev. 7:9-10, 20:7-15). But it goes further than that. The Scriptures explain the roots of racism in the sinful hearts of men (Isa. 59:7-8; Jer. 17:9; Matt. 12:34; Luke 6:45; James 2:9) and how Christ redeems racists through the Gospel to become multi-ethnic bricks in the building of His Church (Eph. 2:11-21; Gal. 3:25-28; 1 Peter 2:4-5). God's Word goes further still to instruct those bricks how to stick together in love and unity (Acts 10:28; Matt. 5-7; Eph. 4:1-16; Phil. 1:27-2:10; Rom. 12:1-21), how to bring comfort to those who are suffering (Job; Psalm 13, 42; 2 Cor. 1:3-7, 4:16-18; 1 Thess. 5:14; 1 Peter 1:6-9), and how to confront sin in the heart (Psalm 51; Rom. 8:13; 1 Cor. 6:18-20, 10:1-13; 2 Cor. 7:10; Rev. 2-3). And maybe best of all, the Bible teaches us about the forgiveness of the cross of Christ, which enables us to step confidently into the lives of our fellow believers without guilt or fear, knowing that even if we say the wrong thing or fail to say the right thing, Jesus will not only reconcile us to Himself but will ultimately unite each of us to each other in perfect harmony (Matt. 18:21-35; Rom. 3:21-26, 14:1-23; 2 Cor. 5:16-21; Col. 1:19-20, 2:6-15; Heb. 10:18-25). Oh, how we need to hear the Word!

Think about how radically united the Church would be if we actually just obeyed the commands of Scripture to "do nothing from selfish ambition or conceit, but in humility count others more significant than yourselves" (Phil. 2:3)! Think about how charitably we could disagree if we first were obedient to "welcome [the one who is weak in faith], but not to quarrel over opinions" (Rom. 14:1). Just think how conspicuously harmonious would be our fellowship halls if we fixed our eyes on our glorious Savior in Heaven and, in so doing, obeyed Paul's commands to the Colossians:

> Put on then, as God's chosen ones, holy and beloved, compassionate hearts, kindness, humility, meekness, and patience, bearing with one another and, if one has a complaint against another, forgiving each other; as the Lord has forgiven you, so you also must forgive. And above all these put on love, which binds everything together in perfect harmony. And let the peace of Christ rule in your hearts, to which indeed you were called in one body (Col. 3:12-15).

Oh, Believer, if only we were bonded together in obedience to God's Word! Then we wouldn't have to look to the world's wisdom to staple us together in a flimsy fraternity of dying causes. If we would privilege God's voice above any others, we would be one under the authority of the Lord Jesus Christ, and that's just where we want to be.

To put it simply: the Bible is sufficient for every matter of the heart, and that matters for Christian hearts. We don't live in fear of not knowing, but we humbly listen and confidently speak as those who have been given "all things that pertain to life and godliness, through the knowledge of him who called us to his own glory and excellence" (2 Peter 1:3). As the apostle John writes:

> I write to you, not because you do not know the truth, but because you know it, and because no lie is of the truth . . . But the anointing [of the Holy Spirit] that you received from him abides in you, and you have no need that anyone should teach you. But as his anointing teaches you about everything, and is true, and is no lie—just as it has taught you, abide in him" (1 John 2:21, 27).

## THE WORD AND OUR WORDS

Remember Jake? I remember him often. And the more I meditate on Jake's objection to biblical truth, the more I recognize the same blind spot in other conversations. When someone says in response to an explanation of Scripture, "That's just your interpretation," or "You couldn't possibly understand," or "Who are you to say?," I've come to realize that the issue isn't my lack of credentials. It's their refusal to acknowledge that God is in the room.

See, when a Christian expounds on the inspired Word, we're no longer just dealing with two finite creatures and their dueling perspectives. God Himself has condescended in His Spirit to attend the delivery of His Divine revelation, whether He is acknowledged or ignored. That's not to say that our interpretations are infallible or free from error—we're always learning and growing by God's grace. But it does mean that the Bible isn't just another book like the one you're reading right now. The eternal Author Who inspired the biblical letters, sentences, paragraphs, and books makes them come powerfully alive in hearts where He dwells. "For the word of God is living and active, sharper than any two-edged sword, piercing to the division of soul and of spirit, of joints and of marrow, and discerning the thoughts and intentions of the heart" (Heb. 4:12).

If that's the truth about the Word, then there can be no true unity without it. Unity in the Church can only come when the people of God share one mind—the mind of Christ, the Word of God. The Bible is absolutely indispensable and uniquely sufficient in our struggle toward ethnic harmony in the Church. While other voices may give us perspectives that help us empathize with those of other ethnicities, only Scripture can unite us in the unchanging truth of God.

I would be remiss if I didn't give God the final word in this chapter. David writes about the inerrant, infallible, sufficient Word of God in Psalms:

> The law of the LORD is perfect, reviving the soul; the testimony
> of the LORD is sure, making wise the simple; the precepts of
> the LORD are right, rejoicing the heart; the commandment of
> the LORD is pure, enlightening the eyes; the fear of the LORD
> is clean, enduring forever; the rules of the LORD are true, and

righteous altogether. More to be desired are they than gold, even much fine gold; sweeter also than honey and drippings of the honeycomb. Moreover, by them is your servant warned; in keeping them there is great reward" (Psalm 19:7-11).

## DISCUSSION QUESTIONS

1.  Do you believe that the Bible is sufficient to address all the pain that racism has caused in your life and in the lives of your fellow Church members?

2.  In what ways, if any, have you substituted merely human voices for the Divine voice of God in the Scriptures? Do you look to the world to teach you about racism and unity? Do you define concepts like racism and unity according to man's definitions or God's?

3.  Read 1 Corinthians 2:14-16. What's the difference between reading the Bible as a non-believer and as a believer? What does the Holy Spirit enable Christians to do in Bible reading? How should that affect your Bible reading?

4.  Are you reading God's Word regularly and sitting under the preaching of God's Word weekly, so that you can be equipped with its sufficient truth? What does a healthy devotional life look like?

5.  How might an unwavering confidence in the power of the Word of God change your conversations about ethnicity? What texts can you think of that apply to the topics of racism, justice, ethnic harmony, and the Church? What would it look like for you to apply those texts to your life this week?

CHAPTER 3

# ETHNICITY AND RACE

## GALATIANS VERSUS ROMANS

After the two best weeks of summer, I despised my best friends.

Summer's Best Two Weeks is the name of a Christian summer camp in southwestern Pennsylvania, where I spent fourteen days as a young teenager learning the limits of my awkward, overweight frame and the power of collective identity. At SB2W (as they call it), I would run around in the woods, struggle through a variety of athletic competitions, stamp my leather lanyard, fear the unknowns of a forty-feet zipline, gorge myself on galley-style camp food, and sing along to the cheesiest nineties' Christian music available. I loved it and hated it all at once and wouldn't for a minute quibble with the camp's overconfident title.

Like anything involving coming-of-age adolescents, SB2W faced the challenge of how to motivate participation in their variety of activities beyond the uncomfortable promise of "purpling"—that is, boys and girls talking. So, campers would be awarded different ranks of S's for successful performance on the soccer field, in the swimming pool, or even in the craft tent. We were already indoctrinated by our school systems into the pursuit of meaningless letters, so it made perfect sense. The year I attended was the opening year for the camp's new site, the "Que" at Quemahoning Reservoir, so we were further incentivized by the regular reminder that we would be the first at everything. And to their credit, I do remember blowing out my hamstring while strenuously trying to be the first chubby kid to complete the long-jump. I honestly don't remember if I did.

But ask any former camper—the ultimate form of motivation at SB2W came from our new tribal identities: the Galatians and the Romans. Upon arrival, we were immediately told which of the two teams we would belong to for the remainder of the camp and issued a blue (Galatians) or red (Romans) t-shirt that would be worn for two weeks without laundering. I was blue. My best friends were red. And the games began.

Regardless of our previous relationships, our newfound group associations defined our enemies and our allies. To the camp's credit, they clearly wanted to foster a spirit of unity among all the campers under the banner of Christ, but we and the college-aged counselors had other ideas. Before long, I had learned our newly minted Galatian team chant (something about *sola fide*), developed secret handshakes with my blue-shirted brethren, and organized clandestine, Galatian-only meetings to plot our ascendancy over the barbaric red army. Blue face paint, blue ribbons, blue shorts, and even blue juice in the dining hall became the placards of our team pride. We competed together; we dined together; and we would die together. The Galatians were my people.

As you can imagine, my unbridled team spirit had a negative impact on my friendships. At first, it was just playful jabs here and there—"Blue rules; red drools," or some other verse of inspired poetry. But eventually it became genuine disinterest, then suspicion, then rejection. The inter-team prank wars escalated, and shaving cream became the vehicle for our angst. The divergence between the teams was so pronounced at points that the Galatian boys even forbade each other from fraternizing with Roman girls. That's right: our group identity actually outweighed the untamed power of teenage hormones.

In the end, I think the Romans won. We got back on the bus, and we acted like none of it had ever happened, our friendships (mostly) restored. No more Galatians or Romans—just some sweaty kids and a potent memory.

## DEFINED BY FICTION

Given the title of this chapter, you've probably already guessed why I dragged you back with me to the heat of a Pennsylvania summer. What I experienced in those two weeks as a team-divided camper parallels our country's far more serious and more deeply divided history of race. Mistrust, anger, aggression, isolation, exclusion, and hatred have characterized the American inter-ethnic experience since before Plymouth Rock. In the historical prelude, we already looked at just a few snapshots of the barbaric treatment of African Americans in our nation's history. The evidence is overwhelming—these United States has been anything but ethnically united. And the debris from our struggle still litters the ethnic landscape of our country, even the hallowed halls of our churches.

But I wanted to take you to my teenage camp warfare days to draw out a more important similarity to the concept of race today, one that we need to come to terms with in order to move forward in the conversation about race. Here it is; are you ready?

The whole thing is made up.

I wasn't born a summer camp Galatian. Nothing about my lineage, my academic performance, my DNA, my external appearance, or even my own preference determined which group of two-week warriors I'd be affixed to. Some camp administrator just put me in one column instead of another; I was handed blue apparel; and my identity was set in polyester.

So it is with race. Race is completely made up. It's an arbitrary group designation assigned by others on the basis of prejudice. It's entirely without grounding in physical reality. In point of fact, there is no such thing as a black person or a white person. Biologically speaking, we're all just different shades of brown, based, in part, on the amount of the pigment melanin in our skin. Race exists only as long as we perpetuate the social designations that comprise it.

Race is a fiction, through and through, designed historically to deny people of dignity, rights, and worth. From its inception, the construct of race has been an instrument of division, oppression, and genocide unlike any other ideological force. Undeniably and horrifically, the fabrication of race has destroyed whole families, cultures, and countries for the last four hundred years of world history, propped up by faulty pseudo-science and bigoted lies.

Friends, race is nothing more than a sweaty camp t-shirt, and we need to throw it out.

Now, those may sound like strong claims, but stay with me, and I'll show you why we need this racial reality check. I want to go back and look at some of the architects behind the construct of race and how the concept of race developed over time. Then I want to show you how the Bible defines humanity and how Christ redeems a new people for Himself from every tribe and tongue and nation of humanity. What we'll find (in the book of Galatians, oddly enough) is that while the wicked forces behind the construct of race continue to alienate believers today, Jesus keeps tearing down every wall that would divide His diverse Bride. In Christ, our fictional groupings give way to our spiritual family, and the lies of race are replaced with harmonious, multi-ethnic worship to Jesus.

We won't be defined by race, but we also can't be ignorant to its long wake of destruction. Out of the ashes of racial division, Christ will bring multi-ethnic unity to His Church.

## ORIGINS ERASED

Before jumping into the history of the concept of race, let me clearly state the truth about human origins from Scripture. God tells us in the first chapter of the Bible that mankind came from God's creative act, that we were spoken into existence in an instant by the transcendent, benevolent Creator (Gen. 1:26-27). And when God created mankind, He did not create separate species or races, but He made one man and one woman—Adam and Eve (Gen. 2:7-22) who are everyone's ancestors (Gen. 3:20). Every single

ETHNICITY AND RACE 95

person who has ever existed came from Adam and Eve, and Eve came from Adam's rib (Gen. 2:21-22). That's why Paul says to the Athenians, "And he made from one man every nation of mankind to live on all the face of the earth" (Acts 17:26). So, any method of grouping human beings that doesn't start from this simple, fundamental, historical, biological reality is building on a foundation of sand.

The first sandcastle architect to propose the concept of race was Carl Linnaeus (or Carl von Linné), a Swedish botanist and zoologist who has been called "the father of modern taxonomy." He was considered by his contemporaries to be one of the most brilliant, influential scientists of his day.[96] In his 1735 work *Systema Naturae*, Linnaeus laid out the biological hierarchy system that we still teach in elementary science class today—Kingdom, Phylum, Class, Order, etc.—which in his day was revolutionary.[97][k]

Unfortunately, Linnaeus also tried to apply this same taxonomic framework to people. Linnaeus coined the term "homo sapiens" to describe the human species but went on to divide humans into four subspecies: *europeaus, afer, asiaticus*, and *americanus*.[98] He described the members of *homo europeaus* as "of fair complexion, sanguine temperament and becoming form . . . of gentle manners, acute in judgment . . . governed by fixed laws," while he described members of *homo afer* as of "black complexion, phlegmatic temperament . . . crafty, indolent . . . governed in their actions by caprice."[99] And don't miss this—Linnaeus presented his racial categorization of human beings as *scientific* explanations grounded in *biological* reality. So began the twisted history of the construct of race.[100][l]

---

k   Not only did Linnaeus' system gain prominence in Europe, but it also made its way across the ocean to the colonies and profoundly impacted how the fathers of the American Revolution thought about race.

l   I'm aware that Francois Bernier is recognized as the first to group humanity on the basis of scientific classifications akin to race in 1684 and that even before him, in 1453, Gomes de Zurara began grouping people into something like racial categories in order to justify slavery. But Linnaeus' work became the source material for "race science" in the following centuries, and so it makes sense to start with him. Also, I will inevitably leave out many of significant figures in my brief survey on the history of race.

Linnaeus' human taxonomy quickly snowballed into further attempts to scientifically categorize different races of humans. In the late eighteenth century, Johann Blumenbach picked up Linnaeus' bucket of sand and poured out a fifth racial classification based on craniology, the study of skull size. His five categories were: Caucasians, Mongolians, Ethiopians, Americans, and Malays. Blumenbach coined the term Caucasians to describe the subgroup of humanity that, according to him, originated in the Caucasus Mountain range in Eastern Europe. He called the Caucasian skull "most handsome and becoming" and argued that their fair skin color "we may fairly assume to have been the primitive colour[sic] of mankind."[101] Samuel George Morton took the torch of craniology from Blumenbach into the nineteenth century and continued to assert that racial differences could be proven by differences in skull size, which he correlated to brain size and, thereby, intelligence. Caucasians, he determined, had the largest skulls.[102]

With the foundations of sand cranially established, the race-based fiction of evolution could begin construction. Charles Darwin's predecessor, Robert Chambers, anonymously published a work titled *Vestiges of the Natural History of Creation* in 1844, in which he used Blumenbach's racial categories to argue for hierarchies of more—and less-evolved—human races.[103] Chambers wrote:

> Our brain . . . passes through the characters in which it appears in the Negro, Malay, American and Mongolian nations, and finally is Caucasian. The leading characters, in short, of the various races of mankind, are simply representatives of particular stages in the development of the highest or Caucasian type . . . The Mongolian is an arrested infant, newly born.[104]

Fifteen years later, English biologist Charles Darwin cemented the hierarchical understanding of race as an evolutionary necessity in his famous work, *On the Origin of Species*. The full title of that still-celebrated book is *On the Origin of Species by Means of Natural Selection, or the Preservation of Favoured Races in the Struggle for Life*. In it, Darwin argued that the astounding diversity of life that we see on earth is not the product of the creative act of a Divine being but of natural processes like selection, mutation, isolation, and environmental factors.[105] Knowing how potentially volatile his ideas could be, Darwin only briefly referenced humanity in connection with his evolutionary theory but cryptically noted that in time, "Light will be thrown on the origin of man and his history."[106]

According to Darwin, that light came in 1871 with the publication of his own volume entitled *The Descent of Man, and Selection in Relation to Sex*. In this work, Darwin took Blumenbach's racial classifications and blended them with his theories about biological evolution to further entwine the construct of race with faulty scientific explanations.[107] Because mankind had evolved from simian ancestors, argued Darwin, the "lower" or "savage" races were simply less-evolved and, therefore, in many ways, more ape-like than human. According to Darwin:

> At some future period, not very distant as measured by centuries, the civilized races of man will almost certainly exterminate and replace the savage races throughout the world. At the same time, the anthropomorphous apes . . . will no doubt be exterminated. The break between man and his nearest allies will then be wider, for it will intervene between man in a more civilized state, as we may hope, even . . . than the Caucasian, and some ape as low as a baboon, instead of as now between the negro or Australian and the gorilla.[108]

To clarify, Darwin imagined a future where certain races of man continue to evolve to such a degree that they have as much in common with other less-evolved human races as Europeans have with apes, instead of being close in Darwin's evolutionary development like Africans, Aboriginal Australians, and gorillas. And just in case it's still not clear how shockingly racist Darwin's views were, look at his own words in the conclusion of *The Descent of Man*: "For my own part, I would as soon be descended from that heroic little monkey . . . or from that old baboon . . . as from a savage."[109] Given the option,

Darwin would have preferred that his grandparents were monkeys rather than Africans.

These are the architects of the shifting sandcastle of race. Beginning from the premise that God did not make man, they followed their speculations to their logical, hateful conclusions. But they weren't motivated by scientific curiosity alone; they were unmistakably shaped by their own racist worldview. Their own prejudices gave birth to the lies of racial categorizations that have so painfully affected our world. They fabricated a whole subset of pseudo-science to justify their supremacist bigotry. As Ta-Nehisi Coates puts it, "Race is the child of racism, not the father."[110]

## EVOLUTION EMBRACED

It shouldn't surprise us, then, that the rotten roots of race in our history continued to bear the bitter fruits of racial hatred, partiality, and bigotry. Stephen Jay Gould, an evolutionist, wrote, "Biological arguments for racism may have been common before 1859 [the year that Darwin published *On the Origin of Species*], but they increased by orders of magnitude following the acceptance of evolutionary theory."[111] And its violent impact has proven to be ghastly.

Perhaps more than any other premise, evolution fueled the fires of racism into an inferno that has engulfed the last 150 years of human relations. Charles Darwin's own half-cousin, Francis Galton, the man who first used fingerprints to trace criminals, was also the founder of the harrowing study of eugenics. Galton said that the goal of eugenics was "to check the birth rate of the Unfit and improve the race by furthering the productivity of the fit by early marriages of the best stocks."[112] He wanted to ensure that the "right" races kept procreating and that the "wrong" races died childless.

In the early twentieth century, Galton's work, along with Darwin's, became the basis for German embryologist Ernst Haeckel's efforts to apply the ideas of evolution to social change in Germany. In contrast to his predecessors, he saw Germans specifically as the apex of the evolutionary chain. Haeckel wrote, "The Germans have deviated furthest from the common form of ape-like men . . . The lower races are psychologically nearer to the animals than to civilized Europeans. We must, therefore, assign a totally different value to their lives."[113] Elsewhere, Haeckel also wrote, "I consider the Negro to be a lower species of man and cannot make up my mind to look upon him as 'a man and a brother,' for the gorilla would then also have to be admitted into the family."[114]

Haeckel's views influenced a generation of young Germans, among whom was an art student named Adolf Hitler. Hitler's manifesto *Mein Kampf* (translated *My Struggle*) stated:

> It will be the task of the People's State to make the [preferred German] race the centre[sic] of the life of the community. It must make sure that the purity of the racial strain will be preserved . . . It must see to it that only those who are healthy shall beget children; that there is only one infamy, namely, for parents that are ill or show hereditary defects to bring children into the world and that in such cases it is a high honour[sic] to refrain from doing so.[115]

By 1936, under the direction of Hitler and his Nazi Party, the German Society for Race Hygiene implemented eugenics practices[116] that would evolve into the unthinkable, systematic murder of millions of Jews. And the basis of the entire argument was the preservation of the purity of a fictional category called race.

America wasn't immune to the sickness of these same evolutionary ideas. Dr. Hornady, the director of the Bronx Zoological Gardens in 1906, displayed a captured Central African man named Ota Benga in the same cage as the apes because in his view, there was "a close analogy of the African savage to the apes"[117] based on "a hierarchical view of the races." By 1914, children across America were being taught these racist ideologies through their textbooks, like George William Hunter's *A Civic Biology Presented in Problems*, which said,

"At the present time there exists upon the earth five races . . . the highest type of all, the Caucasians, represented by the civilized white inhabitants of Europe and America."[118] The Jim Crow laws themselves were born out of the desire to preserve the "purity" of the races and that wicked ideology kept African and European Americans segregated for over a century.

Perhaps the saddest impact of evolutionary concepts of race has been in the professing Christian world. For instance, in 1956, a traveling evangelist named John Rice argued against interracial marriage, saying, "Socially, it is better for both Negroes and whites to run with their own kind and intermarry with their own kind. The mixing of races widely differing is almost never wise."[119] Bob Jones University, founded as a fundamentalist Christian college, went so far as to prohibit interracial dating from its inception in 1927 until 2000.[120] Former school president Bob Jones III said in defense of the policy, "There are three basic races—Oriental, Caucasian, and Negroid. At BJU, everybody dates within those basic three races." And in 1998, just before the policy was changed, a spokesman for BJU said, "God has made people different from one another and intends those differences to remain. Bob Jones University is opposed to intermarriage of the races because it breaks down the barriers God has established."[121]

Using God and the Bible as a justification for racist ideologies was nothing new. The biblical boogieman in much of America's history of racial slavery was the so-called "Curse of Ham" from Genesis 9:25. In that passage, Noah pronounces a curse on Ham's son, Canaan, saying, "Cursed be Canaan; a servant of servants shall he be to his brothers." On the basis of this verse, slave-owners would postulate that all their African slaves were descendants of Ham (they were not) and must therefore continue to be slaves per Noah's pronouncement. It was in their blood to remain enslaved, slave-owners argued. The vice president of the Confederacy, Alexander Stephens, claimed in a speech that "the negro by nature, or by the curse against Canaan, is fitted for that condition which he occupies in our system."[122] This erroneous exegesis and evolutionary thinking promoted division, racism, and hatred, rather than the biblical mandates of unity, humility, and love. And they did it all on a foundation of sand: the myth of race.

## SCIENTIFICALLY BASELESS

As Christians, we need to respond to the lies of the construct of race with the truth of the Word of God. As we've already noted, Moses tells us in Genesis exactly where man came from (God's creation of Adam and Eve), which means that man did not evolve in separate races over the course of millions of years but descends from one man. According to Scripture, we are all from the same gene pool, and there is no such thing as a biologically superior race—or race at all. So, if the Bible says there's no such thing as biological race, then that's it. Case closed, right?

Well, the story of mankind's profound racial lie didn't end with the Civil Rights Act. Though the UNESCO statement of July 1950 pronounced race as a social category,[123] it's only been in the past few decades that scientists have begun to condemn the concept of race as fictional, factional, and unhelpful. This advance has largely come through the field of genetics. In 2000, the Human Genome Project declared that on the basis of "the entire sequence of the human genome . . . there is only one race—the human race."[124] Other scientists have since chimed in, saying, "The concept of 'race' from a genetic standpoint has been abolished,"[125] and "there is absolutely no genetic or evolutionary justification for 'racial' categories of humans."[126] In fact, one scientist argues, "The genetic variation within each of the various ethnic groups of *Homo sapiens* is greater than that between the various ethnic groups."[127]

Did you catch that? At the level of our DNA, we have more in common with people from other ethnic groups than we do from people in our own ethnic groups. Genetically speaking, we're only .1 to .2 percent genetically different from any other human being on the planet anyway, and even those differences don't fall along the lines of socially constructed races.[128] That is

102 A HOUSE WITHOUT WALLS

to say, skin color, hair texture, nose width, eye shape, and thousands of other physical traits are not distributed neatly into arbitrary group designations like "white," "black," and "Asian." Despite the persistence of those categories in our national census,[129] they are essentially meaningless when it comes to defining who we are physically! Even an evolution-affirming science journalist contends, "The true human story . . . appears to be not of pure races rooted in one place for tens of thousands of years, but of ongoing mixing, with migration constantly changing geographical directions . . . Almost everyone on the planet is the descendent of a migrant somewhere."[130]

So, if that's true, how *do* secular scientists conceive of race? The American Association for the Advancement of Science put out a statement in 1997 saying, "Race is a social construct derived mainly from the perceptions conditioned by events of recorded history, and it has no basic biological reality."[131] For scientists who study genetics more broadly, they've noticed that genetic variation occurs much more widely among other species, like invertebrates and apes. Remarking on this phenomena, geneticist Steve Jones writes, "For a snail or an orangutan it makes good biological sense to be a racist, but humans have to accept the fact they belong to a tediously uniform species."[132] That is to say, racism makes less sense than snail prejudice.

One brief story can illustrate the absurdity of trying to use meaningless categories of race in our society. In 1987, a woman from Virginia sued the company where she worked because she perceived that they were discriminating against her because she was black. The judge didn't buy her argument because she had red hair, so she lost the case. Later, while working for a black employer, she sued him for racist behavior against her because she was white. She lost that case as well because the court said that as an alumna of a historically black school, she couldn't possibly be white.[133] Apparently, even legal definitions of race aren't so black and white.

Defining ethnicities or people groups is a notoriously difficult task without widespread agreement. Some contend that there's much overlap between the terms "race" and "ethnicity," while others say they are entirely distinct. Several definitions of ethnicity even include the word "race." Because Scripture frequently uses the Greek word *ethnos* to refer to people groups identified as nations, for our purposes we will use the *Oxford English Dictionary's* definition, which says that ethnicity is "the fact or state of belonging to a social group that has a common national or cultural tradition."[134]

To call race "scientifically baseless" is accurate but an understatement. Because of the long history of false scientific justifications defending racial categories and because of the incalculable damage these lies have caused, the propagation of the concept of race as an instrument of division is not only baseless but outright immoral. Instead, we ought to recognize cultural, religious, linguistic, and geographic differences as *ethnic*, meaning tied to self-identified people groups.[135] Though humans come from distant countries, adopt distinct fashions, and worship in disparate ways, we are all one biological race descended from Adam, who was made by God. All people share in a profound heritage, and according to Scripture, that has profound implications for human dignity.

## DIGNITY FROM THE DIVINE

Now, once we begin to talk about dignity, we've moved out of the realm of what scientists and sociologists can explain. Human dignity can only come from God. Inherent worth and value, the basis of human dignity, can't come from mankind because we don't define what's inherently valuable. God does. And in Scripture, God shows us that human beings have two fundamental reasons to affirm our individual dignity—our source and our purpose.

First, people have dignity because we are made by God. Not only were the first human beings created by God from dust and rib, but the Bible says that God is sovereignly responsible for the procreation of every single person. David writes in Psalm 139:13-14, "For you formed my inward parts; you knitted me together in my mother's womb. I praise you, for I am fearfully and wonderfully made. Wonderful are your works; my soul knows it very well." Job likewise calls out to God, saying, "You clothed me with skin and flesh, and knit me together with bones and sinews. You have granted me life and steadfast love, and your care has preserved my spirit" (Job 10:11-12). God is intimately involved in the construction of every human being, from the first to the last. He's the source, ever and always.

Knowing that God is responsible for giving us life grants each person astounding dignity and worth. Here's how Job works out this reasoning:

> "If I have rejected the cause of my manservant or my maidservant, when they brought a complaint against me, what then shall I do when God rises up? When he makes inquiry, what shall I answer him? Did not he who made me in the womb make him? And did not one fashion us in the womb?" (Job 31:13-15).

How stinging a rebuke would this verse have been to American slave-owners abusing their fellow man! God is the slave-owner's Source, *and* God is the slave's Source; and that, Job argues, means that nobody is permitted before God to mistreat anyone else. When God judges us ("rises up," "makes inquiry"), He will hold us accountable for how we treated all those whom He made in the womb.

It's like when I play blocks with my son; he could care less what happens with the wooden block towers that I build. But if I so much as breathe on the heap of bricks he's meticulously ordered, the sheriff comes to town. We care more about what we ourselves have made. All people have inherent dignity because they aren't just the fizz from a cosmic belch but the masterfully designed, carefully assembled handiwork of the Creator, and He cares deeply for His own craftsmanship.

Second, our dignity comes from our purpose—that we were made by God to reflect God as His image-bearers. This is one of the first things we hear about mankind in the Bible before we even learn about Adam being sculpted from the dust. Moses writes, "So God created man in his own image, in the image of God he created him; male and female he created them" (Gen. 1:27). Much ink has been spilled on what the *imago dei*, or image of God, actually means;[m] but regardless of the full extent, we can at least assert two truths about it:

1.   Man is supposed to, in some way, show or reflect or display something about God; that's just what "image" means.[136]

2.   Man has inherent worth as the handiwork of God, such that people deserve to be treated with respect and protected from violence.

I arrive at that second conclusion from two passages. When Noah steps off the ark and God establishes a new world for him and his descendants to inhabit, God explains to Noah, "From his fellow man I will require a reckoning for the life of man. 'Whoever sheds the blood of man, by man shall his blood be shed, for God made man in his own image'" (Gen. 9:5-6). Notice God's logic in establishing this basic principle of retributive justice: Because people are made in the image of God, their life is of such a value that to sinfully steal it requires an equal restitution. You take a life; your life is taken; and this principle is grounded in the image of God in man.

The second passage that substantiates the worth of man in the image of God takes the argument a step further. James writes, "But no human being can tame the tongue. It is a restless evil, full of deadly poison. With it we bless our Lord and Father, and with it we curse people who are made in the likeness of God" (James 3:8-9). While James is less explicit with his language, the implication is hard to miss. Because people are made in the image of God, even just trash-talking someone is an evil act. So, it's not only murder that the image of God prohibits, but also malicious insults and gossip. The dignity afforded to people through the Divine imprint is so all-encompassing that it naturally opposes not only the physical violence of manslaughter but also the spiritual violence of slander.

---

m   For more on this, see Anthony Hoekema's excellent book on the topic, *Created in God's Image*.

Here's another illustration with my son to clarify. We've got dozens of books on a shelf in our living room that are just for my son. If he looks through one of those books—say, *The Lorax*—and bends the pages, bends the cover, or even doodles on the illustrations, I won't make a big deal about it. If he tried to rip the thing in two or throw it in the trash, I'd intervene, but he can mark up his books all he wants because they're cheap and they're for him to enjoy, anyway. But when my son grabs my Bible—the one with all my notes in the margins from most of my Christian life, the one I had rebound a few years ago just so I could keep using it—and comes at it with a crayon and a wild glint in his eye, I'm shutting him down. In fact, whenever he looks through my Bible (which I love for him to do!), I'm watching him carefully the entire time just to make sure he doesn't rip the pages. I'm careful with my Bible because that book is precious to me.

James says that the image of God in man is such a pervasive source of value, worth, and dignity that we need to take extraordinary care not to hurt or damage our fellow image-bearers, even in the slightest way. Animals, though also crafted by God's hand, don't receive this same level of value and worth in the eyes of God. Neither do plants. But God sees fit to issue orders to protect human beings because our whole person is so inherently valuable.

And this dignity afforded to mankind goes beyond just physical protection; it extends to the protection of our hearts. We dare not assault even with our words a vessel so precious! Instead, we handle each other with care. We affirm the dignity inherent in man through the image of God by treating each other with respect, speaking to each other with kindness, and treating our fellow image-bearers as valuable in the sight of God.

This dignity transcends ethnic boundaries, cultural distinctions, and countries of origin. It transcends preferences, friend groups, and political alliances. It even transcends the Church. All people, believers and unbelievers alike are deserving of this basic kindness, love, and deference because all people are created in the image of God. Nobody has more of God's image or less, but all are equal as created vessels for God to display His own glory. A DNA panel can't teach you about this profound dignity baked into humanity any more than a demographic survey or a racial label. Our worth comes from God, is explained by God's Word, and is even written by God on our hearts. These truths are indeed self-evident.

## BABEL'S DIVIDING DIASPORA

What may be less self-evident, however, is how the image-bearers of God came to take on such a wide variety of appearances, languages, cultures, and political identities. Why are so many on earth so different from each other if we all came from one man? To explain where ethnic differences came from, we need to go back to Genesis, before Abraham and Isaac and Jacob but after the worldwide flood. We need to find out what happened at the Tower of Babel.

> And the LORD said, "Behold, they are one people, and they have all one language, and this is only the beginning of what they will do. And nothing that they propose to do will now be impossible for them. Come, let us go down and there confuse their language, so that they may not understand one another's speech." So the LORD dispersed them from there over the face of all the earth, and they left off building the city. Therefore its name was called Babel, because there the LORD confused the language of all the earth. And from there the LORD dispersed them over the face of all the earth (Gen. 11:6-9).

Almost eighteen hundred years after the global judgment of the flood, mankind had once again grown numerous and once again turned their backs to God. A unique feature of this time is that there didn't appear to be anything like distinct nations, people groups, or cultures because, as God said, "'They are one people, and they have all one language.'" I imagine this was about as close as humanity came to living out John Lennon's version of utopia from his song, "Imagine." There were no ethnic or racial tensions because there were no ethnicities or racial constructs. And in a world without sinners, that might have actually worked well. But like our world today, Babel was full of sinners. In their pride, they sought to oppose God and build a brick structure that could outlast another cataclysmic flood by rising above the waters, thereby surprising and outsmarting God.

God is never surprised.

Rather than knocking down their sand construction project, however, God had another plan. This plan was complex beyond imagining, global in its scope, and long-term in its payoff. God divided up all people on earth by scattering them across the continents and separating them with a new barrier—languages. So, God drove the people apart, confounded their communication, and distributed them across globe.

The Tower of Babel reminds us that God is sovereign, God created languages, and in so doing, God established ethnicity. To be sure, the sin of man was the presenting reason that provoked God to action, but God had determined before time to deal with mankind in this way. He knew that ethnic distinctions would lead to an almost un-paused history of warfare on the earth. He knew that men would pervert these distinctions to design social constructs for the purposes of oppression. He knew that America today would be divided by ethnicity, and yet He made it, anyway. Surely, then, he must have had a grander plan in mind that could somehow make all of this pain and division worth it.

And, of course, He did.

## YOU CAN BE A NEW MAN

In the Jewish calendar, Pentecost marked the end of the barley harvest and the beginning of the wheat harvest. In Exodus 34:22, it was called "The Feast of Weeks" because it occurred seven weeks after Passover, when the barley harvest would begin. Pentecost marked the end of a season and the beginning of a new one.[137] In His sovereign plan, God ordained that one

Pentecost in particular would signal the beginning of something altogether new in the story of God's redemption—the Church.

Nine days after Jesus' ascension to the right hand of the Father, His disciples were waiting for the Holy Spirit to come. And in a moment, flaming tongues fell on the believers, and they received the gift of speaking in foreign languages they otherwise had never known (Acts 2:1-4). So, they took to the streets of Jerusalem, which were filled with Jews from all over the Roman Empire because of the feast, and they began to speak. As they spoke, Egyptian Jews and Phrygian Jews and Roman Jews all heard these disciples declaring the power of Jesus Christ in their own native languages (Acts 2:5-11). Despite the incredulity of the crowd, Peter preached Christ crucified; three thousand were saved; and the Church was born (Acts 2:12-47).

When you've read about what happened at Pentecost, have you ever wondered, "Why tongues?" Of all the miraculous signs that God could use to authenticate the witness of His Son's disciples, why break the language barrier?

At Pentecost, God empowered His nascent Church with His Spirit to signal that the time had come to reverse the judgment of Babel. The New Covenant Church, unlike Old Covenant Israel, would not be ethnocentric. God's people would no longer be nationally, geographically, and politically one. Joining the Church wouldn't require a green card. The Church would be made up of people from every ethnicity. Language would no longer separate God's people from the world. Now, God's people would unite across language differences in the common bond of Christ. One author writes:

> At Pentecost, the festival of the firstfruits of the harvest, the church received the firstfruits of cosmic redemption when the Holy Spirit was poured out equally upon all flesh (Acts 2:1-4). The miracle of tongues, where everyone heard the Gospel in his own language (v. 5-11), provided evidence God was breaking down the cultural and ethnic division imposed at Babel . . . [defining the church] not by tongue or culture but by common faith in the Messiah.[138]

At last, in the Church, we begin to see the fulfillment of Psalm 67:5: "Let the peoples praise you, O God; let all the peoples praise you!" In the Church, God brings together what He tore apart at Babel. Through the sending of His Spirit, God draws together those who were sent apart and creates one new man out of the many. God gathers multilingual praise to Himself through the establishment of the multiethnic Church, such that the whole earth begins to resound with worship to their Creator. In the Church, God glorifies Himself through a rich tapestry of precious image-bearers from every ethnicity, and He does all of it in the person of Jesus Christ.

In fact, Paul explains God's grand plan for ethnicity in His letter to the Galatian church when he writes, "For as many of you as were baptized into Christ have put on Christ. There is neither Jew nor Greek, there is neither slave nor free, there is no male and female, for you are all one in Christ Jesus" (Gal. 3:27-28). Paul's phrase "baptized into Christ" literally means "immersed into Christ." This is not the language of water baptism (though water baptism symbolizes this) but of spiritual union. And for those who have been united to Christ through faith, they have "put on," or "dressed themselves," in Christ. Jesus uses this word in a direct reference to Pentecost, that the disciples would be "clothed with power from on high" (Luke 24:49). Our new clothing, that which adorns and defines us in the Church, is Christ. All other categories become, at best, secondary.

Paul uses the same word for "put on" in Colossians 3:10-11 in a similar way:

> And [you all] have *put on* the new self, which is being renewed in knowledge after the image of its creator. Here there is not Greek and Jew, circumcised and uncircumcised, barbarian, Scythian, slave, free; but Christ is all, and in all.

Notice how, once again, Paul connects the "putting on" of a new identity with the demotion of our other identifiers. Certainly, Paul isn't arguing here that ethnic differences are entirely erased in Christ—he recounts his own Jewish pedigree to the Philippians (Phil. 3:5). But in comparison with his new

ETHNICITY AND RACE 111

identity in Christ, Paul says that it's almost as if those cultural distinctions don't exist at all. Elsewhere, he even counts those associations as "loss" (Phil. 3:7).

Paul declares that Christ is the Christian's all-consuming reality. Our internal, spiritual union with Christ outranks our external, human associations. Ethnic alignment, religious background, language groups, social class, and even biological sex become the background for Christ's glorious work in the foreground. "Christian" tells you far more about who I truly am than "American." Today, we might say of the Church, "Here there is not black and white, majority and minority, Spanish-speaker, Korean-speaker, rich, or poor; but Christ is all, and in all."

Did you catch Paul's reference to the image of God in Colossians 3:10? Not only does our new identity in Christ supersede everything else about us, but it's also the canvas where God masterfully restores His own image in us. That which sin has marred in us, God will renew in us. And He'll continue to restore that image in each of His people from every ethnicity until the choir of Heaven is filled with a rainbow of redeemed sinners conformed perfectly to the image of Christ (Rom. 8:28-29; 1 John 3:2).

This was God's plan for ethnicity from the beginning. From Babel to Pentecost, from Pentecost to Glory. One race of mankind from thousands of language groups and cultures glorifying the Lamb Who was slain because He has ransomed for Himself a people from every tribe and tongue and nation to be a kingdom and priests to God as they reign on the earth (Rev. 5:9-10). And right now, in this era of redemptive history, those people are called the Church. H. B. Charles writes:

> The blood of Jesus Christ has created a new race of man. It is called the church. Christian baptism identifies us with this new race . . . This does not mean Christians ignore, deny, or trivialize ethnic identity. It means our ethnic identity does not define us.[139]

Christ defines Christians, not ethnicity. But the gift of this astounding new identity raises one more important question that we need to address.

## COLOR-BLIND AND COLOR-CONSCIOUS

Conversations about race in America can often end with a sentence that sounds like this: "I just don't see people like that. I don't think of my friends as black or white or Latino. They're just my friends." Maybe you've been in one of those conversations, or maybe you yourself have said something like that. Allow me to argue for a little bit of nuance.

As we just read, in Christ, "there is neither Jew nor Greek." Our identification with Christ is so significant and life-defining that our ethnicities, according to Paul, are nearly non-existent by comparison. So, in a sense, it's right and appropriate to be "color-blind," insofar as we recognize and rejoice in our new identity in Christ as primary. When Christians see other Christians, they should see past skin color, nationality, language, clothing, and cultural expressions to value their fellow image-bearers and love their fellow new creations in Christ (2 Cor. 5:17). Even more than that, we ought to refuse to define each other on the basis of "color" (which I take to mean "race") because, as we've discussed, race is a biological fiction and an arbitrary, oppressive social construct. Christians logically should refuse to buy into the world's evolutionary system of human categorization because we know it's made up and harmful.

If we fail to treat each other's *spiritual* condition as primary, we also run the risk of overemphasizing our differences, and that can have dire consequences. Segregated churches, for example, can arise from outright racism or, more subtly, from placing an inordinate importance on ethnic distinction and undervaluing our common redemption. In this vein, it makes sense for Christians to look beyond our social and cultural differences to revel in the union we share in Christ. If color-blindness means close, familial love that sees each other as brothers and sisters rather than racial representatives, then color-blindness is not only preferable but biblical (Matt. 12:46-50).

In recent years, however, color-blind Christians have been criticized for ignoring the obvious and, in some cases, rightly so. Wholesale, willful ignorance about another person's racial categorization isn't holy; it's naive.

To acknowledge that the world sees everyone through an unhelpful racial lens isn't necessarily an endorsement of race as a concept. I can weep with you when you've been slandered without giving credence to the lies that hurt you. But I'll be hard-pressed to empathize with your pain if I'm unwilling to acknowledge that slander has happened. We all want to love our brothers and sisters in Christ with Christlike affection, but how can we sympathize like our Savior if we intentionally ignore a significant, shaping influence like race in our fellow Christian's lives?

Imagine for a second that you grew up in a family that always wore teal turtlenecks in public. No matter the season, no matter the venue, when people saw you, they saw you in your teal turtleneck. Over time, you would probably get some nicknames, undoubtedly some comments about your wardrobe choices, and maybe even some odd fashion hostility from the less sensitive. It may even change who would be willing to date you or spend time with you because you're "that weird turtleneck person." That teal turtleneck would have a meaningful impact on your life, even though it came from your family's arbitrary, made-up clothing preferences.

So it is with race. We are born into a society that treats you differently based on how you look, not on who you are. Some of the consequences of the socio-political construct of race are insignificant, but some are devastating. Imagine trying to tell W.E.B. Dubois that you "just don't see race" as he's being forcibly ejected from a "whites only" restaurant. If you ignore race altogether, how could you empathize with Booker T. Washington climbing up out of slavery? How could you even begin to minister to Elie Wiesel, an Auschwitz survivor, unless you agree that racial categories have significant meaning in his life? We hate it, but the lie of race has had and continues to have a profound impact on people from every background. It can hurt our brothers and sisters when we refuse to acknowledge such a formative force in their walk on this earth. We would be fools to bury our heads in colorless sand. Isaac Adams puts it this way:

Complete colorblindness cannot be the final step in our love because it requires ignoring God-ordained realities about people—realities that shape our joys, fears, experiences, and make us who we are. We love when people share themselves with us, and their experiences enable them to do so. Thus, Christians do need some balance of color-consciousness in the church because God does see and value the worlds he's made us to live in. He created our colors. He loves them! They bring him great glory in all the earth, and his glorification is what he wants.[140]

That being said, we ought to be careful to not let color-consciousness overtake and undermine our biblical anthropology. While we recognize the influence of the social concepts of race, we must deny its grounding in physical reality and reject subtle attempts to reinforce racial ideologies in the Church. It's possible, in the name of humble sensitivity and Christlike love, to so emphasize the effects of racism that we inadvertently entrench ourselves deeper in the racial rut. For example, when our calls for "racial reconciliation" involve lifelong cycles of white awareness and white repentance or black dignity and black action, we will (perhaps unwittingly) train each other to make race our primary identity. If our framework for unity in Christ means focusing on fictional human categories, we've missed something truly fundamental. H.B. Charles writes:

> To the degree we have allowed secondary things . . . to become primary, we inevitably see corresponding degrees of division. The truth is that it is impossible for us to be one if we are focusing on anything but the Lord Jesus Christ.[141]

So, I would argue that we ought to be both color-blind and color-conscious. Though it's possible to go too far in either direction, we can't afford to be ignorant of race or focused on it. We reject the fiction of racial distinctions and warmly run to embrace each other primarily as fellow Christ-followers. And we do it because we believe that Christ will continue to build His multi-ethnic Church, to tear down the walls that divide her, and to bring us all to Himself as one body by His death on the cross.

## ZOO DOCTRINE OR DIVINE ADOPTION

Recently, my wife and I took our kids to gawk at the animals at the National Zoo in Northwest D.C., as people do. The lions slept; the panda played; and the zebra trotted along. My son's favorite animals were the monkeys, most of whom were housed in a brick building called the "Think Tank," along with dozens of brains of varying sizes. Fin whale brains, shrew brains, Asian elephant brains, orangutan brains, and yes, human brains, too.

I stopped to read a prominent bulletin board inside the Think Tank labeled "What's Size Got to Do with It?" featuring various pictures of animals and their brain sizes. *In our racially sensible age*, I thought, *surely, the nation's leading zoologists and anthropologists will clarify that brain size does not, in fact, correlate with intelligence. That's in the past, buried with eugenics and the Third Reich. Nobody believes any of that today.* I was wrong.

Despite the rightful death of race science at the hands of genetics, scientists have pried open its coffin, exhumed Darwin's racial skeletons, and displayed once again the Frankenstein of scientific racism to justify their dogmatic faith in evolution. Canadian researchers claimed in 2002 that "brain size-related variables provide the most likely biological mediators of the race differences in intelligence."[142] Another study published in 2005 by the American Psychological Association stated that "the new evidence reviewed . . . points to some genetic component in Black–White differences in mean IQ."[143] And as recently as 2016, Scientific American boldly asserted that "brain size accounts for between 9 and 16 percent of the overall variability in general intelligence,"[144] with brain size demarcated along racial lines. Faulty "scientific findings" like these continue to prop up baseless, racist arguments like *Mankind Quarterly's*[n] recent paper declaring that higher COVID-19 mortality rates among black people can be attributed to their genetically-determined

---

n    The history of *Mankind Quarterly* goes back to 1961 and ties directly into multiple white supremacist, alt-right groups known for their notorious racism. Angela Saini tracks the development of *Mankind Quarterly* and its impact in America in her book Superior: The Return of Race Science.

lesser intelligence.[145] The zoo taught me that unconscionable scientific racism never really died; it just rebranded. Race still plagues our country today, forever wed to Darwin's theory.

Scientists committed to evolution can't let go of the fiction of race, and the natural conclusion of this naturalistic worldview is racism. It's curious that many scholars today don't see the inherent connection between evolution and racism and even try to distance the two. However, Dr. James Watson (a geneticist who, with Francis Crick, won the Nobel Prize for discovering DNA's double-helix structure) exposed this inconsistency in 2007 when he claimed that "there is no firm reason to anticipate that the intellectual capacities of peoples geographically separated in their evolution should prove to have evolved identically."[146][o] In other words, evolution can't account for the ethnic diversity that we see around us without calling some ethnicities smarter than others. Evolution will always lead to racism. In fact, despite the protests of its apologists, evolution demands racism, and in many ways, racism demands evolution. As long as the myth of evolution persists, so will the myth of race.

So, a starting point for ethnic unity in the Church needs to be the round, biblical rejection of evolution and all of its pseudo-science stepchildren. Evolved apes will always divide based on divergent ancestry, but image-bearers can unite based on our common Creator. The image of God in man grounds our shared dignity and composes the most fundamental truths about what it means to be human. As opposed to evolutionary theories, a biblical understanding of ethnicity also sheds light on where languages, nations, and people groups came from and what God intends to do with our differences. Through the Gospel of Jesus Christ and in the Church, God glorifies Himself by uniting people from ethnic groups far and wide in the joyful, harmonious

---

o    It should be acknowledged that evolutionists differ on how to account for human difference, some arguing for monogenesis (origin from one location) and others for polygenesis (origins from multiple locations simultaneously). But neither theory fully answers the question of ubiquitous genetic commonality between Homo sapiens. Instead, as evolutionary argumentation always does, it simply pushes the question into the unknown ether of thousands of years.

life of the Spirit. Wisely, lovingly navigating this common life in the Church requires nuance and humility, but as we look to Christ together, we find His power sufficient to bring us together when we are divided in weakness.

Unity only comes through our shared identity in Christ, not a simultaneous acknowledgement of our differences. The biblical metaphor of the family of God in the Church illustrates the intimacy and fellowship that can be found through the commonality of Christ alone. Trillia Newbell captures this concept well when she writes:

> Understanding the family of God is yet another weapon against racial intolerance in the church. As we recognize, accept, and embrace our new family, the walls of hostility will crumble. We are indeed different because God's creation is unique, but we are much more the same than we are different.[147]

Our uniting similarity in the Church is the person and work of Jesus Christ. Noting this, Anthony Carter writes:

> The black experience and the white experience in America are different and often in conflict. We need not deny this. As Christians, however, we can affirm that though our experiences may be contextually different, our membership—indeed our citizenship—is in the same kingdom, the kingdom of God. It is the eternal kingdom where the citizens are called and united under the same Spirit, the same Lord, and the same faith.[148]

Whether you're Galatian, Roman, barbarian, Scythian, American, Syrian, slave, or free, the blood of Christ can be the ink on your adoption papers (Gal. 4:1-7). His is a family and a kingdom that will not erase your ethnicity but will bend it in service to worship of the King. All of Jesus' brothers and sisters love each other, and they love Him even more. In Christ's house, we aren't defined by race, and we aren't ignorant of Satan's designs in it. But we trust in the God Who raised up a Church from Babel and Who designed our skin tones for His eternal glory.

God glorifies Himself by making us one through His Son. In Jesus, we are "a chosen race, a royal priesthood, a holy nation, a people for his own possession, that you may proclaim the excellencies of him who called you out of darkness into his marvelous light" (1 Peter 2:9). There's nothing fictional about the unity of the "chosen race" of the Church. We come from one bloodline—the cross of Jesus Christ—and we are citizens of one nation—the kingdom of Heaven. There's only one Man who can bring together His multi-ethnic Church in this kind of beautiful, harmonious, diverse unity: the God-man Jesus Christ.

Isaac Watts closed one of his most-powerful, least-known hymns, "How Sweet and Aweful is the Place," with the following stanza, a glorious image of the undivided Church that we all want to see:

We long to see Thy churches full

That all the chosen race

May with one voice, and heart and soul

Sing Thy redeeming grace.[p]

## DISCUSSION QUESTIONS

1. If race is fictional, why does it so powerfully define our social consciousness as a country? Where did the concept of race come from, and what keeps it going?

2. Why is evolution so inextricably tied with the concept of race? How should rightly understanding Creation help us rightly understand our inter-ethnic relationships?

3. Where does human dignity come from? What are some of the implications of universal dignity for all people? How would acknowledging the image of God in other people actually help our relationships?

---

p    Isaac Watts, "How Sweet and Aweful Is the Place," 1707, Public Domain.

4. How is God glorified through ethnic differences? How should that affect our church?

5. Galatians 3:27-28 and Colossians 3:10-11 both replace a Christian's former identity with a new identity in Christ as a distant, significant priority. How should we talk about ourselves as Christians from different ethnic backgrounds? How should we respond to the desire to elevate our ethnic identities above our Christian identities? What kind of life flows out of these new identities?

CHAPTER 4

# ETHNICITY AND SIN

## STATUES AND STATUTES

Under the bronze gaze of Abraham Lincoln, Frederick Douglass reasoned with protestors. On July 24, 2020, in Lincoln Park in Washington, D. C., a Douglass reenactor addressed the crowd with the same words that the famous freedman abolitionist spoke in that same spot on April 14, 1876.[149] The subject of his address, then and again in 2020, was the Freedman's Memorial, a statue of Abraham Lincoln holding the Emancipation Proclamation while standing over a freed slave. In the summer of 2020, protestors had called for the statue's removal because of its "degrading racial undertones,"[150] by which they meant the implications of a well-dressed white man standing as in authority over a poorly clothed black man. The reenactor countered that the statue still had value, being mostly funded by freed slaves as an homage to the admittedly complicated legacy of the first assassinated president. At the time of writing (I went there and checked), the statue still stands.

Lincoln's metallic likeness is just one example of American statuary currently facing opposition. All over the country, statues of Confederate generals and plantation owners are being torn down, burned, decapitated, and even, curiously, drowned in the name of ethnic equality.[151] Monument toppling is certainly nothing new in world history, but it is relatively new on

121

this scale in American history.[152] [q] The idea behind deposing these stone and steel reminders, according to historian Julian Hayter, is that "the symbols of white supremacy . . . are inextricably linked for many people to *institutionalized* bigotry in the twenty-first century."[153] In other words, when the statues come down, so do the racist systems they represent. At least, that's the hope.

Now, to be clear, I'm not arguing for or against the removal of statues. I can see the wisdom in removing a statue of, say, Nathan Bedford Forrest, the first Grand Wizard of the Ku Klux Klan.[154] However, there may also be historical value in keeping the statues up or even just moved into a museum as some have advocated.[155]

My point is not to render a verdict on all statues in the United States either way. That's not what concerns me. What's concerning to me is that our country is after the Tin Man instead of his heart. We're aimed at the wrong target. We're tearing down structures instead of strongholds (2 Cor. 10:4). We've villainized institutions instead of dispositions. We're trying to change the world without changing the man. Our enemy has become policy on the books and not partiality in the heart. We're fighting systemic racism instead of fighting the racism at its root. What concerns me far more than a debate about statues is our nation's collective effort to eradicate sin by erasing its effects—treating the symptoms but not the disease. It's a treatment plan that's doomed to fail.

There's only one solution for the sin of racism, and it's not in a figure toppled down but in another raised up. A country, a city, and a church divided by ethnic partiality can't be united by graffiti-covered statues but only by the sin-covering blood of Jesus Christ.

## REDEFINING RACISM

If our divided country has one common enemy today, it's racism. Racism has been called a public health crisis.[156] The hashtag #endracism has trended on

---

q   During the time of the American Revolution, the colonialists toppled a handful of statues of British figures, like King George III, but in isolated instances.

Twitter and Instagram. As I write, eight of the top ten *New York Times* bestselling paperback non-fiction books are all treatises against racism.[r] The Senate convened hearings to talk about issues of racism; the streets resound with cries of racism; and even first grade classrooms are beginning to receive curriculum on how to combat racism.[157] Everyone, it seems, is opposed to racism.

What racism is and how to eliminate it, however, is up for debate. According to many today, racism is a systemic, institutional problem that needs dismantling. An article from the American Friends Service Committee, a loosely Quaker activist group, boasts "We Won't Stop Until We Dismantle the Whole Racist System."[158] According to *NPR*, Layla Saad's *New York Times* best-selling book *Me and White Supremacy* "helps you do the work of dismantling racism."[159] *The Washington Post* has recently offered counsel on "How We Can Start Dismantling Systemic Racism."[160] Author Joseph Barndt even titled his book *Understanding and Dismantling Racism.*

Here's the question we need to ask: can racism even be dismantled? I don't mean to ask whether or not we have the intestinal fortitude. I mean, is racism the kind of thing to which the verb "dismantle" even applies? You can dismantle an engine, or furniture, or, abstractly, a collection of laws, taking it apart piece by piece. But is racism really like a brick building that can be deconstructed one chunk at a time? Can racism be dismantled like a skyscraper? Like a slave ship? Like a statue?

Again, it depends on who you ask and especially on their definitions. Ever since the word "racism" entered the English vocabulary in the early 1900s, its definition has remained relatively the same: partiality based on race. This definition implied, or sometimes stated, that racism involved conscious, willful feelings of superiority over another person on the basis of the fictional category of race. Racism, historically, was something that people did, like lynching an African American freedman during the Reconstruction era,

---

r   They are *White Fragility, So You Want to Talk About Race, The Warmth of Other Suns, Born a Crime, Just Mercy, The Color of Law, Stamped from the Beginning,* and *The New Jim Crow.*

like angrily shouting a racial slur at Japanese Americans during World War II, or like refusing to serve a Mexican American man at a deli counter during the Civil Rights era. In the past, a *person* could be racist, but not a *system*.

But that all began to change in the latter half of the twentieth century. American author and linguist John McWhorter writes:

> [The word] racist has morphed to refer to animus beyond the conscious and deliberate. A great deal of the race debate since the 1960s has revolved around a quest to teach Mr. and Mrs. America that racism can be covert, and can be as harmful as the old-school kind.[161]

Throughout the sixties and seventies, the definition of racism was slowly depersonalized and systematized. No longer were people responsible for racist thoughts, actions, or words, but they could be guilty of racism without even knowing it. Positively commenting on someone's hair, cooking, or clothing could be taken as a slight and therefore deemed racist, despite the well-meaning (if uninformed) intention of the commenter. Enter the era of the microaggression.

By the time George Floyd was killed in May 2020, the definition of "racism" had almost completely evolved. Since then, a new definition has taken hold of our cultural consciousness. Racism is no longer a synonym of prejudice. Today, racism is "prejudice + power."[162] Racism is "a system of oppression based on race."[163] Racism "occurs when a racial group's prejudice is backed by legal authority and institutional control."[164] Racism is "a system of advantage based on race, involving cultural messages, misuse of power, and institutional bias, in addition to the racist beliefs and actions of individuals."[165] One college graduate even lobbied for *Merriam-Webster* to update their definition of "racism" to include this new, systemic definition.[166] As of September 3, 2020, the *Merriam-Webster* definition for racism includes "the systemic oppression of a racial group to the social, economic, and political advantage of another."[167] Now, racism is defined both personally and impersonally.

Author Ibram Kendi argues in his book *How to Be an Antiracist* that the definition for racism needs to be taken one step further. According to Kendi, not only does the definition of "racism" necessarily include some systemic component, but it also *cannot include* a personal component, at least at its root. Kendi writes, "This is the consistent function of racist ideas—and of any kind of bigotry more broadly: to manipulate us into seeing people as the problem, instead of the policies that ensnare them."[168] He goes on to define a racist as "one who is supporting a racist policy through their actions or inaction or expressing a racist idea,"[169] and a racist policy as "any measure that produces or sustains racial inequity between racial groups."[170] For example, a policy that maintains the status quo of differing levels of income between African Americans and European Americans, according to Kendi, would be a source of racism, not the human heart. Kendi even goes so far as to say that "racial discrimination [what a person does] is an immediate and visible manifestation of an underlying racial policy."[171]

By his definitions, policies *make* people prejudiced, not the other way around. According to this new definition, the only true fountains of racism are systems, not people. Or, as Jean-Jacques Rousseau put it, "Man is born free, but he is everywhere in chains."

In case this new definition of racism isn't clear enough, here's Kendi's clarification:

> If racial discrimination is defined as treating, considering, or making a distinction in favor or against an individual based on that person's race, then racial discrimination is not inherently racist. The defining question is whether the discrimination is creating equity or inequity. If discrimination is creating equity, then it is antiracist. If discrimination is creating inequity, then it is racist.[172]

Given a worldview where all racism is systemic, not personal, I can understand why the statues would need to come down. If the source of racism is a system that promotes inequity, then our solution needs to be systemic change to promote equity. If the issue isn't people's hearts but society's ills, then protests and policies may indeed be the right remedy. If our greatest enemy right now is unequal access to money and power, then you can understand why so many want so badly to dismantle our statues, our suburbs, and even our fundamental governing structures. If bronze Lincoln is the real racist, after all, then down he goes! But is he—I mean, *it*—the real racist?

As unfair as our national structures may be, and as much untold suffering as unjust laws have caused in the history of our country, and as much as reform may be needed throughout our criminal justice system, no system is as powerful, deadly, or responsible as the real culprit behind racism. I desperately want to alleviate the pain that my brothers and sisters of all ethnicities feel, and I want our lawmakers to govern with righteousness and justice as God designed them to do. But if you tore down every last brick of the American experiment in the name of antiracism, you still wouldn't touch the rot in our foundation. The greatest enemy to our country, Church, and us today is not our systems but our sin.

## REDIRECTING ATTENTION

The word "racism" isn't in the Bible, so as a Bible teacher, I'm hesitant to make that one word the battleground for truth. A more stable, biblical term for personal racism would be "ethnic partiality." It may be a mouthful, but at least we can defend it with the Word of God. That being said, we still need to reckon with this current conversation about "racism" as such.

My reason for recounting evolving definitions of "racism" is that I want us to see what's happening in our world and how that's connected with sin. The conversation is being moved away from sin and toward systems, and it's happening by redefinition. Cultural revolutions are always accompanied by redefinitions—it's one particularly powerful way of changing public perception. Ibram Kendi acknowledges this cultural influence of definitions when he writes, "To be an antiracist is to set lucid definitions of racism/antiracism."[173] Definitions, and especially redefinitions, control conversations like a ship's rudder. Slight adjustments here and there lead to entirely different destinations.

So, where is this new, systemic definition of "racism" taking us? Again, Kendi's brutal honesty is both refreshing and saddening:

> "The only remedy to racist discrimination is antiracist discrimination. The only remedy to past discrimination is present discrimination. The only remedy to present discrimination is future discrimination."[174]

Now, at this point in the conversation, we might be tempted to engage in a back-and-forth political discourse on the merits of the kinds of discrimination to which Kendi's referring—reparations, criminal justice reform, and diversity initiatives in America. Many brilliant men and women have continued those debates, and I'm grateful for wise people who do so and bring clarity where it's needed. There's no doubt that some of our country's laws, either in spirit or in practice, unfairly and maybe even unintentionally disadvantage whole groups of people. Our hearts long for the justice of Christ's rule on earth, even while many labor for proximate justice in our land today. And those conversations are valuable in the right context.

But if our discussion about racism primarily emphasizes its systemic implications, then we would implicitly agree with Kendi that our chief problem and its solutions lie on a political plane. But I don't believe that, and neither should you.

While governmental, policy changes can and should increase righteous rewards and decrease innocent suffering, they can't penetrate the outer shell of a man to the more pervasive, more fundamental issues of the heart. Our ethnic divisions can't be hammered out by the Supreme Court. The issue of our day is not the issues of our day. We face a greater foe, so we need a greater ally. We don't look to the Senate, the House, or anyone on the Hill to solve humanity's most basic problem—we must look to a higher court. "Some trust in chariots and some in horses, but we trust in the name of the LORD our God" (Psalm 20:7).

## REFOCUSING ON SIN

Ask yourself this question: If oppressive laws that discriminate against certain ethnicities are the prime offender in inter-ethnic relations, where did those laws come from? The Bible actually gives us the answer in Psalm 94:20-21 as the psalmist addresses God: "Can wicked rulers be allied with you, those who frame injustice by statute? They band together against the life of the righteous and condemn the innocent to death."

The word for "frame" in verse twenty-one is also used for blacksmiths forming armor out of hot metal (Isa. 44:12). The psalmist is saying that unjust statutes and laws—lifeless systems that promote injustice—are formed by wicked people with sinful hearts. "Those who frame injustice" are people making systems, not systems making people. The tail doesn't wag the dog, and the policy doesn't create the sin. All systemic racism is borne in the sinful heart of man, then codified into policies, procedures, value systems, and ideologies. Ultimately, the sin of sinners condemns the innocent. The unconscionable evils legalized by Jim Crow laws would not have existed as such without the man Jim Crow, an actor named Thomas Dartmouth Rice, with his humiliating, black-faced caricature of African Americans.[175] Sin in the sinful heart of man is the source of all injustice and the source of all ethnic division as well.

Al Mohler brings clarity to the origins of systemic racism when he says:

> So, as we think about structural sin or systemic sin, it basically comes down to the fact that when sinners sin, it has consequences in the society around us. Sin corrupts every single human system in one way or another, because it's made up of sinful human beings. Furthermore, sin sometimes even takes

the structural form of laws and policies, rules, and habits and customs. All of these are . . . corrupted by sin.[176]

Brothers and sisters, we shouldn't try to act like "systemic evil" doesn't exist because of course it does. If hate is in the paintbrush, then naturally it's going to get all over the canvas. Structural, institutional evils are a ubiquitous reality in the human experience. The question is not whether systemic evil exists but why it exists. The answer is sin.

Take, for example, the systemic evil of abortion. America's official protection of the ghastly murder of infants in abortion has its poisonous roots in sin, just like all other evil. *Roe v. Wade* is a structural problem, a horrific blight enshrined in our legal precedence. But there would be no legalized infanticide without Justice Harry Blackmun and six other Supreme Court justices who sinfully condoned murder in their own hearts before voting for its systemic protection. Sin is the architect; people are the builders; and an unjust law is the jail that sin builds.

It may seem patently obvious that all evil in the world is the result of sin. But do you see, then, how redefining racism away from sinful hearts and toward impersonal systems moves us further from the source of the problem? And if we wrongly identify the disease producing the deadly symptoms of injustice, then we'll prescribe the wrong treatment as well. If we point to the wrong source, we'll have the wrong solution.

Allow me to reiterate so as not to be misunderstood: as Christians compelled by holistic compassion, we ought to care deeply about systematized injustice in all of its forms because we serve a God of justice and we empathize with those who have been hurt by injustice. But if our compassion is truly holistic, then we'll see the far greater need for deliverance from sin. We aren't forced to choose between political and spiritual engagement, but if you had to choose, it would have to be the spiritual. Not only do our societal ills all have the same patient zero—the sinful human heart—but more than that, the consequences for our sin before a holy God are more deadly than any partial policy. We want people to be delivered from sin more than we want them to be delivered from systemic suffering because we know that sin earns eternal suffering.

To clarify, I'm not advocating for the "miracle motif" approach to societal issues that all Christians need to do to eradicate systemic evil is to tell people about Jesus, and when everyone gets converted, they'll just change the laws out of Christian love. After all, who's to say that God will change those particular lawmakers? No, what I'm advocating is that trying to eradicate systemic evil is the wrong goal entirely. In his book on race and racism, John Piper explains why Christians must prioritize heart change over policy change:

> My concern is not that the political and social ideas of the right and the left are not often true, as far as they go. My concern is that these ideas are spiritually hollow and impotent. The gospel[sic] of Jesus does not come to the controversy between personal accountability and structural intervention and take sides. It calls both sides to repent and believe in Jesus and be born again and make the glory of Jesus the supreme issue in life. The gospel[sic] is not a political adviser standing to the side waiting to be asked for guidance. It is the arrival of God saving people from their sin and from the everlasting wrath of God, giving them the Holy Spirit, and bringing their lives progressively into conformity to Jesus.[177]

Undoubtedly, when we grow in Christlikeness, we'll be more aligned with policies that reflect biblical ethics. But when we talk about sin and its consequence, we're dealing with untouchable holiness, infinite wrath, and eternal death. My heart is more broken over a racist policymaker facing his fearsome Judge than his racist policies oppressing me and the people I love. Again, I don't actually think I have to choose; as a Christian, I care about all suffering. But in trying to redefine the Church's priority with respect to racism, this war of definitions demands that we be clear about the Church's

God-given priority. If we want multi-ethnic unity in the Church, we won't find it at the voting booth but in the atoning cross. Only the death of Jesus can kill our sin because only He can get at its source.

## THE ORIGIN OF EVIL

In order to understand how Christ defeats our sin, even the sin of ethnic partiality, we need to trace sin's biography back to the beginning. Once we have the context for our malicious condition, we can face our foe with confidence in our Savior's full forgiveness. Then, as redeemed rebels, we are freed to show compassion and long-suffering to our fellow sinners. Our heart problems need distinctly Christian answers, and those answers send us back to the first pages of Scripture.

Oddly enough, today, you can hear a uniquely Christian phrase tumbling from the lips of social activists and pundits: original sin. Usually, it's modified to *"America's* original sin." The conceit goes that the American experiment, from its moment of inception, has been inherently and systemically racist and that racism is the source of most or all of the problems we see today. Racism is in America's DNA. Racial discrimination and violence are inextricable from America's most fundamental institutions, the BBC has argued,[178] going back even earlier than the exclusion of Jefferson's slavery clause from the Declaration of Independence.[179] The phrase "America's original sin" has been used in recent years to emphasize the pervasive, endemic, and often unseen nature of institutional racism in American history.[s] Many assert that from day one, America's main problem is the racist superstructure of white supremacy.

As Christians, we ought to be attentive when the world starts using Bible language like "original sin." And we ought to ask some clarifying questions, too. Is racism America's most fundamental sin? Is racism anyone's original sin? Where did sin come from to begin with? And why?

---

s    Jim Wallis popularized this concept in his 2017 book, *America's Original Sin.*

Here's the truth: sinners started America, but America didn't start sin. Evil predates the thirteen colonies by millennia. Sin is an ancient corruption, festering in human hearts since the dawn of humanity. Sin didn't begin in 1619 any more than 1492. It started in the garden with Adam and Eve.

In the Garden of His very good, newly minted world, God gave the first human beings one rule: "'You may surely eat of every tree of the garden, but of the tree of the knowledge of good and evil you shall not eat, for in the day that you eat of it you shall surely die'" (Gen. 2:16-17). Deceived by the Satan-serpent, Eve and then Adam, in the first ever acts of human sin, disobeyed God's rule and ate from the forbidden tree (Gen. 3:1-6). The Bible doesn't leave us to wonder what was in the hearts of the first sinners. "So when the woman saw that the tree was good for food, and that it was a delight to the eyes, and that the tree was to be desired to make one wise" (Gen. 3:6). The apostle John calls this "the desires of the flesh and the desires of the eyes and the pride of life" (1 John 2:16).

Notice what's absent from the Bible's description of the origin of sin: ethnic partiality. In the Garden, where sin was born, there were no ethnicities. It was impossible for racism to be the original sin. If we can categorize the first sin as anything, we would call it pride. Adam and Eve wanted to be like God instead of worshipping God. They weren't content to be creatures serving their Creator, so they chose to believe a lie instead of the truth, and they sinned. Our first parents weren't constrained by an oppressive environment into transgressing the loving warning of their benevolent God; they literally lived in paradise! And yet, they still sinned because sin comes from within.

Now, someone could respond that while Adam and Eve may have fallen into sin because of their own corrupt hearts, that's not necessarily true for the rest of humanity. All the evil in America could still be the product of racist policies, per Ibram Kendi, and not the human heart. To that charge, we turn to Paul in his letter to the Romans. Paul writes, "Therefore, just as sin came into the world through one man, and death through sin, and so death spread to all men because all sinned" (Rom. 5:12).

This verse explains for us the biblical doctrine of original sin. Paul clarifies in verse fourteen that this "one man" is Adam and that his sin is the first sin from which all other sin came. "Sin came into the world through one man." That is, sin came through a person, a human agent. Not a system. Not institutional racism. Not inequity. A human heart that gave itself over to sin is responsible for all the subsequent sin in the world. John Calvin writes in his *Institutes*:

> By his own evil intention, then, man corrupted the pure nature he had received from the Lord; and by his fall drew all his posterity with him into destruction. Accordingly, we should contemplate the evident cause of condemnation in the corrupt nature of humanity.[180]

Calvin observes what Paul says plainly—that through Adam, "death spread to all men because all sinned." Every person who comes from Adam— every person to ever live—inherits a sin nature, original sin, from Adam (except, of course, Jesus Christ). Sin is passed down spiritually like DNA is passed down genetically. Even the sweetest little baby girl possesses a sinful, corrupt heart, and she is enslaved to her own evil desires (Titus 3:3) and is held accountable by God for her sin. In fact, God's individual judgment on each human being for his or her own sin proves that the buck stops with us, not our systems. Augustine writes:

> Evil could not occur without an author. But if you ask who the author is, no answer can be given, for there is not just a single author; rather, evil people are the authors of their evildoing . . . Evildoings are redressed by God's justice. It would not be just to redress them unless they come about through the will.[181]

Our corrupt hearts are responsible for every shape and shade of sin in this world. Sin didn't enter the world through American chattel slavery any more than it came through Israel's pagan child sacrifices or Rome's cult prostitution. As heinous and pervasive as our sins may be, as tempting an environment as our vices may produce, and as crystallized as our transgressions may become in our laws, there's only one first sin, and it happened in a utopia.

When we know the true origin of sin—originally Adam, now original sin in our sinful hearts—we can respond with biblical clarity to some accusations about ethnicity today.

For instance, many today have set their sights on "whiteness" as the primary source of evil, pain, and injustice in the world. One author contends that to be white is to be racist, without exclusion or exception.[182] The architects of critical race theory claim that "racism is pervasive, systemic, and deeply ingrained. If we take this perspective, then no white member of society seems quite so innocent."[183] The Smithsonian even produced a chart (that has since been removed from their website) villainizing "whiteness" for its promotion of "rugged individualism," "the scientific method," "the Protestant work ethic," and a concept of justice in which "intent counts."[184] The social categorization of whiteness—which, remember, is fictional to the core—has been charged, tried, and sentenced as the criminal responsible for injustice and inequity in America.

While I would unflinchingly agree that wicked thoughts and feelings of light-skinned, European American superiority have been used to justify countless, unspeakable acts of racism in our country's history and today, the real culprit is not "whiteness" but sinful hearts. Sin finds any and every excuse to manifest itself, be it skin color, financial status, or political affiliation. But if someone hates you because you're liberal, wealthy, or have caramel-colored skin, that doesn't make any of those facts about you evil any more than you hating those who don't share your qualities. The human heart, where sin is born and multiplies, produces ethnic partiality. Sin comes from inside of us, not outside.

## WHAT SIN IS

Up until this point, we've just been assuming a generally accepted definition of sin. But as we've already noted, definitions matter, especially in conversations about ethnicity. Depending on the definition of sin itself, evil may reside in the human heart or in human systems. A biblical understanding of sin will show us that though the Bible affirms sin's structural scope, its source is always the heart.

The Old Testament word usually translated "sin" famously means "to miss the mark."[185] This meaning is apparent from its literal usage in Judges 20:16 (emphasis mine): "Among all these were 700 chosen men who were left-handed; every one could sling a stone at a hair and not *miss*." Applied to a spiritual sphere, the word means to miss the mark of God's moral standard. For example, "Saul said to Samuel, 'I have sinned, for I have transgressed the commandment of the LORD and your words'" (1 Sam. 15:24).

Theologians have described sin historically as "any want of conformity unto, or transgression of, the law of God."[186] Most of the other words that the Scriptures use to describe sin (usually translated "evil," "transgression," "iniquity," and similar synonyms) communicate the same concept about moral wrongdoing: sin breaks God's law.[187]

While there's plenty of nuance that we could continue to glean from the biblical language about sin, just this one idea is sufficient to understand the nature of sin for our purposes. Consider, for a second, the speed limit on 495 North near the church where I serve, which is fifty-five miles per hour. Why is there a speed limit there? Of course, it's there to keep people safe, to guard against reckless driving, and so on. But more fundamentally, what is the speed limit meant to accomplish? Laws exist to control people's behavior. It would be nonsense to say that the law is for the car, the road, or the idea of automobile travel in general. Laws are always given to people so that people will keep them.

Sin, then, is failing to meet a standard that God has given to people to keep. Whether that law came posted in the form of the Torah to Israel (Genesis through Deuteronomy), written and spoken in the commands of Christ to His disciples (Matt. 28:18-20), or if it comes hardwired in the conscience of every person on earth (Rom. 2:14-16), the intended audience of the law of God is always people. God's law is a system for people, and we're the human recipients required to obey that law.

So, if sin is breaking God's law and God's law is only directed at people, then it's simply not possible for an impersonal system to sin. Whiteness cannot be the source of sin any more than your car is the source of you speeding (try that excuse the next time you get pulled over). The American government is not the source of sin. Laws about policing procedures and conduct do not make anyone sin, nor are they the source of sin. All of these structures can certainly promote sin, foster sin, enshrine sin, approve of sin, aid sin, and codify sin; but they aren't sin, and they aren't responsible for sin. By definition, we the people are the authors and actors of sin.

## A SAVIOR FOR SINNERS

To some, this repeated emphasis on the personal nature of sin may sound obvious and counterproductive. It's obvious, one might retort, that people do horrible things to themselves and to each other. But that evil is magnified by the formation of systems that multiply those sins—see the Jim Crow laws—and the result is deadly. Shouldn't we also focus, then, on dismantling these oppressive systems for the sake of saving lives? Martin Luther King, Jr. expressed this sentiment in a speech given at Western Michigan University in 1963:

> Certainly, if the problem is to be solved then in the final sense, hearts must be changed . . . But we must go on to say that while it may be true that morality cannot be legislated, behavior can be regulated. It may be true that the law cannot change the

heart but it can restrain the heartless. It may be true that the law cannot make a man love me but it can keep him from lynching me and I think that is pretty important, also.[188]

To Dr. King's sentiment, I give a hearty "amen." It would be impossible to quantify just how important it is to keep our fellow citizens from being violently, wickedly, unjustly killed. God hates unjust scales (Prov. 11:1), and so do we. Because we love every image-bearer God has made, we should always be strongly concerned when they are mistreated, maligned, and murdered. And that burden will naturally manifest itself in a desire to change the laws that protect such evil.

Notice, though, Dr. King's first statement. Better laws will not bring the solution that we need the most. We can constrain and restrain racist behavior, but our final hope comes only through heart change. And heart change doesn't come through new and better laws.

We know that better laws won't make better people because we've seen the effects of perfect laws. Adam and Eve were given one unmistakable, all-good, and loving command from God, and they broke that law and sinned against God (Gen. 1-3). The people of Israel were given a comprehensive governmental, social, societal system of laws to govern their entire lives from cradle to grave. Every last comma of that Mosaic Law was perfect, and they broke that law again and again, sinning against God. Then the Lawmaker Himself came to earth to explain the law and all of its implications (Matt. 5-7), speaking with perfect justice and righteousness, and what was the result? "'Crucify, crucify him!'" (Luke 23:21). Sinful men rejected the embodiment of God's law in the person of Jesus Christ, murdered him unjustly, and sinned against God.

Just laws can help, but they can't change the heart. If sinful hearts want to break a good law, they will. And the penalty for sinning and breaking God's perfect law, written on our hearts, is eternal death. "For the law brings wrath . . . " (Rom. 4:15). "For the wages of sin is death . . . " (Rom. 6:23). "What then shall we say? That the law is sin? By no means . . . For sin, seizing an opportunity through the commandment, deceived me and through it killed me" (Rom. 7:7, 11).

If we want to escape a deserved fate worse than death—the second death of eternal Hell—then we ought to cry out like Paul, "Wretched man that I am! Who will deliver me from this body of death?" (Rom. 7:24). And Paul's answer is not more or better laws. It's Christ. "Thanks be to God through Jesus Christ our Lord!" (Rom. 7:25).

Oh, what we need more than righteous laws is a righteous Lord! We need Jesus, the Son of God, Who will die in our place on the cross to die our deserved death and rescue us from our lawlessness. The chief reason why we should be concerned primarily with sin in human hearts over laws in man-made systems is the cross of Jesus Christ! Jesus didn't suffer, bleed, and die to dismantle broken systems but to save wicked sinners. Our names are written on His hands (Isa. 49:16)—the names of vile lawbreakers like me. Jesus didn't die for America; He died for you! Or, as Pastor Virgil Walker puts it, "Jesus didn't come to save society,[sic] he came to save sinners."[189]

The apostle Paul writes:

> For if, because of one man's trespass, death reigned through that one man, much more will those who receive the abundance of grace and the free gift of righteousness reign in life through the one man Jesus Christ. Therefore, as one trespass led to condemnation for all men, so one act of righteousness leads to justification and life for all men. For as by the one man's disobedience the many were made sinners, so by the one man's obedience the many will be made righteous (Rom. 5:17-19).

The Gospel of Jesus Christ is Good News for sinful people. Though we have inherited original sin through Adam which should lead to our unending pain, Jesus bore those marks in His body on the tree so that we might live to righteousness with Him. Though the gavel has fallen on Adam and his tree, the sentence has fallen on Christ on His tree. Though our first father made us law-breakers, our Savior's law-keeping makes us innocent in the court of Heaven, and His Spirit changes our hearts here on earth.

He has given justification and life to "all men," meaning every kind or ethnicity of man. The cross of Christ breaks through the ethnic barriers we construct to give us the righteousness we so desperately need. Once rebels to God's law, now obedient servants from every ethnicity to our Lord Jesus Christ. The Gospel rescues all kinds of sinful people *in* a cursed, broken world, but not *from* it (John 17:14-19).

So, systemic injustice should send us to the cross. It's not naive or unsophisticated to say that heart-generated evils need heart-healing answers, and the Gospel of Jesus Christ is the only medicine that can cure our sin-sick hearts. For those who have the opportunity to advocate for just laws and the protection of life in our governmental systems, please do that. Our country obviously needs it. But for those of us whose hands aren't on the steering wheel of society, what can we possibly do in the face of such apparently widespread racism? Tell people about the One Who saves racists and adulterers and tax collectors alike and plead with Him to transform sinful hearts.

## SADNESS FOR SIN

In order to round out our discussion about sin and racism, we need to address two more questions about ethnic partiality in our complex and changing society. First, if it's true that the sin of ethnic partiality underlies our broken systems, how ought we to respond? Second, what does ethnic partiality actually look like today?

While there are many appropriate and biblical responses to the sin of ethnic partiality in our world, one of those responses must be sadness. When we hear on the news about another shooting, another riot, or another ethnically-motivated act of violence, our souls ought to feel heavy. When wicked white supremacist groups hold a rally down the street, oh, how we ought to mourn! When politicians, pundits, and celebrities spout racist filth about the inherent evil of whiteness and moral superiority of blackness, may we hang our heads in another silent prayer: "How long, O Lord?" (Psalm 13:1).

The Scriptures teach us that a right response to sin in its many and various forms is sadness. Tears befit suffering, and sin begets sighs. Cries of "how long shall the wicked exult?" (Psalm 94:3) and "Be not silent, O God of my praise!" (Psalm 109:1) go hand in glove with the suffering of a sin-soaked world. We "weep with those who weep" (Rom. 12:15) and not just superficially. Jesus Himself wept on this earth in the face of sin, death, sorrow, and unbelief (John 11:35). While we should be prudent to reserve judgment where we can't see someone's motives, the pain and death that sin produces are always to be lamented. Sadness necessarily follows sin and its effects.

Allow me to add one dimension to our mourning—sadness over our own sin. One of the obvious objectives of redefining racism to a systemic problem is to escape personal culpability. When the source of all problems are outside of me, then I don't need to examine myself. In fact, if all my sin, including racist thoughts and feelings, are just the result of external forces pressing in on me, then I'm not responsible for my sin at all. Changing the source of sin to the systems outside of us makes us the victims, not the culprits.

But the Bible doesn't remove our culpability for sin or our need to sorrowfully repent of it. David writes concerning his own sin, "For when I kept silent, my bones wasted away through my groaning all day long" (Psalm 32:3). Like all of us, David keenly felt the sting of each sin in his own heart, and especially so when he wouldn't bring it before the Lord. That sadness over his sin drove him to repentance: "I acknowledged my sin to you, and I did not cover my iniquity; I said, 'I will confess my transgressions to the LORD,' and you forgave the iniquity of my sin" (Psalm 32:5). There's a freedom for those who trust in the Lord that if in godly sorrow we confess our sin to Him, we will find forgiveness in the cross of Jesus Christ.

But not all sadness over sin is helpful sadness. Paul says of the Corinthians, "As it is, I rejoice, not because you were grieved, but because you were grieved into repenting. For you felt a godly grief, so that you suffered no loss through us" (2 Cor. 7:9). Sadness over sin and its effects is godly when it leads to repentance, greater love for God, and more holiness. "For godly grief produces a repentance that leads to salvation without regret, whereas worldly grief produces death" (2 Cor. 7:10). Worldly grief only cares about worldly consequences—what's going to happen to me and the people I love? Godly grief is burdened by sin's offense to God. That's why David says to God in his psalm of repentance, "Against you, you only, have I sinned and done what is evil in your sight, so that you may be justified in your words and blameless in your judgment" (Psalm 51:4). Our sin is always and primarily against God. The greatest sadness about sin is that it lies about God. Therefore, godly sadness over our sin has both eyes fixed on the cross of Jesus Christ, where we simultaneously see the heights of our transgression and the depths of God's mercy to forgive.

In a world plagued and divided by ethnic partiality, sadness is a necessary response for the Christian, but it shouldn't be our last response. Our sorrow over sin ought to bring us to the feet of Christ over and over again. Not only has He conquered sin on His cross, but He also understands our sorrow about sin in His heart. Mark Vroegop exhorts those who weep over sin: "Run to him. Use your pain to drive you toward the Savior. Don't allow sorrow to win. Let grief lead you to renew your love for the man of sorrows."[190]

## BIASED BIAS

Secondly, I want to address the question of what ethnic partiality actually looks like in America today.

To begin with, we should affirm that a system of government that doesn't evenly distribute wealth and opportunity to all its citizens is not necessarily racist. Inequity does not prove personal racism. Disparity of outcomes, even when correlated to ethnic groups, doesn't mandate the existence of sinful motives today. Evil, violent racism has certainly shaped our country, and that has lingering effects; but that doesn't prove that our current system of laws is inherently racist. In fact, the hard work of reform carried out in the turbulent decades of the twentieth century has effectively eliminated overt, intentional racism from our legal statutes.

But willful, hateful, knowing racism is no longer our public enemy. The battlefield has moved to the subtle, subterranean subterfuge of the unaware. To hear our politicians and social scientists explain partiality today, the enemy now has a new name: *implicit bias.*

This discussion about implicit bias needs to be treated biblically at much greater length, but a short summary will suffice for now. If you've never heard of implicit or unconscious bias, it's usually defined as a psychological category of thoughts, opinions, and preferences that go unnoticed but nonetheless affect our conscious speech and action.[191] Critical theorists have described implicit bias as "the near-automatic connections that almost every person who grows up in American society draws between race and personal qualities."[192] Others have called it a kind of "socialization" that causes everyone to unknowingly make certain subconscious judgments about people, particularly on the basis of race.[193] These oblivious assumptions can range from an innocuous culinary stereotype to outright bigotry. The unifying factor, however, is that they remain below the conscious surface— we don't know we have them.

One embattled example of a judgment made with unconscious bias is the stereotypic association between an African American person and violent crime.[194] This bias, it's argued, causes police officers to unintentionally be more suspicious of people with darker skin, which leads to police shootings of unarmed African American men. If this bias can be curbed, then, the assumption is that these tragic instances would lessen and potentially disappear altogether.

That being said, the claims of unconscious biases are not applied only to police officers but to everyone. According to Harvard researchers, anyone can discover their unconscious bias by taking an Implicit Association Test (IAT), which measures in milliseconds the associations between various categories like race and goodness.[195] Since 1998, this test has become a popular referent in studies dealing with unconscious bias, cited over four thousand times and used almost ubiquitously in diversity and bias training classes.[196] If you took the IAT right now, you would be statistically likely to receive feedback indicating that you possess at least a slight unconscious preference for one race over another.[197] Using biblical definitions, that means you would be guilty of an unconscious sin of ethnic partiality. And, in fact, that's just what the academics have asserted. With regard to unconscious racial bias, one scholar writes, "It is impossible for any white person to claim to be innocent."[198]

Now, if you're European American, before you get defensive, let's go to the Bible to see if there's legitimacy to this notion of unconscious bias. First, we should observe that Scripture does affirm a category of unconscious sin. Leviticus 4:27-28 deals with unwitting error in the context of the sacrificial law:

> "If anyone of the common people sins unintentionally in doing any one of the things that by the LORD's commandments ought not to be done, and realizes his guilt, or the sin which he has committed is made known to him, he shall bring for his offering a goat, a female without blemish, for his sin which he has committed."

The word translated "sins unintentionally" is elsewhere translated "mistake" (Num. 15:25), "without intent" (Josh. 20:3), and "error" (Eccl. 10:5). Note that this unintentional sin demands a real, intentional response once it comes to light and that God says the person has really committed the sin, however unconsciously. So, for example, if an Israelite borrowed his friends' only coat and genuinely forgot to return it before sundown, he would be guilty of having sinned and broken God's law (Exod. 22:26). If he realizes in the morning what he's done, he would need to return the coat, ask his cold friend for forgiveness, then head to the tabernacle with a goat to offer it in sacrifice for his oversight. Even though the act wasn't intentionally malicious or unloving, he still sinned and would have to pay the price for it. You and I are guilty of all kinds of similar unaware sins every day, and it's God's incredible grace that He reveals them to us slowly.

A handful of other passages in Scripture confirm that we do, indeed, sin unintentionally. David prays, "Who can discern his errors? Declare me innocent from hidden faults" (Psalm 19:12). King Josiah seems to have been unaware, at least to some degree, of the sinfulness of Israel's pagan practices until hearing the Book of the Law, at which point he repents and institutes nationwide reform (2 Kings 22-23). The author of the letter to the Hebrews warns that "if we go on sinning deliberately after receiving the knowledge of the truth, there no longer remains a sacrifice for sins" (Heb. 10:26). Deliberate, premeditated, ongoing sins are here distinguished from unintentional, momentary, unconscious sin, the former carrying with it an eternal consequence. So, unconscious sin exists, and when we become conscious of that sin, we're responsible to repent of it.

So, how does unintentional sin relate to unconscious bias? As it turns out, not much. Despite the clear existence of unconscious sin, the argument for a nearly universal existence of implicit racial bias doesn't hold up under scrutiny. The IAT, for example, has been roundly rebuffed as an inaccurate, arbitrary exercise with no real connection to conscious bias or action.[199] One of the original psychologists behind the IAT (which, again, is cited in nearly all of the research in support of implicit bias) has admitted the flaws of the test and criticized implicit bias training as mere "window dressing" without the capacity to actually change thoughts or behaviors in a substantive, measurable way.[200] None of that should surprise us because the assumptions behind the IAT and similar tests come from an incorrect, materialistic, evolutionary worldview that sees human beings as the sum of our environmental influences. We know better.

But what about the biblical data that seems to support this notion that we all have unconscious sin? Isn't it in some way related to stereotyping and implicit bias? Let me give three brief, biblical responses.

First, it is demonstrably the case in Scripture that we are more sinful in our motives than we even know, but not with every type of sin. Paul says in Romans 7:15, "For I do not understand my own actions. For I do not do what I want, but I do the very thing I hate." This dynamic seems to even be in play behind the cry, "'I believe, help my unbelief!'" (Mark 9:24). That's why John Owen wrote, "Spiritual wisdom consists in finding out the subtleties, policies, and depths of any indwelling sin . . . to trace this serpent in all its turnings and windings."[201] Scriptural insight would teach us that our unconscious motives are often more selfish and sinful than we'd like to admit.

However, the Bible nowhere argues that all or most people suffer from a particular, deeply embedded, unconscious ethnic partiality that is unraveling society at the seams. The "unconscious racial bias" argued for today is radically different from an admission that our hearts are subtly sinful. Of course, all kinds of people have formed opinions about different ethnicities over their lives; but those aren't always morally right or wrong, and they aren't necessarily subconscious either. For those opinions that are subconscious, there's no indication in Scripture that we're ruled by these unseen assumptions. Though we would be fools to ignore our world's impact on us, we aren't robotically controlled by the racial environments in which we grew up. We consciously choose what we do with those assumptions. Unconscious bias, as a psychological framework, is simply in a different category from the biblical concept of unintentional sin. Stereotypes don't dominate mankind; sin does.

If unconscious racial bias were really the sinful puppet-master behind our societal woes, you'd expect that the biblical authors would clearly unmask this villain and make the invisible culprit known. They do not. The hunt for unconscious racial bias is a modern invention—and an unhelpful one at that. Often, it seems, these "hidden forces" take the blame for all kinds of horrible things that can and should be explained by thousands of other complex factors. So, in affirming the seditious subtleties of our sinful flesh, the Bible does not support the notion that everyone is actually a racist deep, deep down.

That doesn't rule out, though, the possibility that anyone reading this may indeed be in need of a serious heart check in their relationships with people from other ethnicities. For example, if you are just reading this book looking for ammo so you can slam-dunk on your co-workers in conversations about race, it's likely that you're being guided more by pride than you might think. If you tend to make negative judgments about individual people based on what you think about their ethnic group, that's sin.[202] Have the humility to acknowledge that you may be more animated by sin than you think, and always be watchful over your own motives. "Therefore let anyone who thinks that he stands take heed lest he fall" (1 Cor. 10:12).

Second, multiple figures in the Bible claim a kind of innocence of false motives that contradicts the modern narrative about unconscious racial bias. For example, David defends his clean intentions when he writes, "Vindicate me, O LORD, for I have walked in my integrity, and I have trusted in the LORD without wavering" (Psalm 26:1). Paul says to the Corinthians, "For I am not aware of anything against myself" (1 Cor. 4:4). Elsewhere, both men clearly acknowledge their sinfulness, yet they are comfortable calling themselves "innocent" and "blameless," at least in some general way. We wouldn't say that every person is a pedophile deep down in their heart, so why would we say everyone's a racist deep down? A believer isn't necessarily naive, then, for claiming innocence with respect to a certain sin.

Christians have the ability to not be dominated by sin. It may genuinely be that someone has, by the power of the Spirit, overcome their greed, lust, partiality, or anger in such a way that it has no demonstrable impact on their thoughts, words, or actions anymore. If sinful cultural stereotypes have affected them in some way, the effect could be so minor that it's essentially non-existent, or it could just genuinely be non-existent. With appropriate humility, believers can honestly say, "I am not ethnically partial," without lying or admitting to some weird form of sinless perfectionism. Else, how could Paul say, "Be imitators of me, as I am of Christ" (1 Cor. 11:1)?

Third, for the unconscious sin that does linger in our hearts, the Bible would enjoin us to run to the Lord, not psychology, to expose it. Both of the passages I referenced earlier are followed with appeals to God as the one who sees our hearts. "Prove me, O LORD, and try me; test my heart and my mind" (Psalm 26:2). "For I am not aware of anything against myself, but I am not thereby acquitted. It is the Lord who judges me" (1 Cor. 4:4). God's Word is the sharp sword we need to expose our hidden motives (Heb. 4:11-13), not a flawed psych test based on millisecond response times. Go to Jesus with your fears about your heart.

If you're concerned that you may have unknowingly imbibed racist ideas, then pray and ask our gracious heavenly Father to show you where you may be in error. And here's the great part—not only will He answer that prayer, but if you're in sin, He'll also give you the power to change. No randomized, double-blind study can do the same. Only Christ can show us our sin by the power of His Spirit, and only Christ can free us from that sin. Our goal should not be to prove our blamelessness but to actually be blameless and to let God defend or expose us where we err.

## MICROACCUSATIONS

We haven't entirely answered our second question: What does ethnic partiality look like today? Certainly, there's still conscious, overt, despicable racism all over the world, and even in our own country. But I fear that there may be a more pervasive form of partiality that has taken hold in our day—the accusation of microaggressions.

Columbia University Professor Derald Wing Sue defines microaggressions as "brief, everyday exchanges that send denigrating messages to certain individuals because of their group membership."[203] In an article for *Psychology Today*, Sue gives a few examples of these microaggressions:

- When a white couple (man and woman) passes a black man on the sidewalk, the woman automatically clutches her purse more tightly, while the white man checks for his wallet in the back pocket. (Hidden message: Blacks are prone to crime and up to no good.)
- Police stop a Latino male driver for no apparent reason but to subtly check his driver's license to determine immigration status. (Hidden message: Latinas/os are illegal aliens.)
- American Indian students at the University of Illinois see Native American symbols and mascots, exemplified by Chief Illiniwek dancing and whooping fiercely during football games. (Hidden message: American Indians are savages, blood-thirsty, and their culture and traditions are demeaned.)[204]

Sue goes on in the same article to indicate that each of these microaggressions comes from a "well-intentioned white person"—"well-intentioned" meaning "without evil intent." Therefore, the source of microaggressions, according to Sue and other sociologists, is unconscious or implicit biases. By its definition, these little ethnic *faux pas* don't register on the level of willful decision-making but function below the surface. So, someone may say or do something ethnically offensive without realizing it, which would then get labeled a microaggression based on unconscious racial bias. Regardless of actual motives, the microaggressive act has now been labeled as racism.

Play this out. Who is in the wrong if your friend uses a word that unintentionally offends you, like, say, "twinkie?" He may think he's talking about the Hostess brand, apocalypse-proof snack cake; but you may think he's using a derogatory, racist slang term for Asian-Americans who have fully embraced Western culture.[205] Has he sinned against you? No, because the sin of ethnic partiality necessarily includes valuing and devaluing of people on the basis of ethnicity. If he didn't even know his words had anything to do with ethnicity, it's hard to substantiate a claim of ethnic partiality against him. One's offense does not prove another's fault.

But let's take this a step further. Suppose that, in response to his unwitting use of the term "twinkie," you post on social media about the racist oppression you endure every day from people like him. No doubt you'd find a sympathetic ear online. But what's just happened? At worst, you have just sinfully slandered your friend's motives on the basis of an assumption about his use of words. At best, you have called his ignorance racism.

DesiringGod.org staff writer Greg Morse, who is African American, explains the sad implications of this micro-accusing mindset. His article on the topic is worth quoting at length:

> When the suspicious lens filters everything into black and white, we interpret bad interactions with white people as racism. The habit of explaining many of our interpersonal problems, setbacks, or disparities with other ethnicities through the simplistic answer of assumed racism harms us the most. When skin color becomes the go-to explanation, you begin to live a life of seeing ghosts, often when they aren't there. Defective motives lurk behind every interaction. Suspicion feeds suspicion; the web tightens the more you roll around in it. Soon, you become suspicious of even your previously positive relationships with others. You are tempted to grow angry or tired with those who can't see what you see to the degree to which you see it. You may become divisive to fellow believers and absurd on social media. This becomes to you the all-important issue. The more you assume, the more racism you will believe you've found, and the smaller and darker your world becomes. Your Christianity, should you get lost in such an all-consuming racialized

> worldview, will become increasingly earthly. What really
> matters becomes the immediate: the next injustice, the next
> protest, the next confirmation of how you see things—and how
> others simply refuse to see it . . . You start to overcompensate
> and fellowship only with those who confirm your assumptions.
> The soul becomes embittered, angry, and suspicious of those
> you once called friends and brothers and pastors.[206]

Paul writes, "Love bears all things, believes all things, hopes all things, endures all things" (1 Cor. 13:7). If you say you love your fellow believers, then the slanderous assumptions and micro-aggressive accusations have got to go. We don't respond to ignorance with specious accusations but with lovingly spoken truth. We're not omniscient, and we don't see into hearts, so we dare not pronounce judgment on hidden motives and thoughts. If we see overt, unmistakable racism (like a knowing use of a racial slur), then we confront it for what it is: the sin of ethnic partiality. But Christian love will not permit us to play judge, jury, and executioner with other image-bearers, lawmakers, or law enforcers without evidence of sin.

So, what does ethnic partiality look like today? Certainly, it looks like white supremacist rallies and inter-ethnic violence. Sometimes, it looks like dismissive remarks about "those people" or simply preferring groups that look more like us. Often, it looks like loveless accusations of racism that are more slander than substance. If the Church is going to be a beacon of ethnic unity, then we must condemn divisive sin in all of its manifestations and seek forgiveness with God and each other for our own evil intentions. And as those who have been forgiven much, we are ready and eager to forgive much as well (Luke 7:47). The cross of Jesus Christ has purchased our freedom to forgive.

## RACISM AND RELATIONSHIPS

Which brings us back to Lincoln Park. Can we meaningfully charge bronze Lincoln with racist intent? What sin lurks inside that weathered edifice that it should earn the label "racist?" Are our structures the real racists after all?

The answer, of course, is no. There may be some benefit to removing those embattled figures from our public square, but eradicating racism will not be one of them. Jesus alone can tear down the idols of ethnic partiality enshrined in our hearts, and He does it by His uniting Gospel. Sinners from every ethnicity stand equally condemned at the foot of the cross, and there we receive lavish, undeserved grace from Jesus Christ. The law can only discourage sin, but Jesus destroys it.

Outside of Christ, sin always leads to bitterness, anger, and division. Just turn on the news, and you'll see what I mean. Without the Spirit, there's no way for our selfish, prideful hearts to back down, own up, or stop when we've sinned against each other.

But in Christ, sin always gives way to repentance, forgiveness, and restoration. The Spirit causes us to grieve for our own sins, like ethnic partiality, and leads us to God in repentance (2 Cor. 7:10). And having received fresh assurance of our forgiveness in the cross of Christ through confession (1 John 1:9), we then turn to forgive our brothers and sisters over and over and over again (Matt. 18:22). Out of that forgiveness flows a renewed trust, joy, and openness to correction that would be impossible without the sin-slaying influence of the Spirit of Christ (Rom. 8:13). We go on to love each other without suspicion, believing the best rather than assuming the worst (1 Cor. 13:7), because Christ has freed us from the sin of slander.

The Church, then, becomes the garden of redeemed relationships that blossom together into spiritual fruit. As our proximity breeds empathy, God uses our Christian brothers and sisters to grow us in selflessness, patience, and maturity for the glory of Christ. Our friendships in the Church make us more like Christ. Author Trillia Newbell writes:

> By building into diverse relationships, we display the reconcili-
> ation and redemption of Christ to a world that is broken and

divided. True unity is found first through being reconciled to God and then to each other. To walk in that unity arm in arm with people of every tribe and race is to declare to the world that Christ's blood is enough.[207]

Newbell's point is that often the reality of ethnic unity in the Church grows in the rather ordinary soil of Christian relationships. A few years back, I got into a heated discussion with one of my African American brothers in Christ about racism. He was kind to me throughout, but I was frustrated at points and tried harder to win the argument than to understand and care for my friend. Later that night, after the dust had settled and I had time to reflect on how I had treated my brother in Christ, I felt those precious pangs of sorrow for sin that drove me to God in confessing prayer. Shortly thereafter, the work of the Spirit on my heart also drove me back to my friend to repent and ask for forgiveness, which he warmly received and graciously granted. Our relationship has grown in understanding and joy from that day. He even helped me name my son.

The sins of ethnic partiality, pride, and presumption threaten to rip the Church apart. We've been told that to defeat racism, our country needs to be pulled up from the roots. To do anything less, some say, is to join the racist system, to join the enemy. But don't be fooled. Our enemy is sin, and our champion is Christ. When He defeated sin on the cross, He broke sin's yoke of slavery in our lives and freed us to care for one another with selfless, impartial love. Christ alone can topple our greatest obstacle to ethnic unity in the Church, and it's not a rusted statue, an antiquated law, or an outdated police code. Through the tree and the tomb, Jesus pardons our partial hearts.

## DISCUSSION QUESTIONS

1. How have you seen the sin of explicit ethnic partiality or racism in your life? Where does ethnic partiality come from? How does it affect relationships?

2.  In Romans 5:12-21, Paul reminds us where sin originated and how Christ has conquered that sin for His people. How can a biblical concept of original sin help us fight our sin? How can it help us to care for other sinners?

3.  How does the Gospel of Jesus Christ answer the sin of ethnic partiality?

4.  What should it look like for Christians to "weep with those who weep" because of sin and its effects in our world? How can we be both discerning about the legitimate causes of suffering and empathetic to those who are suffering?

5.  What does Paul mean in 1 Corinthians 13:7 when he writes that "love believes all things?" How would an active application of that principle transform the way that you relate to your brothers and sisters in Christ? In particular, how might it change your conversations about race and ethnicity?

## CHAPTER 5
# ETHNICITY AND GUILT

## VICARIOUS APOLOGIES

The pope said, "Forgive us." The primate of Italy wasn't reciting the Lord's Prayer or a catchy Christian tune. Throughout his tenure as the bishop of Rome, Pope John Paul II issued several official, pontifical, corporate apologies, all of which roused rapt media attention and garnered widespread support. His penitential life was prolific. By the end of it, John Paul managed to apologize more than any other pope in the history of the Roman Catholic Church and not just for himself. He had asked God to forgive millions of guilty sinners for countless sins he himself did not commit.

For example, in 1985, John Paul flew to Douala in the Central African Republic to apologize for "Christian nations" and their sinful participation with the "trade in blacks."[208] In 1992, the pope addressed the Pontifical Academy with an apology for the Catholic Church's mistreatment of Galileo for asserting that the Earth revolved around the sun.[209] And in 1999, he expressed his "deep regret for the cruel death inflicted on John Hus," an early Bohemian Reformer who was burned at the stake by the Catholic Church for stating that Christ, not the pope, is the head of the Church.[210] To God, in front of all these people hurt by Roman Catholics throughout the history of the church, the pope said, "Forgive us."

The terrifying truth is that God did not answer John Paul's prayers. I understand that it may sound harsh to say that God didn't answer the pope's prayer for forgiveness, but there are a number of theological reasons for saying so; and one in particular is important for our study of ethnic division in the Church. God didn't answer John Paul II's prayers for forgiveness because the offenders he prayed for were already dead. The judgment for their guilt had already been pronounced. In the court of Heaven, the verdict had been rendered, the gavel dropped, and the sentence delivered. Despite his claims to the contrary, the pope's prayers did not erase any guilt from the ledger of Heaven because, in fact, they could not.

What I'm getting at is that there exists an unbreakable connection between the guilty and their guilt. Man cannot violate that connection, pope or not. It's an inviolable principle of the justice of our Lord. God doesn't forgive me for your sins or you for mine. We're all equally and individually accountable at the throne of judgment. I can only be forgiven for the crime I am guilty of committing. Try as I might to seek forgiveness for the sins of others (like American chattel slavery, Jim Crow laws, and all other manifestations of racism through the centuries), my apology won't remove anyone else's guilt before God or man. I've got my own guilt that needs removing, and I'm powerless to remove it. And that guilt can't be taken away by just anyone.

Our guilt has limits. A positive way to say it is that guilt has scope. The debt for sin committed doesn't extend indefinitely or indiscriminately from one person to another. We're not guilty for the sins of all Christians, and all Christians aren't guilty for our sins. God doesn't hold us responsible for all the sins of those that have come before any more than he held them accountable for our future sins. Our Lord has not granted anyone limitless power to vicariously apologize for the sins of our man-made groups. While the effects of sin may linger long in this world, the guilt of sin is settled in the next.

No one, not even a pope, can take guilt from a grave. No one, that is, except Jesus.

## WHITE REPENTANCE

Guilt, repentance, and forgiveness—thoroughly Christian terms—now fall frequently from non-Christian lips decrying racism on our shores. For example, in conversations today about ethnic unity, one of the most popular mandates littering antiracist books, signs, and slogans is the call to white repentance.[211] That is, European Americans (both inside and outside of the Church) are called upon to turn the tide of white supremacy by various means: to study the many unheard stories of America's racist crimes against African Americans in history, to acknowledge their own complicity in the continuing oppression of racist societal structures, and to ask African Americans for forgiveness and insight into how to make reparations.[212] The argument goes that white people today are on the social and moral hook for the sins of their racial contemporaries and ancestors, and the only path forward begins with tangible repentance for those sins.

In the world, this process of white repentance usually takes on political, sociological, and psychological dimensions. European Americans must reform the criminal justice system, reverse neighborhoods' demographics, and reorient attitudes about race.[213] We're told that Americans with lighter skin should prostrate themselves before Americans with darker skin in demonstrations of contrition for ancestral sins.[214] Some writers and politicians have also advocated for financial reparations to African Americans as another step in righting the wrongs of American slavery.[215] For example, author Jim Wallis (a European American theologian and the founder of *Sojourners*) writes:

> It's time to repent from our original sin of racism by repairing our racialized policing and criminal justice system, by restoring voting rights to all Americans, by striving to undo the profound inequities in our education system, and by ensuring that the same economic opportunities are available to people of all races.[216]

Our newsfeeds and social media pages have been filled with arguments vehemently for or against these approaches to ethnic harmony. The cultural debate continues.

Inside the Church, the mantra of white repentance sounds a little different. European American Christians are charged to employ biblical categories like lament, repentance, and reconciliation to forge multiethnic relationships and reform Church practices that have purportedly reinforced racist ideologies.[217] According to a number of prominent church leaders, churches who want multi-ethnic harmony must hire more minority culture pastors; sing more ethnically diverse songs; and promote more books, materials, and sermons by authors and speakers who are not of European descent.[218] Bible studies about race and racism have become the new norm in the American church, searching for some way to heal the obvious and painful racial wounds in the body. Many center on the repentant posture that European American Christians must take toward African American Christians with respect to past systems of oppression like American slavery.

My guess is that this call for white repentance sounds pretty familiar to you at this point. If you've been tuning into the evening news, scrolling through Facebook, or even just driving down your neighborhood streets, you've likely heard these calls for justice, equity, and a settling of ethnic accounts. It's everywhere. Popular Christian author Max Lucado held a prayer rally to ask for forgiveness for racism, past and present.[219] Minneapolis Christians knelt before their African American neighbors and prayed, seeking their forgiveness for systemic racism.[220] Spiritual gurus have penned penitent prayers to African Americans like the following:

> On behalf of myself and on behalf of my country, to you and all African Americans, from the beginning of our nation's history, in honor of your ancestors and for the sake of your children, please hear this from my heart . . . I apologize, please forgive us.[221]

The message of these gestures is unmistakable: white people need to seek forgiveness from God and their black neighbors for their own racism and that of their white predecessors. White guilt is a foregone conclusion, and the logical next step is white repentance.

Now, you may have a variety of reactions to the call for white repentance. Maybe you yourself have championed these ideas and desperately want to see them come to fruition. Maybe you recoil at the thought of apologizing for colonial sins and argue that "I wasn't there, so I'm not responsible." Maybe you wish the whole conversation would just go away. However you respond to the language of white repentance, you probably know how critical this conversation is to the multi-ethnic unity of the Church.

The Church cannot enjoy harmonious freedom in Christ as long as ethnic guilt hangs over our heads, real or not. If you believe you're owed an apology for racist sins against you and you're not hearing that apology, that must be incredibly frustrating and disheartening. If you contend that there's no racism you need to apologize for, then you're also probably frustrated at the consistent call to repent of racist crimes you've never committed. We will stay at each other's throats as long as there is this outstanding, unresolved guilt, and the peace of the body of Christ will remain ruptured. The sin of ethnic partiality unquestionably splits the Church (and has for centuries), and so does lingering shame for ethnic partiality. A wall of white guilt has and will divide the body of Christ.

So, the question that we need to answer is at once profoundly simple and complex: who is guilty of what? Is there unrepentant racism festering unchecked in our midst? Are there unfounded accusations holding unpayable debts over our heads? Who is responsible for the sins of the past, and how do we deal with that as a Church? Does anyone have the kind of vicarious authority the pope claims for himself to remove guilt on behalf of another? Will God forgive not just you, not just me, but *us*?

As always, we need to look to God's Word for clarity. In it, God shows us how guilt works, how the price is paid, and how we can be finally forgiven.

## GUILT IS WHAT SIN OWES

Answering a simple question like "Who is guilty?" has become increasingly difficult in our ethnically divided age. To pierce through this fog, we would do well to begin with some first principles, some guiding lights, then explore the nuances from there. We'll start by defining guilt from a biblical perspective, establishing that individual people are held accountable for their own sins.

We need to rightly define "guilt." The biblical concept of guilt comes from a Hebrew word that focuses on the consequence of an evil act, the debt that sin incurs.[222] In its 102 uses in the Old Testament, this word never refers to guilt as a subjective "sense of guilt"—a feeling about wrongdoing—but always deals with an objective reality. Guilt, according to the biblical authors, is the objective liability, the necessary payment, or the restitution required to repair a ruptured relationship.[223] The primary Hebrew word for "guilt" is used interchangeably with "guilt offering," the actual payment rendered for that objective liability. In fact, the English Standard Version sometimes translates the Hebrew word for "guilt" as "compensation," mostly in the book of Leviticus, where the word is used forty-two times to refer to the payment of a debt through the sacrificial system. Put simply, guilt is not what sinners feel but what sin owes.

So, for example, if I stole thirty dollars from your wallet, I would be guilty of stealing, and that guilt would have an obvious price tag: thirty dollars. Even in that simple example, we should note one of the foundational assumptions in the idea of guilt: the justice principle known as "lex talionis," or more famously, the "eye-for-an-eye" principle. Moses writes in Exodus 21:23, "But if there is harm, then you shall pay life for life, eye for eye, tooth for tooth, hand for hand, foot for foot, burn for burn, wound for wound, stripe for stripe." This "tit-for-tat" concept holds that the appropriate restitution for an offense must match the nature and extent of the offense.[224]

Numbers 5:6-7 confirms that this is indeed the nature of the biblical concept of guilt. God tells Moses to instruct the Israelites regarding their own guilt, saying:

> "Speak to the people of Israel, When a man or woman commits any of the sins that people commit by breaking faith with the LORD, and that person realizes his guilt, he shall confess his sin that he has committed. And he shall make full restitution for his wrong, adding a fifth to it and giving it to him to whom he did the wrong."

The phrase "full restitution" in this passage uses the word usually translated as "head" to mean "the complete measure" or "the right amount."[225] If you burn down someone's house, you owe them a house. The weight of your guilt accords with the weight of the sin. The payment of the fifth seems to be an additional compensation for any additional trouble caused by the wrongdoing. So, in the illustration where I stole thirty dollars from your wallet, the Old Testament law would say that the right repayment would include a five dollar fee for damages. This same sentiment shows up in Leviticus 6:1-17 as well, and the point there is the same. Guilt is the debt that sin owes in direct proportion to the sin committed.

This Old Testament concept of guilt remains consistent in the New Testament as well.[226] [t] At Jesus' mock trial, Pilate said to the people that he "found in him no guilt deserving death" (Luke 23:22). Notice the connection in that sentence between guilt and death. In the Roman legal system, as in every law code, there were different levels of punishment for different crimes committed because the guilt of those crimes was proportionate to the harm they inflicted. This justice principle is critical to any functioning society. Without it, you could get the electric chair for jaywalking or a small

---

t     Also note the New Testament concept of "indebtedness" as it related to sin (Matt 6:12-14).

fine for mass murder. Even pagan politicians recognize the need to adhere to this basic principle, that guilt is exactly what sin owes.

Abraham Lincoln understood the price of guilt as well. In his second inaugural address, in the midst of the Civil War, Lincoln declared:

> Fondly do we hope—fervently do we pray—that this mighty scourge of war may speedily pass away. Yet, if God wills that it continue, until all the wealth piled by the bond-man's two hundred and fifty years of unrequited toil shall be sunk, and until every drop of blood drawn with the lash, shall be paid by another drawn with the sword, as was said three thousand years ago, so still it must be said "the judgments of the Lord, are true and righteous altogether."[227]

That's a complex statement, but just observe the direct connection that Lincoln makes with his language between "every drop of blood drawn with the lash . . . paid by another drawn with the sword." A life for a life. Noah received this principle the second he stepped off the ark (Gen. 9:1-6), and it has shaped our understanding of guilt since then. Guilt is what sin owes.

## INDIVIDUAL GUILT IS REAL

While it's absolutely essential to agree to this biblical definition of guilt, we need to go a few steps further. If it's true that guilt is what sin owes, then what does sin owe; who owes it; and to whom do they owe it? This may seem almost too elementary for a conversation about ethnic division, but how we answer these questions will have a massive impact on how Christians from different ethnicities relate to each other in the Church. What do we owe each other, if anything, for our ethnically partial sins and the sins of past generations? Do European Americans owe a debt to African Americans because of the sin of chattel slavery and segregation? What about in the Church? Repentance and reconciliation hang in the balance, so we need to get this right.

I think we can affirm the Scriptural principle of individual guilt without much controversy. When I sin, I'm guilty. My daughter doesn't get disciplined when my son disobeys. The sinner bears the guilt for his own sin before man and before God.

Let's first address sin's guilt before God. On a human level, we have our weights and measures for trying to find proximate justice, to hold law-breakers accountable for their law-breaking. But in the courts of Heaven, God has fixed the perfectly just price for every sin against him (and all sin is against God—Psalm 51:4). Paul says it this way in Romans 6:23: "The wages of sin is death." If guilt is what sin owes, and sin owes God a life, then the life to be paid must be the sinner's life, forever. In the justice of God, I must die the second death in Hell for eternity as the price for my own sin because I am guilty of offending the infinitely holy God.

The prophet Ezekiel further clarifies for us what individual guilt means and doesn't mean. In Ezekiel's day, the exiled Jews accused God of unjustly punishing them for the sins of their fathers. They said, "'The fathers have eaten sour grapes, and the children's teeth are set on edge'" (Ezek. 18:2). In other words, "My dad did bad, but now I'm sad." "My parents were the ones who sinned and I pay the price." But God tells them, "As I live, declares the Lord GOD, this proverb shall no more be used by you in Israel. Behold, all souls are mine; the soul of the father as well as the soul of the son is mine: the soul who sins shall die" (Ezek. 18:3-4).

"The soul who sins shall die." No man will ever die the second death for sins he did not commit. God does not eternally condemn anyone for their parents' sins, though their parents' sins may seriously affect this life (more on this later). At the judgment, we stand before our holy, righteous Judge alone. As vile as the sins of our families or our communities have been, God doesn't damn us for them. He holds you and me to account for you and me. We are guilty of the sin that we commit. Individual guilt is what a sinner owes for his or her own sin.

So, if what someone means by a term like "corporate guilt" is that you can go to Hell for someone else's sin, we must emphatically and sharply disagree.

The line before the Judge's throne is single file. Where you will spend eternity does not depend on your family, your friends, or your ethnic group and what they do or don't do. Your eternal sentence depends on whether or not you receive the free pardon of God in Jesus Christ by faith or if you remain guilty before God in your own, individual sin. God damns persons, not people.

That being said, individual guilt involves more than our eternal destination. There are practical, earthly, temporal consequences for our sin, and the Bible confirms this again and again. Moses' guilt for disbelieving God in the wilderness incurred the cost of his physical exclusion from the Promised Land (Num. 20:10-13). David's guilt for committing adultery and murder earned for him three dead sons (2 Sam. 12:10-12). King Amon's wicked idolatry "incurred guilt more and more. And his servants conspired against him and put him to death in his house" (2 Chron. 33:23-24). Even in the New Testament, we find God putting people in an early grave because of their guilt of sin (Acts 5:1-11; 1 Cor. 11:28-30). Individual guilt often carries with it individual, temporal consequences distinct from the eternal debt that all sin owes. "Know then that God exacts of you less than your guilt deserves" (Job 11:6).

So, there are two dimensions to our individual guilt before God—eternal and temporal. For any one sin, God will, without exception, punish it with His perfect, eternal wrath, either on the sinner in Hell or in Christ on the cross. In addition, God may also bring about a temporal consequence for that sin, though the temporal consequences are varied and often, in God's mercy, foregone altogether.

Before humans, then, we should recognize that there is no eternal dimension of guilt, only a temporal one—namely, a fractured relationship and maybe also an external retribution. So, for instance, when Zacchaeus the thieving tax collector received Jesus, he said, "If I have defrauded anyone of anything, I restore it fourfold" (Luke 19:8). Realizing the guilt of his sin before man, Zacchaeus sought to make it right by repenting and giving back what he had stolen and then adding some extra as a show of good faith. According to Jesus, when we sin against each other, we must quickly repent, seek a restoration of the relationship, and right the wrong we've committed (Matt. 5:21-26). In so doing, we acknowledge that there is a real, temporal dimension to our guilt before man.

One brief application of individual guilt to this conversation, then, would be that if I sin by being ethnically partial, then I need to repent. "But if you show partiality, you are committing sin and are convicted by the law as transgressors" (James 2:9). I'm on the hook for my racist thoughts, words, or deeds—not anyone else. I need to acknowledge that sin and confess it to both God and to those whom I have hurt. "Therefore, confess your sins to one another and pray for one another, that you may be healed" (James 5:16). Healing multi-ethnic wounds in the body of Christ requires our recognition of individual guilt. We should be quick to acknowledge our guilt and eager to repent of it for the sake of unity in the body.

## CORPORATE GUILT IS REAL

If you're a Christian, you're probably comfortable with the idea that you're guilty for your own sins. But is there ever any sense in which we can be guilty together? Can a group be guilty? Is there such a thing as corporate guilt?

Certainly, the world around us has adopted the concept of corporate guilt. In March 2008, German Chancellor Angela Merkel expressed shame on behalf of the German people for "the mass murder of 6 million Jews, carried out in the name of Germany."[228] In March 2019, the Australian government awarded reparations to two Aboriginal tribes for the collective mistreatment of those people groups, especially in removing them from their ancestral lands.[229] Similar apologies and reparations have been called for in the United States, citing the corporate sins of colonial, antebellum, and modern European Americans as the grounds of this guilt. We're familiar with this concept of corporate guilt coming from the world.

Corporate guilt is also a biblical concept, though not in the way that the world defines it. Frequently throughout the Old Testament storyline, we find God holding not just individual Israelites accountable for their own individual sins, but also the entire nation of Israel accountable for all kinds of sins. For example, when Joshua led the people in the conquest of Canaan, their victory march was halted by the sin of one man, Achan, who broke God's rules and kept some of the spoil of war for himself. God spoke to Joshua and said to him, "Israel has sinned; they have transgressed my covenant that I commanded them; they have taken some of the devoted things" (Josh. 7:11). God says "Israel has sinned" when in reality, only Achan had sinned. Why? Corporate guilt.

In 2 Chronicles 19, King Jehoshaphat appointed Levites, priests, and heads of families to judge legal disputes for the people of Israel. In his address to these newly appointed representatives, he said:

> "Whenever a case comes to you from your brothers who live in their cities, concerning bloodshed, law or commandment, statutes or rules, then you shall warn them, that they may not incur guilt before the LORD and wrath may not come upon you and your brothers. Thus you shall do, and you will not incur guilt" (2 Chron. 19:10).

Note that for these judges, a failure to warn the people could result in wrath coming on "you and your brothers." In this instance, the sin of a leader could produce corporate guilt for the whole group. Read the rest of Chronicles to see this same dynamic play out with Judah's kings over and over again.

Often noted today, as well, are the cases of Ezra, Nehemiah, and Daniel's corporate repentance. Ezra, for example, responds to the sinful intermarriage of some of the returned Jewish exiles by praying to God, saying, "Our iniquities have risen higher than our heads, and our guilt has mounted up to the heavens" (Ezra 9:6). Ezra didn't participate in the sin, but he uses the first-person plural pronoun "our" to describe the guilt incurred by that sin.

Responding to a report about the unfinished walls of Jerusalem, Nehemiah "[confesses] the sins of the people of Israel, which we have sinned against you. Even I and my father's house have sinned" (Neh. 1:6). Here, Nehemiah admits his own culpability but still sees fit to confess for the sins of the whole nation, not just his own. Daniel likewise owns the sins of all the exiled Jews when he prays, "All Israel has transgressed your law and turned aside, refusing to obey your voice" (Dan. 9:11). The reality of corporate guilt is confirmed by these corporate prayers of confession.

If individual guilt is what one person owes for his own sin, then corporate guilt would be what a group owes for the sins of some or all of its members. There are a couple of important theological caveats to make, however.

First, corporate guilt in the Bible is never eternal, only temporal; it never refers to the debt of God's infinite wrath against individual sin. Nobody goes to Hell for the sins of their group. We already read, "The soul that sins shall die" (Ezek. 18:20), referring to the second death of the lake of fire (Rev. 20:14). So, the restitution required for corporate guilt in the Bible is not eternal condemnation but temporal consequence. Israel faced political overthrow, military failure, and mass exile as the consequences for their corporate guilt, but not unending torment. Individual guilt earns Hell, but not corporate guilt.

Look, for instance, at Israel's long history of temporal discipline at the hand of Almighty God. Israel was guilty of failing to completely drive out the inhabitants of Canaan, so God punished them with war and enslavement (Judg. 2:1-4, 14-15). Israel was guilty of rejecting God as their king, so God judged them by giving them an unrighteous king who led them into ruin (1 Sam. 8:7, 18). Israel was guilty of worshipping other gods, so God raised up Assyria and Babylon to destroy their homes and lead them into exile (Jer. 22:21-22). We would search in vain for any example in Scripture of God condemning an entire nation to the lake of fire because of the sins of some of its members. Eternal guilt is not imputed (to use a theological word) to others, except in one instance—the cross. Jesus' death is the only instance in the Bible of the guilt of damnation passing from the guilty to the innocent. And praise God it is.

That being said, the biblical concept of corporate guilt is more than just the affirmation that sin has consequences. Of course, that's true, that God has engineered the world to work in such a way that sin often comes back to bite us; and quite often, it sinks its teeth into the people around us as well. But that's not corporate guilt; that's just living in a broken world. Corporate guilt in the Bible means that a group is responsible before God for the sins of some or all of its members. It is an actual debt for which God holds a group accountable. But it has limits.

## CORPORATE GUILT IS COVENANTAL

The key biblical concept to understanding corporate guilt is *covenant*. Covenants define relationships between groups and between individual people and so outline how each will respond when the other breaks the agreement. For example, when Israel entered into a covenant with God at Mount Sinai, God expounded through Moses, in no uncertain terms, the detailed commands that would necessarily govern their relationships with God and with each other in the covenant community. Theologians usually call this the Mosaic Covenant. It defined for Israel not only how they must live as a corporate entity, but also how God would respond to their sins as a group. Corporate guilt was defined for Israel by their covenant with God.

Think about it. Why did all of Israel get punished for Achan's sin? He was just one man! God actually tells us, "Israel has sinned; they have transgressed my covenant that I commanded them" (Josh. 7:11). Why did the whole nation suffer from the sins of Jereboam and Ahaz and all the other individual, wicked kings in Israel's history? Why did God sweep up together innocent children with guilty rulers? Jeremiah explains:

> And many nations will pass by this city, and every man will say to his neighbor, "Why has the LORD dealt thus with this great

city?" And they will answer, "Because they have forsaken the covenant of the LORD their God and worshiped other gods and served them (Jer. 22:8-9).

The expectations and limitations of corporate guilt in Scripture are defined by covenants. God's covenant with Israel set both the standard for their behavior and the boundary of their responsibility. When Moses, along with all the Israelites, stood at the foot of the mountain, under the thundering cloud of Yahweh, and declared, "'All the words that the LORD has spoken we will do'" (Exod. 24:3), they did not ensure the obedience of the Canaanites, the Girgashites, or the Jebusites. The Mosaic Covenant was only binding for those in the covenant community, and not one person more.

But Israel did commit to the covenantal obedience of every last soul in Israel, from the aged elder to the weaning child. For those who couldn't understand, those who could bore the responsibility. In the act of confirming the Mosaic Covenant, the people of Israel agreed to be responsible for the sins of every member in their group before God. And every successive generation of Israelites raised in that covenant community inherited the same responsibility and thereby the same danger of incurring corporate guilt, even for the sins of a few (Deut. 28:15-68). They also inherited the promise of blessing for the obedience of the covenant community (Deut. 28:1-14). So, the Israelites were covenantally bound to root out sin from their midst, to police their own to protect the promise.

When the people renewed their covenant with God on the plains of Moab, on the verge of the Promised Land, Moses defined the covenant participants with crystal clarity, saying:

> You are standing today, all of you, before the LORD your God: the heads of your tribes, your elders, and your officers, all the men of Israel, your little ones, your wives, and the sojourner who is in your camp, from the one who chops your wood to the one who draws your water, so that you may enter into the

sworn covenant of the LORD your God, which the LORD your God is making with you today, that he may establish you today as his people, and that he may be your God, as he promised you, and as he swore to your fathers, to Abraham, to Isaac, and to Jacob. It is not with you alone that I am making this sworn covenant, but with whoever is standing here with us today before the LORD our God, and with whoever is not here with us today (Deut. 29:10-15).

Here's the point: the limits of corporate guilt in Israel were set by a covenant with God that extended to every Israelite. This meant that Israel couldn't be held liable for the sins of other nations, and they also wouldn't be judged by God for the sins of their forefathers (though there would certainly be fallout from the sins of others). They stood before God as a group on the terms of their covenant with Him. No matter how badly their parents had sinned, no matter how idolatrous the surrounding nations became, God made a covenant promise to Israel, saying, "For the LORD will again take delight in prospering you, as he took delight in your fathers, when you obey the voice of the LORD your God" (Deut. 30:9-10). The guilt of the people depended on their own commitment to the covenant. Nobody else.

## CORPORATE GUILT IS STILL COVENANTAL

Now, let's put this in our context as New Covenant believers. Unlike the Old Covenant, the New Covenant community is not made up of primarily one ethnic group, but includes believers from any and every nation. Like the Old Covenant, however, the New Covenant itself establishes the boundaries for our corporate responsibility. As with Israel, our guilt only extends as far as the members of our immediate covenant community. We usually call it the *local church*.

The New Testament authors, and Jesus Himself, affirmed these ecclesiastical limits to the corporate guilt of the New Covenant community, and they did so through the institution of church discipline. In Matthew

18:15-20, Jesus lays down the covenantal terms of the as-yet-formed New Covenant community, which requires His disciples to confront sin in the lives of fellow disciples. Our Lord commands:

> If your brother sins against you, go and tell him his fault, between you and him alone. If he listens to you, you have gained your brother. But if he does not listen, take one or two others along with you, that every charge may be established by the evidence of two or three witnesses. If he refuses to listen to them, tell it to the church. And if he refuses to listen even to the church, let him be to you as a Gentile and a tax collector (Matt. 18:15-17).

These commands presuppose a couple of things. First, they assume some kind of relational contact with the brother who sins. Second, they assume participation in an assembled group of believers, the Church, by the offended and offending disciples. It would be inappropriate to say that Jesus commands Christians to be responsible for the sins of all other Christians everywhere, but right to say that we are absolutely on the hook for sin in our local bodies.

Paul affirms that the scope of Christian corporate guilt is the local church when he condemns an incestuous Corinthian. Paul writes to the divided church:

> It is actually reported that there is sexual immorality among you, and of a kind that is not tolerated even among pagans, for a man has his father's wife. And you are arrogant! Ought you not rather to mourn? Let him who has done this be removed from among you (1 Cor. 5:1-2).

The sin of the one man—sleeping with his step-mom—led to the guilt of the whole church because they pridefully "tolerated" that sin in their midst. They allowed sin to grow up "among" them. They were responsible to confront a believer living in such gross immorality and remove him from their body. They weren't responsible for every pagan, as Paul puts it, who broke the Roman laws prohibiting incest. The courts would take care of that.

But the Church was bound by the New Covenant in Jesus' blood to obey their Lord and excise sin from their body. The boundary of their corporate guilt was their local church.

Cementing this truth, Jesus gave some instructions regarding corporate guilt to the local church of Pergamum, located in the modern-day city of Bergama, Turkey. Through the apostle John, Jesus declared to this struggling church:

> But I have a few things against you: you have some there who hold the teaching of Balaam, who taught Balak to put a stumbling block before the sons of Israel, so that they might eat food sacrificed to idols and practice sexual immorality. So also you have some who hold the teaching of the Nicolaitans. Therefore repent" (Rev. 2:14-16).

The command to "repent" is actually given in a second-person singular command. Jesus addresses the church at Pergamum as one body, one unit, corporately responsible before Him for the sins of "some" with Balaam's false teaching and "some" Nicolaitan heretics. Because of the sins of a few, the whole church is called to account. That's church-wide, corporate guilt.

## YOUR CHURCH IS YOUR CHARGE

Okay, that's a lot of biblical information. Why does it all matter? Let me put it as simply as I can, Christian: your church is your charge. The scope of your responsibility for the sins of others, in the sense that you are accountable before God and each other for their sins, is your local church. God will not hold you accountable for the church down the street. You certainly aren't guilty for the sins of all Americans or all humans. The members of your church are corporately guilty for the sins of the members of your church that you tolerate. If you practice church discipline per the Lord's instructions, if you repent of arrogance for allowing sin to fester in your midst, if you root out ethnic partiality from your gathered body, then you can stand before the Lord with a clean conscience. If you don't, then together, you will stand accused.

At the church where I serve, all members are required to sign a document called the "Membership Agreement," which is just another name for a covenant. Here are just two of the commitments our members make in signing that paper:

> I understand and agree to abide by the discipline and restoration policy as explained in the church bylaws.

> I will protect the unity of my church by acting in love toward other members, by refusing to gossip and by respecting and following the leaders and the teachings of the church.

In reality, protecting the unity of the church by acting in love and agreeing to confront one another in our sins are two sides of the same coin. If we fail to practice church discipline as our Lord commanded, then division, not unity, will reign in our body.

Without healthy, loving confrontation of sin—and especially ethnic partiality—in our church, we'll look more like a high school cafeteria than a family with cliques, in-groups, out-groups, gossip, suspicion, favoritism, neglect, hatred, and eventually some serious fights. Churches that do not deal with the sin in their midst split. May that never be your story. This is how Jesus protects the harmony of His Church—by giving us clear methods and boundaries for dealing with sin.

## CORPORATE GUILT IS NOT RACIAL

On the other side of corporate, covenantal guilt is a different danger. Though we are susceptible to the sin among us, we are also in danger of succumbing to false forms of guilt from outside of our body. Wearing the shame of unearned guilt can also divide a church, and because of that, we need to be clear about what corporate guilt is not.

Corporate guilt is not racial. The most obvious reason that we aren't guilty for the sins of others in our racial group is that race is a fiction, per our study in chapter three. If you got a letter in the mail tomorrow congratulating you on your involuntary membership in the Good Neighbor Group, a neighborhood collective to promote friendliness on your block, you might be kind of excited but a little confused. But if the following day, you received a notice that you owed four thousand dollars to another neighborhood because one of the members of the Good Neighbor Group littered a few streets over, you would be understandably vexed and indignant. If racial groups are likewise involuntary and made-up, then corporate guilt doesn't extend to every member of those groups in any legitimate way.

Let's say, then, for the sake of the argument, that we're not dealing with racial groups but ethnic groups. Are we corporately responsible for the sins of others in our ethnic groups?

Well, if the scope of your responsibility before God is defined by the covenant community, then no. Unlike Old Covenant Israel, Christians have no covenant with all the members of our ethnic group. So, that means there are at least two groups of people whose sins are not on your shoulders— living people from your ethnic group and dead people from your ethnic group. Of course, if you choose to participate in the sins of others from your ethnic group, then you're guilty of those sins. But it is biblically illegitimate to argue that all people of an ethnic group are guilty of the sins of others from that group simply by association. Here are a couple of implications of this truth:

- All African Americans are not guilty of promoting transgenderism because the organization Black Lives Matter promotes transgenderism.
- All European Americans are not guilty of inciting race war because the Aryan Brotherhood incites race war.
- All Chinese citizens are not guilty of waging ethnocide against the Uyghurs because the Chinese government has waged ethnocide against the Uyghurs.

- All Mexicans are not guilty of "ethnic cleansing" in their neighborhoods because the Avenues, a Mexican mafia gang, has been guilty of targeting African Americans in efforts to "ethnically cleanse" their neighborhoods.

And if it's true that we're not guilty of the sins of every member in our ethnic group today, then certainly it's also true that we're not corporately or individually guilty for the sins of our ethnic group in the past. European Americans today are not guilty before God for the evils of American slavery, Jim Crow laws, or any other historical systems of racism, oppression, and ethnic violence. Whether or not those people carried your blood, your pigmentation, or your family name is absolutely irrelevant when you stand at the bar of heavenly justice, eternally or temporally. God will not hold any of us accountable for the transgressions of former generations unless we continue in them. And may that never be.

In contrast, a popular argument in favor of corporate racial guilt attempts to link Ezra and Daniel's penitential prayers with white repentance. For example, Tim Keller says:

> In Daniel 9, now we're talking about corporate guilt and responsibility inside a whole race or a culture . . . Here is Daniel feeling a responsibility for and repenting for things his ancestors did. Why? Because he knows that the culture that he's part of produced the sins of the past and he's still part of that culture. He senses the responsibility and the Bible senses the responsibility. He senses the connection.[230]

Also on the basis of Daniel's prayer, Jemar Tisby concludes that "Within Christianity . . . is a sense of corporate and communal participation" such that "it is up to the current generation to interrupt the cycle of racial compromise and confront it with courage."[231] Likewise on the basis of these prayers, Mark Vroegop contends, "We can lament the extent to which we have contributed to and been a part of a culture that allows, sanctions, or benefits from the sinful actions of others—both past and present."[232] Latasha Morrison makes this racial understanding of corporate guilt explicit:

> Like Ezra, Daniel had been personally innocent of the offenses against God, but he did not try to distance himself from the collective sin of his people. He owned his part in it as a member of the community . . . When we honestly acknowledge and lament the truth of our sins (especially our racial sins), we will come face to face with the shame and guilt of our collective past.[233]

What each of these authors does not acknowledge is the covenantal context of Ezra and Daniel's repentance. Kevin DeYoung writes, "The Jews were not lumped together because of race, ethnicity, geography, education level, or socio-economic status. The Israelites had freely entered into a covenant relationship with each other and with their God."[234] Daniel was not repenting for the sins of his ethnic family tree but for the sins of his covenant community. We cannot support the idea of corporate racial or ethnic guilt from the Bible, despite many recent, well-meaning attempts to do so.

Therefore, do not use the Bible to justify unbiblical ideas like "white guilt." There is no such thing as white guilt; it does not exist. Do not say that Nehemiah 1 is a model for white repentance. There is no such thing as white repentance. The Bible does not model ethnic repentance, but covenantal repentance. If the world wants to come up with sociological categories and terms to group and guilt people from different ethnicities, so be it. We stand on God's Word alone, and we preach Christ alone.

Though we long to see our government, our businesses, and our neighborhoods turn from evil and conform to the righteousness of Christ, that's not the assignment God has given to us. Our corporate guilt is limited to the sin we tolerate in our churches and our own failure to preach the Gospel to a dying world. May we say with the apostle Paul, "Therefore I testify to you this day that I am innocent of the blood of all, for I did not shrink from declaring to you the whole counsel of God" (Acts 20:26–27). Our charge is not the reformation of society but of the household of God. Your church is your charge.

Again, Kevin DeYoung confirms this limited extent of biblical, corporate guilt when he writes:

> The category of corporate responsibility can easily be stretched too far. The Jews of the diaspora were not guilty of killing Jesus just because they were Jews. Neither were later Jews in Jerusalem charged with that crime just because they lived in the place where the crucifixion took place. And we must differentiate between other-designated identity blocs and freely chosen covenantal communities. Moral complicity is not strictly individualistic, but it has its limits. All white people today are not automatically guilty of the racist sins of other white people.[235][u]

My hope in this chapter is not to answer every question that could be raised about corporate guilt, but instead to show where we need to turn our focus. If we're fixed on getting ethnic groups to repent of past sins they didn't commit or owning present sins of people who look like them, then we're probably ignoring present sins in our own spiritual family and holding people accountable for that which God does not. Instead, we ought to be preaching the guilt-bearing cross to each other and to the world so that once and for all, we can be free from the guilt of our own sin.

## MY GUILT, HIS NAILS

Believer, we've got good news about guilt, don't we? The pope's prayers can't remove it. Ethnic repentance can't erase it. Reparations can't pay it. But

---

u   In his article, DeYoung references Peter's speeches in Acts 2-3 as examples of corporate guilt, that all the Jews in Jerusalem are charged with the murder of Jesus. However, it would be better to understand these statements as rhetorical simplification for the sake of effect rather than an establishment of a new category of corporate guilt. That being said, DeYoung's point is well-taken—that Peter does address differently the Jews in Jerusalem and those outside of Jerusalem, thereby undermining any claims to corporate ethnic guilt in the case of Jesus' murder.

we know the One Who can, Who did, and Who has. On a bloody cross, "Jesus paid it all."

Paul presents this glorious good news about guilt in his letter to the Colossian church when he writes:

> And you, who were dead in your trespasses and the uncircumcision of your flesh, God made alive together with him, having forgiven us all our trespasses, by canceling the record of debt that stood against us with its legal demands. This he set aside, nailing it to the cross (Col. 2:13-14).

Just look at how Paul describes guilt in this passage—it's exactly how we've seen it defined elsewhere in Scripture. He calls our guilt "the record of debt that stood against us with its legal demands." Our trespasses, our rejections of God's law, require eternal restitution. The holy Judge of Heaven waves His gavel in the air, ready to pronounce condemnation on us for our sins. His sentence of death will be exactly what we deserve. And we're powerless to pay the price ourselves.

But then we look to the hill outside Jerusalem, and we see the nails. According to Paul, those metal spikes that pinned our Lord Jesus Christ to a Roman cross pinned the outstanding payment of our sin to Jesus Christ. In Jesus' beaten body hung the treasure of Heaven, brought out from the bank of eternal glory to exchange our balance for His. When Christ died, he absorbed our debt, took our guilt, and satisfied God's wrath against us. As we receive Him, we get His righteous credit, blameless record, and guiltless life. And we respond with worship. "Oh praise the one who paid my debt and raised this life up from the dead!"[v]

The answer to the guilt of despicable racism, past and present, is not hollow, ineffective apology on behalf of your race but the cold steel of Calvary's nails. Jesus has borne your guilt, Brothers and Sisters! He has buried your debt

---

v    Elvina M. Hall, "Jesus Paid It All," 1865, Public Domain.

in His tomb, and when He left that tomb, it was empty. No more guilt to be found. No more price to be paid. Only paradise to receive.

If we can't be united around this Good News, then how can we be one? We, the guilty, have been pardoned. He, the Innocent, has been crushed. Will we, then, demand satisfaction for that which has been satisfied? Will we continue in unforgiveness as those who have been forgiven much? Will we believe the world's lies about corporate guilt and ethnic repentance, or will we stand together on equal ground at the foot of the cross? Will we live as guilty or free?

## THE LINGERING EFFECTS OF SIN

Now, I don't mean to imply by this reminder of the glorious Gospel of our guilt-bearing Savior or by our survey of individual and corporate guilt in the Bible that all we need to do to deal with ethnic partiality is sing about the cross. We ought to acknowledge that sin, though conquered in Christ, has not been erased from this earth yet, nor have its effects. And that pushes us back to Scripture.

On Mount Sinai, where God gave His law that constituted the terms of His covenant with His people, Moses asked to see God's glory (Exod. 33:18). God denied his request but said that He would pass by and reveal Himself (Exod. 33:21-23). Hiding Moses in a crag in the mountainside, Moses heard God describe Himself in one of the most-quoted and most glorious Old Testament passages in Scripture:

> The LORD passed before him and proclaimed, "The LORD, the LORD, a God merciful and gracious, slow to anger, and abounding in steadfast love and faithfulness, keeping steadfast love for thousands, forgiving iniquity and transgression and sin, but who will by no means clear the guilty, visiting the iniquity of the fathers on the children and the children's children, to the third and the fourth generation" (Exod. 34:6-7).

Of particular interest to our study of guilt is the last phrase in that sentence, the one about "visiting the iniquity." What this passage is *not* saying, which we noted earlier, is that God condemns people to eternal Hell for the sins of their parents. Apart from Christ, we stand condemned before God on the basis of our own sin. We don't need any help creating an eternal debt; we're quite capable on our own.

What this passage *does* mean is that the character of God is such that He allows the sins of one generation to influence the next in this broken, cursed world. "Visiting" in this verse doesn't refer to guilt distribution but to corrupting influence. If the parents worship idols, it's likely that their kids will worship idols, too. Liars beget liars. Swindlers bear swindlers. Racists raise racists. God allows this to happen in His world as a natural consequence of sin.

So, it should not surprise us, then, that as Israel transmitted its sins to the children's children, so, too, has America. Fourth generation plantation owners didn't invent the system of slave-ownership; they just inherited and embraced it. In a way, racism yesterday begets racism today. The ethnic partiality behind these ideas has been passed down to children through their parents. Throughout the history of our country, ethnic partiality has been propagated at the dinner table. Sin that starts in the heart multiplies in the home. The Bible acknowledges this reality, and we should, too.

We should, then, make a distinction between the effects of sin in our homes and our embrace of that sin. If, for example, your parents used racist slurs casually during your childhood, you're not guilty for that. We will all answer to God for our own sinful words, not those of our parents.

But we also shouldn't be ignorant to how our family's sin, and particularly the sin of ethnic partiality, can affect us. Tortured justifications for slavery were formed in colonial European American children at a young age as they watched African American children work while they were tutored inside. Kids learn the language of racism from their grandparents and parents. Even an indifference to inter-ethnic issues slides from the nonchalance of one generation to the next. Generally speaking, we receive the interpretations of the world that our parents present to us, and that has lasting implications. As the cast of the 1958 Rodgers and Hammerstein musical *South Pacific* sang it, "To hate all the people your relatives hate, you've got to be carefully taught."[236]

Don't assume, then, that you were handed a morally clean slate. Our minds need to be transformed into the mind of Christ, not conformed to the world of our forebearers' design. If your parents gave you a biblical ethic of ethnicity, praise God. But if your parents repeated cultural mantras more than biblical convictions, it may be time to take a hard look at your own inherited attitudes about race and ethnicity.

For those who are parents right now, let me hasten to add that we have an incredible opportunity. We can raise our children in a home that communicates an assumed equality and value of all people based in Scripture, but it won't happen accidentally. Of course, we need to teach our kids about the image of God in man, the origin of different ethnicities at Babel, and the beauty of the united multi-ethnic Bride of Christ. But we need to take it a step further.

Do we invite people from different ethnicities into our homes? Do we take time to learn and to teach about different cultures? Do we acknowledge the hardships faced by people from different ethnic groups and help our kids to form a biblical worldview about those issues? Do we show our children how Jesus Christ brings together people from radically different cultures to worship him as one? Because of the lingering effects of sin, our history has a racist momentum that won't be stopped without a counter effort, and that effort begins in our hearts and our homes.

## UNRIGHTEOUS MAMMON

One last concern we need to address on the topic of ethnicity and guilt is white privilege. If it's true that corporate guilt is not racial, but at the same time, white people are actively complicit in on-going systemic racism by virtue of their willing reception of benefits gained by oppression (i.e., white privilege), then white people stand guilty of a form of racism. And if there are guilty debts to be paid or benefits to be exchanged because of white privilege, that would naturally affect our inter-ethnic relationships in the church. Again, if ethnic guilt remains, multi-ethnic harmony cannot. So, we must consider the claims of white privilege.

The concept of white privilege found its early formulation in the essays of W.E.B. Du Bois. In *The Souls of White Folk* (1920), Du Bois summarizes the concept of white privilege as "the white man's title to certain alleged bequests of the Fathers in wage and position, authority and training."[237] In the late 1960s, Theodore Allen's pamphlet, *White Blindspot*, called it "white skin privilege."[238] Allen continued to write on the topic, particularly focusing on the ways in which white privilege, developed during the Colonial era, served to maintain social hierarchies, oppress African Americans, and confer benefits on the European American working class.[239]

The most widespread formulation of the idea of white privilege came through the writing of a feminist scholar, Peggy McIntosh. In 1987, McIntosh published the now-famous article titled "White Privilege: Unpacking the Invisible Knapsack" in which she originally listed twenty-six benefits that she experiences by virtue of being a white person. Here are some of McIntosh's examples of her own white privilege, which are still cited today as representations of this dynamic:

> 1. I can if I wish arrange to be in the company of people of my race most of the time.

> 5. I can turn on the television or open to the front page of the paper and see people of my race widely represented.

> 9. I can go into a music shop and count on finding the music of my race represented, into a supermarket and find the staple

foods that fit with my cultural traditions, into a hairdresser's shop and find someone who can cut my hair.

19. If a traffic cop pulls me over or if the IRS audits my tax return, I can be sure I haven't been singled out because of my race.[240]

The problem, however, with these white privileges is not that they are, as McIntosh notes, "unearned," but that they are placed into the laps of white people by means of the oppression of non-white people. And therefore, according to writers like Ron Sider, participation in the benefits of white privilege produces real guilt. Sider writes, "If one is involved in unjust social structures . . . and does nothing to try to change them, then one is personally guilty in the same way that one is guilty if one commits an act of adultery or tells a lie."[241]

Perhaps most frustrating of all for white privilege advocates, it seems that many white people are unaware of these unique privileges. Professor George Yancey explains the intractable issue of white privilege this way:

> Often I hear whites say that they should not be blamed for the injustices of the past. They personally never owned slaves, killed Indians, stole land from Hispanics or put Asians in internment centers. They are quite right, but their assertions miss the bigger picture. While these majority group members did not directly participate in past racial sins, they have benefited from those sins. They enjoy their present economic standing partly because their ancestors were spared from racial discrimination. That fact raises a moral question for majority group Christians. Should Christians accept wealth that was stolen, even if they did not do the stealing?[242]

Do you see the ethical quandary? If you wouldn't accept a Snickers bar that was just stolen from the convenience store, then why would you (speaking to a European American person) accept security, comfort, wealth, and land that was all at some point stolen from other people groups by other European Americans? Isn't it just a matter of degrees of difference?

Allow me to respond with one affirmation and three clarifications. To begin with, we ought to affirm that there is such a thing as white privilege, even if that title is overly simplistic,[243] or you'd prefer to call it something else.[244] Since the inception of the category of "white people" four hundred years ago, the concept of race has been used to deprive people of God-given rights in order to gain financial, political, and social benefit for those with the power to take it. Since the horrors of American racism have been so widespread for so long, a lasting legacy was inevitable. Our world is what it racially is today because of the past that brought us here. Historically speaking, most of the societal advantages in America have gone to white people, and most of the disadvantages to non-white people. Consider, for a simple example, that it wasn't until 2009 that a non-white president sat in the Oval Office, preceded by forty-three white presidents who were not precluded from the office by their race. White privilege exists and meaningfully affects our lives.

Now, some clarifications. First, I would contend that receiving stolen candy and stolen land sovereignty are categorically different, and that difference matters. Technically speaking, property inheritance isn't white privilege, but it is closely related. Yancey implies by his language that white privilege is a kind of indirect participation in past racial sins, that a white person's home today is, so to speak, drenched in non-white, colonial blood. However, in so implying, Yancey confuses cause and effect, essentially erasing the distinction between sinning and benefitting from someone else's sin. And that's an important distinction.

What I mean is that sin is active, while privilege is passive. If I were to knowingly receive a candy bar that's just been stolen, I'd be guilty of actively entering into the possession of the benefit by ill-gotten means. That would be sin. However, if I grow up in a family that owns a house because my grandfathers and great-grandfathers also owned houses and passed down that wealth to my family, I haven't done anything to actively participate in receiving that home. Even if my ancestors violently asserted their ownership of that home, I was involuntarily born into it. White privilege, as I understand it, falls into this second category of benefits that come about not by voluntary action but by involuntary inheritance. One version deserves Hell; the other deserves circumspect reflection.

Second, I would point out that many white privileges simply constitute appropriate, respectful human interaction, the way all people should treat each other. McIntosh herself describes the unearned advantages of white privilege as "exemption from discrimination."[245] Not receiving suspicious looks on public transportation should be a universal standard, though, of course, we recognize that it sadly is not. But to call whites to repent of their complicity in systemic racism or "contribution to the maintenance of the status quo"[246] because they were shown common decency is utterly backward. Receiving kindness is not a sin to be repented of but a blessing to be enjoyed! It also is no excuse to ignore the plight of those who don't receive the same kindness. In such cases, white privilege should be an opportunity to reaffirm the value, dignity, and worth of all people because all people are equally made in the image of God.

Finally, Jesus Himself spoke to the issue of unearned advantages. In Luke 16:1-8, Jesus told a parable about a wicked, thieving manager who conned his master out of money in order to shrewdly ingratiate himself to other businessmen and thus secure his future. In a fascinating turn, Jesus actually commends this dishonest huckster, not for his forked tongue but for his serpentine prudence (Luke 16:8). Then Jesus says to His disciples, "And I tell you, make friends for yourselves by means of unrighteous wealth, so that when it fails they may receive you into the eternal dwellings" (Luke 16:9). What's going on here?

In a nutshell, Jesus is advocating shrewd stewardship. The phrase Jesus uses for "unrighteous wealth" means the corrupted, sin-stained goods of this world. The fact that this "mammon of unrighteousness," as the King James Version translates it, is attached historically to evil does not mean that it's untouchable for Christ's disciples. Quite the contrary. Jesus commands His followers to make prudent use of whatever blood money they possess, which according to Jesus means investing the money in evangelistic relationships in order to form eternal friendships.

Jesus does not say it's a sin to have tainted wealth, though it apparently would be disobedient to misuse it. Having the goods, the advantage, the privilege isn't the issue; what you do with it is. Of course, Jesus is in no way advocating theft or sinful gain, but given that all money and power in this world comes to us on a sea of past sins, our Lord calls us to turn that fake money into relationships without diminishing returns.

So, whatever privilege you have, be it from perceptions about whiteness or from family inheritance or from a lottery win, don't repent of it; instead, use it to win people to Christ. And in whatever disadvantages you suffer, trust in Christ to turn every unjust adversity into heavenly glory beyond comparison (2 Cor. 4:16-18). In either circumstance, seek contentment in Christ, empathy for those without, and opportunities to make the Gospel of Jesus known to a dying world.

## REPENTANCE AND FORGIVENESS

The Church doesn't need a pope to clear away our guilty records. He couldn't do it, and we already have forgiveness in our real High Priest, Jesus Christ, through His death and resurrection. And while we desperately need the humility and insight to see our sinful hearts and confess our wicked motives, I hope we can now see more clearly in the limits of our guilt the limits of our repentance. We don't repent for our race or for our privilege, but we do repent for ourselves and sometimes for our church. How much more potent will our contrition and confession be when it's aimed squarely at our sin and not at cultural targets? How much more united will our church stand knowing that our debts have been nailed to the cross, and there, Jesus paid it in full?!

The cancelling of our guilt at Calvary has myriad implications for our multi-ethnic unity in the Church, but maybe one of the most profound is our univocal worship in response. As a musician in the church, I have few greater joys than to lead God's people in singing God's praise together. As those who have been rescued from an eternal price by the blood of Christ, it's appropriate that we would unite our hearts in musical worship to the God Who declares the guilty not guilty.

One of my favorite songs that exults in this truth is Chris Anderson and Greg Habegger's "His Robes for Mine," which I've copied below.[247] May it lead us to higher and deeper love for the Savior who has declared us guiltless in Him.

> His robes for mine: O wonderful exchange!
> Clothed in my sin, Christ suffered 'neath God's rage.
> Draped in His righteousness, I'm justified.
> In Christ I live, for in my place He died.
>
> His robes for mine: what cause have I for dread?
> God's daunting Law Christ mastered in my stead.
> Faultless I stand with righteous works not mine,
> Saved by my Lord's vicarious death and life.
>
> His robes for mine: God's justice is appeased.
> Jesus is crushed, and thus the Father's pleased.
> Christ drank God's wrath on sin, then cried "'Tis done!"
> Sin's wage is paid; propitiation won.
>
> His robes for mine: such anguish none can know.
> Christ, God's beloved, condemned as though His foe.
> He, as though I, accursed and left alone;
> I, as though He, embraced and welcomed home!

*I cling to Christ, and marvel at the cost:*
*Jesus forsaken, God estranged from God.*
*Bought by such love, my life is not my own.*
*My praise—my all—shall be for Christ alone.*

## DISCUSSION QUESTIONS

1.  What's the difference between a feeling of guilt and objective guilt? Should there be a connection between the two? Should we feel guilty at all?

2.  What does it look like to compassionately confront sin for the unity of our local church? How can that process go awry? What fruit do we hope to see in church discipline?

3.  Have you ever felt the weight of guilt for sin on your shoulders? What did you do? How did the Gospel of Jesus intersect with your guilt?

4.  Read Colossians 2:8-15. How does the Gospel of forgiveness in Christ protect us from "empty deceit" and "human traditions?" What does Christ offer that no worldly philosophy can?

5.  Knowing that sin has lingering effects in our broken world, what would it look like to show empathy to your brothers and sisters in Christ who have been hurt by ethnic partiality? How can you support and encourage those still reeling from the effects of sin in their lives?

CHAPTER 6

# ETHNICITY AND JUSTICE

## THE JESUS SAVES GUY

His was the only sign that read "Jesus saves." On the sidewalk outside the Supreme Court in Washington, D. C., an African American street preacher named Sam Bethea held his hallmark placard high. Several other signs surrounded his—some labeled "Justice," others depicting graphic pictures of aborted babies, others calling for "health care justice." The crowds alternated chants, some shouting for "reproductive rights," others shouting pro-life justice mantras. Behind them, the Supreme Court building loomed darkly, its guiding principle signed in stone: "Equal justice under law."[248] A couple of women walking their dogs held their own signs that read, "#justice4life." Bethea's sign, "Jesus saves," stood out bright and beaten in a sea of slogans.

A few nights before, Bethea prayed with mourners outside of the Supreme Court as they paid their respects to the late Supreme Court Justice Ruth Bader Ginsburg.[249] A few nights before that, Black Lives Matter protestors covered Bethea with flour, silly string, and glitter in uptown Charlotte, N.C., his daily mission field.[250] In each circumstance, surrounded by slogans vying for various causes, Bethea held up his little yellow and black sign and called out, "Jesus saves." According to a Charlotte news station, locals affectionately refer to Bethea as "the Jesus saves guy."[251]

There are so many worthy signs the Church could lift up. It wouldn't take much to become known as "the pro-life church" or "the racial justice church."

It'd be relatively easy to champion the good and godly causes of our day, and we'd probably win some favor for it. But in this huddled mass of ideologies, protests, and convictional taglines, I wonder if our churches are willing to be known as "the Jesus saves church."

I don't know how orthodox Sam Bethea's beliefs are, and I'm not necessarily advocating for his evangelistic approach either; but it strikes me that in the midst of widespread Christian compromise, he is at least known for being about the main thing: the message that Jesus saves. Paul calls the Gospel of salvation a message of "first importance" (1 Cor. 15:3-6). Peter says that Jesus' name is the only "name under heaven given among men by which we must be saved" (Acts 4:12). Jesus Himself, whose ministerial life was filled with all kinds of merciful acts like healing and exorcism, said to His disciples, "'Let us go on to the next towns, that I may preach there also, for that is why I came out" (Mark 1:38). Disciple-making through Gospel-preaching stands tall as Christ's commission for His followers, unrivaled in primacy or urgency by all other worthwhile concerns.

In their landmark work on the mission of the Church, Kevin DeYoung and Greg Gilbert define our priority this way:

> "We believe the church is sent into the world to witness to Jesus by proclaiming the gospel[sic] and making disciples of all nations. This is our task. This is our unique and central calling."[252]

In other words, we're supposed to be known as "the Jesus saves church." That is our mission, and that alone is our message to the world. We already affirmed the priority of the Gospel in chapter one, and here we reaffirm and cement it.

And yet, our message of "Jesus saves" must not be torn away from Jesus' character. Sam Bethea demonstrated the inextricable connection between the message of Christ and the heart of Christ when he knelt to pray with the mourning and when he sorrowfully received scorn for Jesus' sake. Jesus, our great Savior Who condescended to reconcile His enemies, came because of His compassion. His life and mission were animated by His gentleness, meekness, and holiness. Jesus, the God of perfect justice, endured the wrath of God at Calvary precisely because He is so committed to His own justice. We dare not separate the message of Christ from the character of Christ.

In this last chapter, then, I want to chart a nuanced path for Christlike ministry to the world. The church's sign is Jesus' sign and her heart is Jesus' heart. As Jesus had compassion for the hurting, so do His people. As Jesus sought to free sinners from eternal condemnation through Gospel preaching, so do His disciples. Evangelism and mercy ministry should co-exist in the life of the Church, though not as equal, symmetrical missions. Jesus' compassion doesn't modify our mission—it explains our message. Jesus saves because Jesus cares. Or, another way to put it, justice spares from justice. And that should have a profound impact on how we relate to each other inter-ethnically in the Church.

## CALLS FOR RACIAL JUSTICE

Now, more than any other time in my life, I hear the cry for racial justice from every corner of American society. A drive down to Black Lives Matter Plaza (a two-block pedestrian section of Sixteenth Street NW in D.C.) reveals the public demand for justice. Signs, walls, and shirts plead, "Justice for Ahmaud" and "Justice for Breonna." Someone calls out, "No justice, no peace." Everywhere, it seems, from the nightly news to the grocery store, we hear about our country's desperate need for racial reckoning in the form of racial justice.

Religious institutions have begun to echo and adapt this message of racial justice. The United Church of Christ's minister for racial justice (let that sink in) describes the organization's pursuit of justice as an attempt to "disrupt institutions with unjust policies and practices" and to "preach resistance, inclusive identities, and justice for all."[253] The National Association of Evangelicals, representing more than forty thousand churches and forty different denominations, expressed their strong commitment to a "sustained effort toward racial justice and equality."[254] The Ethics and Religious Liberty Commission, the public policy arm of the Southern Baptist Convention, published an article contending plainly that "Christians should be involved in efforts to bring about racial justice" and that "to do so is nothing less than following in the footsteps of Jesus."[255] Church halls ring with cries for racial justice.

So, what precisely is intended by these calls for racial justice, especially within the Church? While the suggestions for how to pursue racial justice vary, author Jemar Tisby summarizes some of the most common justice efforts in his acronym, the ARC (Awareness, Relationships, and Commitment).[256] According to Tisby, racial justice begins with a historical, contextual awareness of the issues. He suggests that Christians take the time to watch documentaries, listen to podcasts, and do internet research on racial history in the United States in order to foster this sense of awareness. He recommends that Christians pour themselves into interracial relationships through intentional conversations, changing the restaurants they frequent, or joining a club or activity with people from a different ethnic group than your own. Tisby goes on to suggest clear, tangible expressions of commitment to racial justice. He advocates that believers act concretely to promote racial justice, like writing a blog post about race, joining a social justice organization, giving money to those who promote racial justice, and voting.[257] He goes on to contend for inventive forms of church-led reparations, the removal of Confederate monuments, public declarations decrying racism, and participation in a new civil rights movement, among other suggestions.[258] The goal of these efforts, according to Tisby, is clear: "Christians must . . . alter how impersonal systems operate so that they might create and extend racial equality."[259]

Several of these proposals are helpful suggestions for Christians to grow in their care and understanding for one another, which should be commended. Empathy for African American Christians is an entirely appropriate and godly response, especially in light of America's abominable sins during the era of slavery, segregation, and civil rights, and the impact that racial bigotry has on people today. May we all strive to "lay down our lives for the brothers"

(1 John 3:16) as Christ laid down His life for us, beginning with the basics of loving, Christian relationships.

But the critical question isn't whether or not we should love our brothers—of course, we should. Here's the question that we need to answer about these calls for racial justice: is that even justice?

As we've already seen, definitions matter, and words can have significant consequences. My hope in asking this question is not to "quarrel about words, which does no good, but only ruins the hearers" (2 Tim. 2:14) to tear down my brothers in Christ over some peccadillo. Rather, I want to "rightly handle the word of truth" (2 Tim. 2:15) so "that the man of God may be complete, equipped for every good work" (2 Tim. 3:17). If we're going to spend significant effort at enacting justice, we ought to be sure we're actually enacting justice and not a counterfeit calling itself justice.

Also, if racial justice is such a critical part of the Christian life, then we need to know how it relates to our primary mission from Jesus—to make disciples by Gospel proclamation. Broad-brush answers will not suffice for an issue this critical to the unity of the Church, so we need to go to the text of Scripture for clarity and truth. In it, we'll discover the God Who is both just and the Justifier, a God Who cares about all human suffering, and a God Who will Himself bring ultimate justice.

## JUSTICE JUST FROM GOD

The biblical language of justice grounds our understanding of this pillar doctrine. The Hebrew root for the word group translated "justice" or "judge" is used 1,057 times in the Old Testament, not including proper nouns. The Greek root for "justice" and "judge" is used 539 times in the New Testament.[w] Both words are used in a variety of contexts, often carrying multiple connotations related to time, action, character, and perception.[260]

---

w  It should be noted that 210 of the uses of κρινω are the verb ἀποκρίνομαι, which just means "to answer or reply," which doesn't fall into the same lexical range as most of the other uses.

So, any attempt to simplify the concept of the word "justice" in Scripture requires significant qualification.

However, if the main idea of the concept of biblical justice can be summarized, we could say that justice is a disposition that desires, as the Puritan Thomas Watson put it, "to give every one[sic] his due."[261] Other voices concur. Tim Keller says that the Old Testament word for justice can be understood as "giving people what they are due, whether punishment or protection or care."[262] Sixth century Roman emperor Justinian defined the concept of justice as "the constant and perpetual will to render to each his due,"[263] and medieval theologian Thomas Aquinas mostly agreed.[264] So, the words for justice are, in some way, related to the idea of rendering to another that which they deserve. Justice gives what's due.

We can also see this understanding of justice supported in Luke's gospel. In describing Jesus' crucifixion, Luke writes:

> One of the criminals who were hanged railed at him, saying, "Are you not the Christ? Save yourself and us!" But the other rebuked him, saying, "Do you not fear God, since you are under the same sentence of condemnation? And we indeed justly, for we are receiving the due reward of our deeds; but this man has done nothing wrong" (Luke 23:39-41).

Justice involves receiving what one is due, either for good or for ill. In the world of legal definitions, as in the Bible, the concept of justice takes on at least two dimensions: commutative and distributive.[265] x Commutative justice deals with individual people giving to each other their rights, while distributive justice deals with an appointed authority's fair treatment of people according to their rights. You can think of commutative justice as general justice and distributive justice as authorized justice. From a biblical perspective, general justice pertains to all individuals respecting each other's

---

x    Keller also uses these two categories but instead calls them "primary justice" and "rectifying justice."

God-given rights as creatures made in His image. On the other hand, the Bible describes authorized justice as coming from God-appointed authorities (like God Himself, parents, and governments) and conforming to God-designed standards of fairness.[266]

We start our study of biblical justice with these concepts because of the infinite importance of those hyphens. The most fundamental thing that can and must be said about justice, before anything else should be said, is that its source is the character of God. God is Justice. Justice does not have a stable definition outside of the character of God. Any idea of rights, fairness, and due all depend on the infinite Almighty, Who has established His own immutable character as the standard by which any concept of justice must be measured. To quote Thomas Watson again, "[God] is not only just, but justice itself."[267]

Scripture confirms that God is the Source and Standard of justice:

- "'The Rock, his work is perfect, for all his ways are justice. A God of faithfulness and without iniquity, just and upright is he'" (Deut. 32:4).
- "Righteousness and justice are the foundation of your throne; steadfast love and faithfulness go before you" (Psalm 89:14).
- "Now then, let the fear of the LORD be upon you. Be careful what you do, for there is no injustice with the LORD our God, or partiality or taking bribes" (2 Chron. 19:7).
- "But the LORD of hosts is exalted in justice, and the Holy God shows himself holy in righteousness" (Isa. 5:16).
- "The LORD within her is righteous; he does no injustice; every morning he shows forth his justice; each dawn he does not fail" (Zeph. 3:5).

Immediately, we should draw out two brief applications from the truth that God's own essence is the Source of all justice in the world. First, to any who long for justice to be done, the Bible would encourage us to ask God for that justice. "Many seek the face of a ruler, but it is from the LORD that a man gets justice" (Prov. 29:26). God may use men to enact justice, but we don't trust in men to give it. We trust that the Lord of all the earth will always do what's right, and we expect that man will often get it wrong. A concern for justice must first drive us to the source of justice in prayer.

Second, to any who question God's justice, recognize who you are and who you're questioning. "What shall we say then? Is there injustice on God's part? By no means . . . But who are you, O man, to answer back to God? Will what is molded say to its molder, 'Why have you made me like this?'" (Rom. 9:14, 20). God Himself answers Job's questions: "'Shall a faultfinder contend with the Almighty?'" (Job 40:2). We don't get to tell God that He's doing a good or bad job, that He's being fair or unfair, that we deserve, or are due, something else than what He has given in Providence. God, not man, is the standard of justice. A thousand theological debates and heart-wrenching questions would mercifully end if we would but follow Job's example and put our hands over our mouths in abased astonishment at the bulletproof justice of God.

Whatever else we have to say about justice, let it begin with the appropriate humility of a creature under the just rule of Justice Himself. Justice matters to us because it matters to God, and justice matters to God because God's character is just. Justice flows from the fountain of God.

## DUE JUSTICE

So, if justice comes from God and looks like people receiving their due, what are people due according to the standard of God's just character? The answer may be more complex than you'd think.[268]

First, all people are due dignity, respect, and life because we're made in the image of God. Those "certain inalienable rights" listed in our Declaration can't be alienated from us because God put His own irrevocable stamp on us at Creation. God has ultimate value, and a failure to treat His image-bearers as bearing value from God perverts justice. All people are due the right to life

(Gen. 9:5-6), the right to worship God (Dan. 3:16-18), and the right to personal property (Exod. 20:15, 17), to name a few of our creaturely endowments. Any refusal to give another person these basic rights, therefore, constitutes injustice, and the protection of those rights is just.

Our due as God's image-bearers bears a variety of implications in our relationships with each other. For example, God says, "For I the LORD love justice; I hate robbery and wrong" (Isa. 61:8), connecting the idea of justice with opposition to theft. Thieving is bad because people are entitled by God to not have their stuff stolen. God owns, so we own; so, don't steal.

Or, as another example, notice the reason why the coming Messianic King protects life: "He has pity on the weak and the needy and saves the lives of the needy. From oppression and violence he redeems their life, and precious is their blood in his sight" (Psalm 72:13-14). Why does this king rescue those who are about to be killed? "For," or "because," their life has value in his eyes. Where does that value come from? The image of God in man.

American slavery violated the justice of God because it denied image-bearers their due dignity. So, too, with Jim Crow laws, "separate but equal" judgments, and other heinous forms of institutionalized racism. When British slavers established the Middle Passage to the colonies, they stole livelihoods, children, dignity, and breath itself from precious African people made to reflect the worth of God. In American slavery, justice was perverted, and God's character was slandered by wicked European colonists. And to take this a step further, any continuing denial of fundamental rights due to African Americans, Mexicans, Koreans, Pakistanis, or the English on the basis of ethnicity spits in the face of a just and generous God and will be met with God's just retribution. God's image-bearers are due life and liberty by God's just design.

Second, all people are due impartial treatment because we are all created with equal rights by God. It's not as if God gave more of his image to Jim and less to Susan and just a dash on top for Kelly. No, all people possess the same amount of the image of God, marred though it is by sin. Therefore, nobody inherently possesses more worth or more rights. The rejection of human equality is called "partiality," and it's a despicable sin and injustice. "It is not good to be partial to the wicked or to deprive the righteous of justice" (Prov. 18:5).

God repeatedly confronts partiality based on disparity in wealth because it implies that someone is due more respect by virtue of being rich. James writes, "My brothers, show no partiality as you hold the faith in our Lord Jesus Christ, the Lord of glory" (James 2:1). He then goes on to give the reason why Christians should show no partiality, saying, "Have you not then made distinctions among yourselves and become judges with evil thoughts?" (James 2:4). The problem with partiality is that it fabricates distinctions in what is due from one person to another, thereby playing the part of God, Who fixes each man's equal due. Partiality toward the rich undermines the image of God in each man.

Of course, if wealth-based partiality is such a great evil, then ethnic partiality is a grave injustice as well. Preferring one race to another sets up a fictional, man-made distinction as determinate of one's due rather than the equal image of God in man. Since we've already discussed the sin of ethnic partiality at length in chapter four, I'll only reiterate that the equally distributed image of God in man provides the reason why preferring one people group to another is so absurd, unjust, and evil.

The epigram etched into the Supreme Court building—"equal justice under law"—enshrines this principle of impartiality in just judgment. In fact, the original use of the phrase by Justice Melville Fuller, borrowing from the Greek statesman Pericles, was "equal and impartial justice under the law" but was shortened to fit on the building's edifice.[269] Impartial justice can also be called "equity," or equality of process. Equity doesn't guarantee that everyone will receive the same outcome or that everyone will start from the same place, but it does mean that all are entitled to the same judicial rules (what we've come to call "due process") under the law. In a just, impartial, equitable society, there isn't one legal system for the poor, another for the rich, another for the black, another for the white. All are judged equitably by the same standard because all are created by God to be equal. "'You shall do no injustice in court. You shall not be partial to the poor or defer to the great, but in righteousness shall you judge your neighbor" (Lev. 19:15).

Third, all people are due compassion in their need because God has compassion on us in our need. While this may seem like a concept more at home in a discussion about generosity, the biblical teaching on justice repeatedly emphasizes this compassionate aspect of justice. Justice helps the hurting. "[God] executes justice for the fatherless and the widow, and loves the sojourner, giving him food and clothing" (Deut. 10:18). "The LORD works righteousness and justice for all who are oppressed" (Psalm 103:6). "It is well with the man who deals generously and lends; who conducts his affairs with justice" (Psalm 112:5). "I will seek the lost, and I will bring back the strayed, and I will bind up the injured, and I will strengthen the weak, and the fat and the strong I will destroy. I will feed them in justice" (Ezek. 34:16). Justice seeks to meet the needs of the needy.

The reason why others are due this kind of generosity in their need is reciprocal—because we ourselves are so often the ones in need who receive God's generosity. Careless and compassionless hearts are not only antithetical to those who wish to emulate their compassionate God, but they're also utterly hypocritical for needy little people like us. Paul writes, "For who sees anything different in you? What do you have that you did not receive? If then you received it, why do you boast as if you did not receive it?" (1 Cor. 4:7). Jesus' parable about the unforgiving servant draws out this same principle, culminating with the line, "And should not you have had mercy on your fellow servant, as I had mercy on you?" (Matt. 18:33).

Of course, this principle of justice can be taken too far, but it can also be taken too lightly. Justice does not require me to donate my way into abject poverty, but it does require me to live with an open hand. Before you start clutching at your wallet, consider that your wallet itself is a gift from God. Then open it up and meet the needs of the people you're closest to who truly need it. God's compassion compels our compassion as a just response.

Fourth, all people are due a reward for righteousness and punishment for wickedness because God has a plan for His image-bearers. I would hasten to clarify that whatever good I do, it is, as Augustine said, "God crowning his own glory," so I should be careful about taking credit where it's not due. However, because of God's plan to bring this world into final judgment and because of His own goodness that He has poured out into the hearts of men, it is just and appropriate for our Judge to both commend the commendable and condemn the condemnable. Elihu affirms this concept of due reward by critiquing its foil: "Shall one who hates justice govern? Will you condemn him who is righteous and mighty?" (Job 34:17).

All of Psalm 112 underlines this same notion, especially verse five and ten: "It is well with the man who deals generously and lends; who conducts his affairs with justice . . . The wicked man sees it and is angry; he gnashes his teeth and melts away; the desire of the wicked will perish!" In fact, the normal course of God's providential justice in the world is such that the "enemy came to an end in everlasting ruins" (Psalm 9:6) and such that David could pray, "Judge me, O LORD, according to my righteousness and according to the integrity that is in me" (Psalm 7:8).

The clearest application of this aspect of justice is in the sphere of government. Paul writes concerning God's design for governing authorities in Romans 13:3-4:

> For rulers are not a terror to good conduct, but to bad. Would you have no fear of the one who is in authority? Then do what is good, and you will receive his approval, for he is God's servant for your good. But if you do wrong, be afraid, for he does not bear the sword in vain. For he is the servant of God, an avenger who carries out God's wrath on the wrongdoer.

Often but not always, God's agents of justice in this world are governments that he has providentially installed to reward righteousness and punish evil. Reward is due to the righteous, and punishment is due to the wicked. Therefore, just judges give to their subjects what they are due for what they do.

Fifth and finally, all people are due eternal condemnation for our treasonous sins against the just Judge of man. If there's anything you and I are due, it's wrath. "For the wrath of God is revealed from heaven against all ungodliness and unrighteousness of men" (Rom. 1:18). "'None is righteous,'" or "just," Paul writes in Romans 3:10, and "the wages of sin is death" (Rom. 6:23). We are due the second death of the eternal wrath of God for the injustice of our snub-nosed sin against the holy, benevolent, just Creator and Ruler of this universe. He made us to worship Him, and we've worshipped ourselves. We've crashed the car; we've sold the farm; we've drunk the poison; we've pulled the trigger; and it's all over but the justice. So, concerning those who have already heard the Gospel, the author of Hebrews warns:

> For if we go on sinning deliberately after receiving the knowledge of the truth, there no longer remains a sacrifice for sins, but a fearful expectation of judgment, and a fury of fire that will consume the adversaries. Anyone who has set aside the law of Moses dies without mercy on the evidence of two or three witnesses. How much worse punishment, do you think, will be deserved by the one who has trampled underfoot the Son of God, and has profaned the blood of the covenant by which he was sanctified, and has outraged the Spirit of grace? For we know him who said, "Vengeance is mine; I will repay." And again, "The Lord will judge his people." It is a fearful thing to fall into the hands of the living God (Heb. 10:26-31).

Our sin is great; our due is death; and our God is just. The flood must drown us, and the cup must kill us; so we cry out with the Philippian jailor, "'What must I do to be saved?'" (Acts 16:30).

## JUST AND JUSTIFIER

God has already answered the cry of His people to be spared from their due. He sent Jesus to pay what we owe, to receive. Paul writes to the church in Rome:

> But now the righteousness [justice] of God has been manifested apart from the law, although the Law and the Prophets bear witness to it—the righteousness of God through faith in Jesus Christ for all who believe. For there is no distinction: for all have sinned and fall short of the glory of God, and are justified by his grace as a gift, through the redemption that is in Christ Jesus, whom God put forward as a propitiation by his blood, to be received by faith. This was to show God's righteousness, because in his divine forbearance he had passed over former sins. It was to show his righteousness at the present time, so that he might be just and the justifier of the one who has faith in Jesus (Rom. 3:21-26).

Peter concurs: "For Christ also suffered once for sins, the righteous for the unrighteous, that he might bring us to God, having been put to death in the flesh but made alive in the spirit" (1 Peter 3:18).

What we find in the Gospel is that for God's people, God's character of justice is all good news. No longer do terror and fear dominate our relationship with God's justice. Instead, we are freed by the death of Christ to revel in the vast, rolling sea of God's great ocean of justice, to ride upon its waves, to take in its thunderings and its tranquility with joyful awe and wonder. No longer do we hate to hear about the judgments and the justice of God—now, we love to tell the story!

What a powerful phrase Paul arranged: "that he might be just and the justifier!" The One Who is Justice makes just. Justice gives justice.

Do you see now why we took the time to examine God's attribute of justice from so many different angles? Because all of them come to bear on the cross of Jesus! The cross affirms the dignity and the sinfulness of men made and marred in the image of God. The cross levels all sinful hierarchies to create equal footing for every sinner united to Christ in His death. The cross is the mountaintop of the compassion of God, the greatest price for the vilest worm. The cross exchanges the reward due to Christ with the punishment due to wretched rebels. And the cross extinguishes the flame of God's justice licking at the sinner's feet and burns with the heat of Hell the Lamb over the Lake of Fire (Rev. 14:10). What an astonishing phrase, "the just and justifier!"

## DO WE DO JUSTICE?

It's appropriate that in our study of God's justice, we move quickly to the Gospel and to worship. But now, we need to move from theology and doxology to orthopraxy—that is, to application. While our grounding in the biblical teaching about God's justice is a critical start, we can't stop there. We've held up our sign that says, "Jesus saves," and we've explained what it means. So, what about all those other justice signs? What about social and racial justice? What about "doing justice?"

If there's any ubiquitous Bible talk that's bandied back and forth in modern discourse on racial justice, it's Micah's now infamous exhortation, "Do justice." It seems straightforward enough. Give to people what they're due—respect, impartiality, and compassion. "Do justice." Simple.

As with other Old Testament justice texts, one of the often-neglected dynamics of Micah 6:8 is its simultaneous continuity and discontinuity with New Testament justice texts. Meaning, there are ways in which "do justice" of course still applies to believers today (2 Tim. 3:16-17), and there are ways in which "do justice" necessarily looks different today. In order to be faithful to Scripture, we need to careful not to superimpose an Old Covenant on a New Covenant, while being clear about the unchangeable nature of the God Who cut them both. And in so doing, we'll discover what it means, and doesn't mean, to "do justice" as a Christian today.

I am acutely aware that there is a much larger hermeneutical and theological debate surrounding the interpretation of Micah 6:8. For our purposes, I'm going to assume (as I would contend) that Old Covenant Israel is a distinct entity from the New Covenant Church, that the Mosaic Law is fulfilled in Christ, that proper interpretation searches for the single meaning of the human author's original intent, and that the Old Covenant is only applicable to Christians today indirectly and not by binding force. If none of this sounds familiar to you, don't worry about it, but just know that there's a broader discussion to be had about some of the issues behind this particular study. If you disagree with me on some of those assumptions, I hope that this study will still be helpful in thinking through how to rightly imitate God's concern for justice in our modern context.

So, what did Micah mean when he said, "Do justice?" In his original context, Micah had already rebuked Israel and Judah's leaders for stealing land from the poor (2:1-2), metaphorically devouring the people by bribes and usury (3:1-3, 11), approving of false peace prophecies (3:5), and spreading violence and injustice throughout the land (3:9-10). Chapter six, then, begins with God setting up the mountains and hills as a jury to hear his case against Israel and Judah in His massive, terrestrial courtroom (6:1-2). God's case begins with a rehearsal of His loving provision and deliverance for His people "that you may know the righteous acts of the LORD" (6:5). Verses six and seven constitute a hypothetical response from Israel, asking if he can simply buy his way out of debt with God via animal sacrifices or even child sacrifice. Then, in verse eight, the exhortation comes: "He has told you, O man, what is good; and what does the LORD require of you but to do justice, and to love kindness, and to walk humbly with your God?" (Micah 6:8).

If justice is giving people their due, then doing justice in Micah's day would certainly look like the leaders of Judah and Israel putting an end to their oppression. They were engaged in the opposite of justice, in injustice, so justice must at least mean stopping the bloodshed, returning the stolen land, silencing the false prophets, and paying back the bribe money. Doing justice unquestionably meant righting the societal ills that these leaders had created. It would go on to include humility and kindness before man and God, to be sure, but the matter of justice itself clearly meant redressing social issues, both positively and negatively.

Kevin DeYoung and Greg Gilbert confirm this understanding of "doing justice" when they write:

> The Old Testament is passionate about doing justice. But Christians haven't always given much thought to what the Bible means by that phrase. Doing justice is not the same as redistribution, nor does it encompass everything a godly Israelite would do in obedience to Yahweh. Injustice refers to those who oppress, cheat, or make judicial decisions with partiality. Doing justice, then, implies fairness, decency, and honesty. Just as importantly, we see that the righteous person does more than simply refrain from evil. He positively seeks to help the weak, give to the needy, and, as he is able, addresses situations of rank injustice.[270]

The way Micah 6:8 is often used today necessarily draws a parallel between the oppression of Israel's leaders and the oppression of systemic racism. If anyone (particularly a white anyone) has benefited from the stealing of land from Native Americans, benefited from the shedding of African American blood from slavery to today, or benefited from the financial ruin of any minority group, they are complicit with injustice and must rectify those wrongs. In particular, because of the long history of African American oppression in the United States, African Americans must be given what is due. Depending on the source, that due may include the unpaid due of ancestors as well. Eventually, the conversation shifts to wholesale redistribution of wealth from wealthy European Americans to poor African Americans in the name of justice. "To do justice," it is argued, "means to do racial justice."

But there's a problem with the way many today apply Micah 6:8 to the modern concept of racial justice. Israel was a nation, and the Church is not. By God's design, "doing justice" in an Old Covenant context regularly included the wholesale reformation of society. Moses said as much in Deuteronomy 4:6-8 when he explained that Israel's nationwide obedience to the Law would result in God's praise among the nations: "What great nation is there that has a god so near to it as the LORD our God is to us, whenever we call upon him? And what great nation is there, that has statutes and rules so righteous as all this law that I set before you today?" Israel was supposed to draw the nations to God through their obedience to the Torah. That often meant that God's people would need to be about the business of redressing social problems. Obedience in the Old Covenant was intended to radically transform Israelite society.

The church works differently, also by God's intentional design. Where God designed the Old Covenant community to be a "come and see" theocratic nation state, he designed the New Covenant community to be a "go and tell" network of disciples from every tribe, tongue, and nation. God never intended for the Church to radically transform societies but to radically transform sinners. The Church's responsibility is not to enforce justice but to explain justice.

God's just character never changes. He was just in Israel and is just in the Church. He hated false scales then, and He hates them now. He defended the weak under Moses, and he defends the weak in Christ. But the Church is a categorically different entity with a different design from God. The composition of the Church, Jesus' commands to the Church, and the goal for the Church are all so distinct from Israel that our application of the just character of God must necessarily look different.

I don't draw people to Christ today by making sure everyone pays their taxes. I draw people to Christ by talking and living like Christ. Pastor Jesse Johnson writes, "The church and Israel are not the same, and they have different tasks, but they have the same goal (the reconciliation of the nations to God), and they have the same motivation (the compassion of God)."[271] God's justice will never change, but its manifestations among His people have changed.

So, if New Covenant believers are not bound, like Old Covenant Israelites, to do justice by transforming their society, how do we "do justice?" We give people their due! The character of God hasn't changed, and the definition of justice hasn't changed, so we still must give to one another our God-given rights. All people still deserve our respect; we still treat each other impartially; and we still show compassion, especially toward those in need. However, we no longer live under the mandate to ensure that those rights are being preserved in our country. God has put our secular government in place to protect social justice, however well or poorly it does its job. That's not the mission of the Church or Christians individually. Social reform is someone else's sign. Ours is "Jesus Saves."

## HEART FOR THE POOR

Here's where we need to add another layer of nuance. While it's true that "doing justice" for Christians today does not involve transforming society, it's also true that our hearts should reflect the unchanging heart of our just God. And throughout Scripture, we find that God has much to say about His heart for the poor, the lowly, the downtrodden, and the outcast. God has a heart for the poor, so as God's people, naturally, we will as well.

How, then, do we put all of that together? Am I supposed to be feeding the poor or not? Am I supposed to be involved in social action to protect the vulnerable or not? Am I supposed to fight for racial justice or not? Since I don't live in Old Covenant Israel, what does compassionate justice positively look like in the Church today?

First, let's establish that all of Scripture confirms God's particular care for the poor. Here are a handful of Old Testament passages confirming God's compassion and its connection to His justice:

- "You shall not pervert the justice due to your poor in his lawsuit" (Exod. 23:6).

- "'If among you, one of your brothers should become poor, in any of your towns within your land that the LORD your God is giving you, you shall not harden your heart or shut your hand against your poor brother, but you shall open your hand to him and lend him sufficient for his need, whatever it may be'" (Deut. 15:7-8).

- "'Cursed be anyone who perverts the justice due to the sojourner, the fatherless, and the widow.' And all the people shall say, 'Amen'" (Deut. 27:19).

- "Learn to do good; seek justice, correct oppression; bring justice to the fatherless, plead the widow's cause" (Isa. 1:17).

This same concern for the most helpless, vulnerable people continues into the Church Age. Here are a handful of New Testament passages echoing God's justice and care for the poor:

- "He said also to the man who had invited him, 'When you give a dinner or a banquet, do not invite your friends or your brothers or your relatives or rich neighbors, lest they also invite you in return and you be repaid. But when you give a feast, invite the poor, the crippled, the lame, the blind, and you will be blessed, because they cannot repay you. For you will be repaid at the resurrection of the just'" (Luke 14:12-14).

- "Only, they asked us to remember the poor, the very thing I was eager to do" (Gal. 2:10).

- "At present, however, I am going to Jerusalem bringing aid to the saints. For Macedonia and Achaia have been pleased to make some contribution for the poor among the saints at Jerusalem" (Rom. 15:25-26).

- "If a brother or sister is poorly clothed and lacking in daily food, and one of you says to them, 'Go in peace, be warmed and filled,' without giving them the things needed for the body, what good is that?" (James 2:15-16).

God sees, hears, and tends dearly to those suffering most in His world. In His justice, He is compassionate, merciful, and gracious. His generosity overflows toward those who need Him most. That's not to say, of course, that God doesn't feel compassion toward the wealthy, but simply to acknowledge that God is near in a special way to the brokenhearted, the downcast, and the helpless.

Since the 1700s, many theologians have seized on God's compassion for the poor as a justification to add to the mission of the Church. From 1970 onward, in particular, a number of scholars and pastors have advocated that because of God's heart for the hurting, social action must naturally accompany evangelism. They have argued, essentially, that the Church should hold up two signs—one that says, "Jesus saves," the other that says, "Jesus cares."

For example, Ron Sider stated the idea that "evangelism and social concern are inseparable and that individual and structural sin are equally abhorrent to Jahweh."[272] According to Sider, "younger evangelicals" followed a "biblical faith" which "reaffirmed the centrality of evangelism but at the same time insisted that social justice is also a central part of our biblical responsibility."[273] John Stott wrote, "Social action is a partner of evangelism. As partners the two belong to each other and yet are independent of each other. Each stands on its own feet in its own right alongside the other. Neither is a means to the other, or even a manifestation of the other. For each is an end in itself."[274] John Perkins followed suit by contending, "If the blood of injustice is economic, we as Christians must seek justice by coming up with means of redistributing goods and wealth to those in need."[275]

However, these social justice side-cars run into two biblical roadblocks. The first is a failure to distinguish between God's design for Israel and God's design for the Church. One is meant to transform society (because it is a society), and the other is meant to transform lives through Gospel-preaching. That doesn't mean that the Church ignores poverty and suffering in the world (more on that in a second). However, it does mean that the Great Commission passages have nothing to say about feeding, clothing, or economically empowering the marginalized in society (Matt. 28:16-20; Mark 13:10, 14:9; Luke 24:44-49; John 20:21; Acts 1:8). The Great Commission is Gospel proclamation, not social transformation.

## PRIORITIZE THE PIOUS POOR

The second biblical roadblock facing the proponents of social justice missiology is the New Testament's prioritization of mercy ministry to believers. That is, the Bible tells believers to meet the needs of other believers before meeting the needs of those in the world.

But the Church's priority to care for the Church hasn't always been affirmed. One author writes, "The Bible is clear from the Old Testament through the New that God's people always had a responsibility to see that everyone in their society was cared for at a basic-needs level."[276] Likewise, Tim Keller argues (unconvincingly, I think) that because the prophet Daniel preached to a pagan king, the Church must, therefore, engage in social justice.[277] But a brief survey of the biblical text will reveal that the Church is not called to be the world's welfare provider. In fact, the New Testament, in particular, makes clear God's priority to care for His spiritual children. At its root, Keller's argument is a dangerous, slippery slope toward liberalism, which argues that "doing justice can make many seek to be justified by faith."[278] He goes on to say that "there is no better way for Christians to lay a foundation for evangelism than by doing justice."[279] The danger in this logic is that it's not contending for simple consistency between message and motive but can actually be a subtle form of manipulation that seeks to give non-believers something they want outside of Christ in order to make Christ seem more appealing. This is the prosperity gospel in justice robes.

In 1 Timothy 5, Paul gives instructions to his young pastor protege about how the Church should help widows. As we see in Acts 6, the Church had become a haven for believing widows, particularly in meeting their daily need for food. But Paul didn't want the Church in Ephesus to turn into a widow soup kitchen, so he gave Timothy specific guidelines for evaluating the genuineness of the widow's profession of faith (1 Tim. 5:5, 9-10). He even goes so far as to say that if a widow has living family members, they should be her primary caretakers. "But if anyone does not provide for his relatives, and especially for members of his household, he has denied the faith and is worse than an unbeliever" (1 Tim. 5:8). Here we see the priority of family provision, followed by the provision of the family of God.

One famous passage on this topic is Matthew 25:31-46, the "least of these" text. In short, Jesus says that genuine believers are those who show hospitality to and meet the physical needs of "the least of these," and anyone who refuses to do so refuses Jesus Himself. The debate about this text lands on the identity of "the least of these." In the text, we have good reasons to affirm that "the least of these" is actually a reference to itinerant disciples of Jesus sent out to preach the Gospel, essentially traveling missionaries. In verse forty, Jesus says, "'Truly, I say to you, as you did it to one of the least of these my brothers, you did it to me.'" Jesus only ever used the word "brothers" to refer to blood family members or spiritual family members. Also, the language in Matthew 25 forms a striking carbon copy of Jesus' instructions for His itinerant disciples, fellow Christians, in Matthew 10. And nowhere else do we hear of Jesus so intimately identifying Himself with the world's poor that He would say ministry to them is as ministry to Him.[280] In contrast, we see multiple commendations of love toward brothers and sisters in Christ as marks of genuine faith, particularly with the practical implication of meeting physical needs (John 13:35; 1 John 3:17-18; James 2:15-17). Some passages explicitly tie this loving ministry to itinerant evangelists, as in Matthew 25 (John 13:20; 3 John 5-8).

In case that's all too complicated, Paul simplifies the matter for us in Galatians 6:10 when he writes, "So then, as we have opportunity, let us do good to everyone, and especially to those who are of the household of faith." The compassionate heart of God in believers doesn't ignore the plight of the poor at the door but puts first the needs of the few in the pew. Paul is describing here a priority of effort. As Israel was meant to eradicate poverty within its borders (but not among the nations), so the Church is called to eradicate poverty in the local body, but not in its wider societal context. The Westminster Confession of Faith confirms this priority:

> Saints by profession are bound to maintain an[sic] holy fellowship and communion in the worship of God, and in performing such other spiritual services as tend to their mutual edification; as also in relieving each other in outward things, according to their several abilities and necessities. Which communion, as God offereth opportunity, is to be extended unto all those who, in every place, call upon the name of the Lord Jesus."[281]

As witnesses to the Gospel of Jesus Christ, commissioned by our Lord and compelled by His Word, we hold one sign, and it reads, "Jesus saves." We hold that sign because we share the compassionate heart of our Savior for true justice. We long to see sinners spared from the eternal weight of just condemnation, so we preach Christ and Him crucified. But the same compassion that moves us to preach moves us to serve—first in the Church, then in the world. We give cheerfully and generously as we're able out of thankfulness for Christ's generosity toward us through the Gospel. We seek to alleviate whatever suffering we can in our immediate spiritual family, then widen that circle as the Lord gives us opportunity. One sign, one heart, and one Lord—one Church united in message, in motive, and in mercy.

## SUBMISSION IN A DEMOCRACY

In order to tie this study of biblical justice back to calls for racial justice, we need to answer two more questions: first, what justice obligations do Christians have in a democratic republic? Second, should our eschatology (understanding of end times events) affect how we approach societal and racial justice? We turn our attention first to political engagement.

Racial justice is not the same as class justice, so the biblical imperatives about giving and the poor don't line up one-to-one with racial justice concerns. As it turns out, financial relief doesn't seem to be the first concern of the racial justice movement, anyway. Instead, those who advocate for racial justice in America today often contend for political change. The call for racial justice is a call to confront laws, policies, and government institutions that unfairly disadvantage people from different racial groups.

For many, racial justice means systemic change. One racial justice advocate writes, "It is only Jesus who can change hearts, and it is only through changed hearts that we can see changed societies. While this is true, we can simultaneously see that laws can and do hurt people around us and as Christians living in a democratic republic, we have not just the ability but the God-given mandate to pursue justice for those being hurt."[282] Jim Wallis takes this a step further when he writes, "The church of Jesus Christ is at war with the systems of the world, not detente, ceasefire, or peaceful coexistence, but at war."[283] Think "Defund the Police." Racial justice for many today means dismantling oppressive governmental systems.

It would be easy to respond to Christian demands to make war on our own government with verses like, "Let every person be subject to the governing authorities" (Rom. 13:1) or "Be subject for the Lord's sake to every human institution" (1 Peter 2:13). And there's a sense in which that is an appropriate response. But did you notice the specific language in the quote above? "As Christians living in a *democratic republic . . .*" The author implies that because our form of government allows us to assert meaningful influence on the relative justness of our laws, we are obligated by God to do so. Is that true?

I would argue that legal political involvement in a democratic republic for the sake of ethnic justice can be a godly effort. Given careful discernment, accurate information, and a biblical worldview, Christian political effort can be a great testimony to the world of God's enduring wisdom among His people. In fact, Christians should be the best political influencers in the world because we know true righteousness in the character of God.

All that being said, in no way is political involvement a "God-given mandate" for Christians. No New Testament author commands Christians to vote, to protest, to write to their congressman, or to post divisive political beliefs on Facebook. We are commanded to submit to the government, but submission and active participation are distinct. To imply or explicitly state that apolitical Christianity is sinful or disobedient would simply be incorrect. Jesus' kingdom is not of this world.

It should also be said, however, that the political opportunities we have been afforded in the United States, which many have fought and died to protect, are an incredible gift of God's Providence and should be seen as a significant stewardship for Christians. Because there's no direct biblical command about political engagement, I'm hesitant to call on all Christians to protest even a horrific, despicable government—the apostle Paul didn't. But I would encourage all Christians to consider the rare opportunity they've been handed to influence our government in some small way toward biblical justice. DeYoung and Gilbert write:

> As we see the physical needs all around us, let's motivate each other by pointing out salt-and-light opportunities instead of going farther than the Bible warrants and shaming each other with do-this-list-or-you're-sinning responsibilities. We would do well to focus less on prophetic "social justice" announcements and more on boring old love.[284]

Indeed, it is love that animates justice. We can start by being clear about a biblical definition of justice and empathizing with those who have been stripped from their due because of their skin color. We should clarify that biblical justice won't always produce the same outcomes but instead is concerned with equity of process. Justice may look rich, and justice may look poor. Biblical justice will always love sacrificially and suffer humbly like Jesus, even as it seeks what is rightfully due.

## CLASH OF KINGDOMS

Here's the last question we need to answer in this chapter on justice: Should our eschatology affect how we approach societal and racial justice? You can probably guess that my answer is yes, but that bears some explanation. Why does eschatology matter for racial justice?

I've heard it said plenty of times by godly men and women, and maybe you've thought it yourself, "I'm a panmillennialist. I think it will all just pan out in the end." Though the humor of this statement may not pun out, the ambivalence toward our promised future is clear. My concern with such indifference toward eschatology is that it is susceptible to vague language about Christ's coming kingdom, particularly in conversations about racial justice. The less clear we are on the end, the more we'll fall for distortions right now.

Here's how this unclear, eschatological language sounds coming from social justice advocates. Edmund Clowney writes:

> We cannot be faithful to the words of Jesus if our deeds do not reflect the compassion of His ministry. Kingdom evangelism is therefore holistic as it transmits by word and deed the promise of Christ for body and soul as well as the demand of Christ for body and soul.[285]

So, what is "the promise of Christ for body and soul?" Has he promised healthy bodies through social justice action right now, or has he promised glorified bodies at the end? You can see how eschatology defines such sweeping statements, one way or another.

Another confusing word comes from theologian Richard Mouw, who writes:

> The payment that Jesus made through his shed blood was a larger payment than many fundamentalists have seemed to

think. For even when they have sung the words with zeal, they
have not seemed to acknowledge in their social/political lives
that Jesus did, indeed, pay it all. He died to remove the stains of
political corruption, and of all forms of human manipulation
and exploitation. And he calls us to witness to and to enjoy the
first fruits of that full redemption.[286]

Again, if it's true that Jesus "died to remove the stains of political
corruption" (which it is, in a sense), then when and how does He actually do
that? Did Jesus intend for His death to become a political rallying cry for the
Church under a government persecution? Or did Jesus die to save sinners from
God's eternal wrath so that they might enter His future, coming kingdom
where all political corruption has ceased? Eschatology matters profoundly to
how we read these words.

Tim Keller, who is absolutely clear about his own eschatology, weds social
justice to eschatology with this brief, bold statement: "The whole purpose of
salvation is to cleanse and purify this material world."[287] "The whole purpose"
of salvation? That may just be hyperbole for effect, but either way, when and
how does God intend to purify this material world? Through the Church today,
or through a seven-year Tribulation, followed by the return of Christ to earth,
followed by a one-thousand-year earthly reign of Christ? You get the point.

If you would call yourself a panmillennialist, such statements may at
first seem inoffensive and straightforward. "First fruits" is a biblical phrase,
and we know that Jesus cares about the body and the soul. And, hey, there's
obviously something important about Jesus coming back to this physical
earth at some point. Vague language can be compelling to vague theology.

But let me show you briefly how having convictions about end times Bible
passages, and particularly premillennial convictions, can help you untangle
social and racial justice from these faulty arguments.

There seems to be general agreement among Christians that Jesus is going
to one day come back and rule over everything with perfect justice. How
we get there, however, differs. Postmillennial theologians (speaking broadly)

would say that the Church will continue to make this world more just and livable until, eventually, it hits a critical mass and Christ returns to claim His kingdom. Premillennialists, on the other hand, contend that conditions on this earth will continue to go from bad to worse until Jesus returns and establishes His kingdom. A postmillennial view, then, sees the Church as cooperating with Christ to usher in a Messianic utopia. A premillennial view understands Jesus as the One Who brings about the dramatic, radical shift into His kingdom. Both end at perfect justice; but one builds into it, while the other suddenly receives it. It probably wouldn't surprise you, then, to learn that postmillennialists are often strong advocates for social and racial justice, and premillennialists are less so.

Premillennialism, however, is the only view that accurately accounts for the biblical and social data and the only realistic hope for true justice. Exhibit A: Turn on the news. Does it look like the world is improving? Are we gradually moving toward utopia? I can imagine the utter frustration of the burden of building the kingdom and seeing it thwarted at every turn. What gains may be made can be lost in an instant, maybe even inside the Church.

Biblically speaking, we protect ourselves from these false hopes when we preserve the distinction between promises and commands. Promises speak about what God will do, and commands speak about what we must do. When we confuse the two, we end up trying to accomplish something only God Himself can do—like bring perfect justice to this earth. A few promises about the coming kingdom in Isaiah will clarify what I mean.

- "Zion shall be redeemed by justice, and those in her who repent, by righteousness" (Isa. 1:27).
- "Of the increase of his government and of peace there will be no end, on the throne of David and over his kingdom, to establish it and to uphold it with justice and with righteousness from this time forth and forevermore. The zeal of the LORD of hosts will do this" (Isa. 9:7).

- "Behold my servant, whom I uphold, my chosen, in whom my soul delights; I have put my Spirit upon him; he will bring forth justice to the nations. He will not cry aloud or lift up his voice, or make it heard in the street; a bruised reed he will not break, and a faintly burning wick he will not quench; he will faithfully bring forth justice. He will not grow faint or be discouraged till he has established justice in the earth; and the coastlands wait for his law" (Isa. 42:1-4).

Jesus will establish true justice on earth, not us. Of course, that shouldn't stop us from stewarding our resources and opportunities to advocate for justice in our government and in our communities, but it does mean we don't bet on a losing horse. And Paul tells us that these kinds of promises about our future hope in Christ's return to rule and reign in justice should be a source of encouragement (1 Thess. 5:11). Even so, we're compelled by compassion now to seek true justice, which is primarily seen through lives changed by the Gospel.

Again, Jesse Johnson writes, "Understanding how the NT commands Christians to show compassion serves as a reminder that the church is called to transform people's lives through the proclamation of the gospel, and not through the ushering in of the kingdom through mercy ministry."[288]

Remember that Jesus said, "'My kingdom is not of this world'" (John 18:36). Like Abraham and Moses before us, we're looking for a better city, one where Justice Himself dwells. In that city, there are no police shootings, racial slurs, or hatred of any kind. Every ethnicity of mankind walks those streets without fear or bitterness. Jesus Himself lights up the sky of that new world to shine His glory all over a curseless, sinless creation. On that day, we won't need to say which lives matter because we'll all believe in our bones that everything touched by the light of Christ matters forever for His exalted praise.

That's the city we're looking for, and Christ Himself will bring it! I trust that as we work now to give each other our due, we will see faint glimmers of a world we could never build and one we don't rightly deserve to see, but one day, we will rule with the just Judge over all.

## BLOOD ON THE SIGN

The darkness of sin is deep, but the light of Christ is bright. We don't expect the world to change for us, but we hold out hope that God will save many in the world through us. We're not pessimistic about the Great Commission, and we're not optimistic about societal transformation. According to H. B. Charles:

> We must be realistic. There are sad realities of this fallen world that will not change until Jesus comes again. As a result, the stain of racism will continue to mark human relationships. No government, education, economy, religion or movement will erase racism. Only the return of Christ will finally make the world as it should be. Yet we should be hopeful. All things will not be right until Jesus comes again. But things can get better.[289]

So, here we stand waving our little sign in a sea of commercials and causes. Our hearts beat with our Father's heart, longing for justice in our states, streets, and homes. And yet we know that our one message silences the loud cries for justice—Abel's blood, and the blood of African slaves, and the blood of countless others—because Jesus' blood speaks a better word: "forgiveness."

The Church will continue to be tempted by voices trying to trade in our message about true justice for another cause. We'll be asked to hold up another slogan, to prioritize unborn lives, to make war on unjust oppressors. Our hearts weep aloud for injustice, and as we mourn, we pray for the courage to keep holding our sign. The oppressed need a greater hope than salvation from injustice. What we need most is salvation from justice.

And Jesus saves.

## DISCUSSION QUESTIONS

1. What did you learn about the biblical concept of justice that you didn't know before reading this chapter? How does that affect how you think about cries for justice in the streets?

2.  What would positive acts of compassionate justice look like in our church context? How does justice meet the needs of our fellow Christians by giving them what they're due?

3.  Read Micah 6:1-8. Noting the differences that exist between Old Covenant Israel and the Church, how do we "do justice?" Also, how can we join that with "[loving] kindness" and "[walking] humbly with [our] God?"

4.  What's your general attitude toward the poor? What's God's attitude toward the poor? How can we bring our hearts in greater alignment with God's heart toward the poor?

5.  How does our eschatology help us to "do justice" biblically? What other practical implications are there for believing in the soon return of Christ to establish His kingdom on earth?

# CONCLUSION

## WHAT DO I DO WITH THESE WALLS?

For most of this book, I've held back from giving lots of specific applications for how to pursue inter-ethnic harmony in our churches, and that omission was intentional. What we need more than a pep talk is to see the truth about our Lord's Church, that "he himself is our peace" (Eph. 2:14). Jesus Christ tears down the dividing wall of hostility in Himself to preserve the unity of His Church. Our joy is to live out our oneness in Christ and see Christ work through our fellow believers to strengthen, encourage, and unify His body. We're not just lifeless stones being forcibly conjoined by a Divine Builder, but we're living stones being built together by the Master Builder Himself. Without the mortar of Christ's blood, all our attempts at ethnic unity in the Church will be superficial at best. Jesus unites His ethnically divided Church, and He works through His Word to do it.

Now that you've taken some time to meditate on these truths about racial justice for yourself, I want to offer my own suggested applications. Of course, these are just my thoughts, so they're not binding on anyone's conscience, but they may help you get started. I'll base these applications on the biblical truth we've already studied, noting the walls that can ethnically divide us and the power of Christ to tear them down.

First, the wall of substitute gospels can keep us divided. Whether it's a message of prosperity, liberation, or plain-old works righteousness, false gospels creep into the corners of the Church, draw believers away from each other, and erect steely walls that segment the Body of Christ. Few things terrify a shepherd more than a wolf in the sheep pen. Counterfeit gospels split churches.

So, how do we preserve the unity of the Church in the face of false gospels? One way is by preaching the true Gospel over and over and over again. Active, ongoing evangelism—particularly to people you've never met—grows Christians closer to each other and closer to Christ like few other ministries. Fighting for souls side by side with your foxhole buddy creates a lasting bond that cannot be broken by man. The frequent reminder of the true Gospel falling from our own lips also protects us from exchanging the Good News for fake news. And evangelism helps us to keep a healthy perspective on issues inside the Church because we see how desperately we need each other to lock arms as we step into our local mission fields. Gospel-preaching not only creates the unity of the Church across ethnic lines, but it can preserve that unity as well.

Second, the wall of competing authorities can keep us divided. While we earnestly want to listen to and empathize with all our fellow believers in their pain, we dare not succumb to victimhood as our source of authoritative truth. Compassion cares about everyone's experience, but wisdom takes it all with a grain of salt. We don't rally behind certain pastors or voices in the Church based on race, but we bow before the one Lord of the Church, Jesus Christ, and His authoritative Word.

We counter the influence of competing authorities by developing a high view of Scripture. We teach the Bible, sing the Bible, pray the Bible, and live the Bible. We wake up to the Bible and memorize the Bible. We reference the Bible and reason from the Bible. We want to so saturate our hearts with the inspired, inerrant, sufficient Word of God that if a competing voice tries to enter the fray, we can tell the difference between a mere man and "one who [has] authority" (Matt. 7:29). No one culture holds more authority to speak than another, and all are level beneath the written Word of God. So, we unite under the truth of God's Word.

Third, the wall of race itself can keep us divided. The made-up categorizations that we call race are not only fallaciously simplistic ways to look at people, but they are rooted in ideologies intended to divide. While ethnicity is a more reliable way to identify our cultural backgrounds, a focus on the myth of race tends to promote enmity rather than charity.

Not surprisingly, then, the wall of race can be torn down with the light of truth. Resolve to not categorize your brothers and sisters in Christ by race but ask them about their ethnic background so you can know them better. Both "white" and "black" people have more interesting family trees than you might think! More than anything, resolve to see your brothers and sisters in Christ as Christ-followers first. Our common life in Christ is at the bedrock of our unity, so we must remind ourselves of those precious bonds as we regularly talk to and care for each other.

Fourth, the wall of ethnic partiality can keep us divided. Maybe you thought this whole book would be about combatting racism in the Church, and in some ways, it is. Centuries of anti-black racism shaped the country we see today, and many of those wounds are still open. Many churches in the U. S. remain, to this day, segregated by ethnicity for a whole host of reasons, and certainly, ethnic partiality is part of the equation.

One of the most transformative ways to combat ethnic partiality in our own hearts and in the Church is to form multi-ethnic Christian friendships. Specifically, invite people from different cultural backgrounds to your house for dinner, and then go to their house. The warmth of hospitality and the intimacy of conversations afforded in someone's living room or kitchen can't be matched by a public meeting space. If you note that there's only ever one ethnicity of people in your home, try to make a friend from a different ethnicity at your church and invite them over. As the saying goes, proximity breeds empathy.

Fifth, the wall of accusations can keep us divided. As easily as racism can cleave our fellowship, so, too, can accusations of partiality, however subtle.

If we contend that our brothers and sisters from another ethnic group owe us something that they are not paying, our Church will be ruptured and our communion cold.

To reverse the effects of these divisive accusations, guard your own thoughts about others and "believe all things, hope all things" (1 Cor. 13:7). Suspicion and doubt will rend any friendship, especially when the suspicion is attached to race in some way. So don't assume anyone else is a racist unless they make that plain, and choose to assume righteous motives over unrighteous. Then, when the sin of ethnic partiality has been clearly exposed, proceed with church discipline in order to win your brother or sister back.

Sixth, the wall of demands can keep us divided. Some would prefer we never talk about race again. Others are convinced that this is the only conversation worth having. Still others could care less about talk and feel a fiery zeal for civic action. Wherever you find yourself, know that our sinful hearts can quickly take good things and turn them into a test of faith.

Rather than giving demands or ultimatums to our brothers and sisters in the Church, let's surpass one another in service. Paul says, "Outdo one another in showing honor" (Rom. 12:10). Instead of outlining the ways your fellow believers need to behave, try to find out what they need and how you can meet that need. It may be as easy as asking, "How can I serve you this week?" Or it may require a little more digging. If we excel still more in service over demands, we will emulate the heart of our Savior, Who came not to be served but to serve (Matt. 20:28). And in so doing, our unity in Christ will blossom into maturity.

## WHAT CHRIST CAN DO

Whatever you do with those suggestions, I hope they cause you to begin thinking biblically and creatively about how best to promote inter-ethnic unity. But I don't want you to just be pushed toward unity—I want you to be pulled into it. If we could imagine together with our sanctified imaginations a picture of what a united, multi-ethnic congregation would look like, what would you see? Would that put gas in your tank for the trip there? Would it encourage you toward living out that vision?

Imagine you pull into your church's parking lot this coming Sunday and are warmly greeted by one of the bundled up, faithful servants in the parking ministry. As you get out of your car, he asks you how your leg is doing, and you say it feels better. You both agree to get together sometime soon, and you make your way inside, stopping at the door to greet a nice elderly couple holding the door for you.

Once inside, you can't take two steps without bumping into another old friend. You hear about the new grandbaby, a teenage daughter's quinceñera, the uncertainties of cancer treatment, and the Yankee's grand slam the other night. One friend in particular stops you, and you quickly dive into deep waters—struggles with contentment, problems at home, and financial uncertainties. You pray with each other right there, hug, and exchange a knowing glance before walking into the service.

You greet a few other folks as you find a seat in the now-crowded pew. You hear a couple of unfamiliar voices behind you speaking a Slavic language you don't know, so you turn around and introduce yourself. It's a couple, and they're visiting for the first time. You ask what language they were speaking, and they say Polish. Before you can ask more, the lights dim, and video announcements flick on. Friendly faces share with the Church about a new food donation program in the Caribbean, a women's ministry coffee social, an opportunity to serve the senior saints by raking their leaves, and a men's discipleship program in the works. You type a few reminders into your calendar, then look up.

One of the elders, a tall, well-dressed man, greets you in the name of the Lord Jesus Christ. He empathizes with everyone's credulity at the sudden drop in temperature, then turns his attention to a slow, deliberate reading of Psalm 67. "Let the nations be glad!" he repeats emphatically. Amens boil over from the pews. The elder prays, and you stand to sing some familiar hymns, some new songs, and some updated arrangements; and almost all are led by a different voice. You stop singing long enough to notice the beautiful pallet of diverse skin colors on the stage leading you in musical worship to Christ.

Your pastor steps into the pulpit, and you open your Bible to the reference that appears on the screen. You hear pages rustling around you and notice a number of children sitting with their parents trying to be the first to find the text in their *Adventure Bibles*. Your pastor preaches an evangelistic sermon calling all to find forgiveness in the cross of Christ. After the sermon and a brief benediction, you say goodbye to the Polish couple you met, and you leave feeling encouraged and convicted to reach out to your co-worker, with whom you've been meaning to share the Gospel. You can't get out the door without several more cheerful conversations, hugs, and handshakes from believers in all walks of life, and you thank God for the blessing to be with the Church again.

Now, why did I drag you through this pretty boring description of a Sunday morning at church? Oh, I hope you see how unspeakably beautiful that boring Sunday is! We ought to be astounded at the normalcy of something so pure and lovely. I wish that all churches would look and feel like this, like home! Do you want that for your church?

Well, in all reality, that story is a composite of a Sunday morning at the church where I serve, Immanuel Bible Church. Our church is far from perfect, but God has richly blessed us to experience an intense love for Christ and for each other that doesn't ignore ethnicity but certainly transcends it.

I hope that when you envision how Christ can unite His church, you do picture some aspect of your church right now. And I hope that image in your mind of a church united in the Spirit of Jesus Christ is wonderfully ordinary.

## WHAT CHRIST WILL DO

As much as we long for knowing fellowship and heartfelt worship in our churches right now, our hearts do yearn for something more, don't they?

As exciting as it is to see a handful of different ethnic groups worshipping together on Sunday mornings, it still feels like someone's missing. And there is. Our souls won't settle for the chapel on the corner. Christ made us for the throne room.

Revelation 5 is one of my absolute favorite passages in the Bible. John hears the earth-shattering words, "Weep no more!" (v. 5) because the Lion of Judah, the Lamb Who was slain, the only One worthy to open the seal and inherit this earth, will open the scrolls. And the multitudes erupt in worship:

> "Worthy are you to take the scroll and to open its seals, for you were slain, and by your blood you ransomed people for God from every tribe and language and people and nation, and you have made them a kingdom and priests to our God, and they shall reign on the earth" (Rev. 5:9-10).

I don't think I could make this scene more dramatic if I tried. The elders and creatures falling before the Lamb. Angels hovering near Him, covering their eyes. Glorified saints as far as the eye can see. A throne pealing with thunder, emitting a rainbow of color. God sitting atop that throne in radiance and fire. A sea like glass littered with kingly crowns, thrown down in fealty and worship. And the repeating chorus, "Worthy is the Lamb!" It's almost too much to take into my mind's eye. The brilliance of my Savior Jesus Christ as He receives the earth and the worship that He has been due from the beginning.

The scene culminates two chapters later with an astonishing addition:

> After this I looked, and behold, a great multitude that no one could number, from every nation, from all tribes and peoples and languages, standing before the throne and before the Lamb, clothed in white robes, with palm branches in their hands, and crying out with a loud voice, "Salvation belongs to our God who sits on the throne, and to the Lamb!" And all the angels were standing around the throne and around the elders and the four living creatures, and they fell on their faces before the throne and worshiped God, saying, "Amen! Blessing and glory and wisdom

and thanksgiving and honor and power and might be to our God forever and ever! Amen" (Rev. 7:9-12).

Can you see it? Can you hear their voices? This is why our skin color is different, why our foods don't taste the same, and why our music styles vary. For all the pain, death, violence, horror, and bloodshed that has been done in the name of ethnic or racial distinction, this moment puts it all in perspective. Every last racist slur and every stolen drop of blood was worth enduring, because the Lamb, Jesus Christ, is worthy of the diverse worship He will then receive! Eternity will not be able to exhaust the cultural expressions and instruments and stories needed to tell of the greatness and majesty of Christ the Almighty. He cannot be summed up by black or brown, African or European, Chinese, Arabic, or Latin. Every unique voice in all of creation joined together in endless harmony will be a gloriously inadequate tribute to the worth of Jesus Christ. And we'll see all of it for endless years upon years. Oh, for that day!

My prayer, Brothers and Sisters, is that this glimpse of the glory of Jesus in the worship of all peoples would help us to see how precious the multi-ethnic unity of His Church is now. May our churches be "a city set on a hill" (Matt. 5:14), a people undivided, and a house without walls. Whether black letters on a white banner, red churchyard bricks against a pale evening sky, or the dark-skinned descendants of slaves holding light-skinned hands in confounding Christian unity, may every trace of colorful beauty in this world be to the eternal praise of Jesus Christ.

# BIBLIOGRAPHY

"2018 Hate Crime Statistics." FBI: UCR. Accessed September 14, 2020. https://ucr.fbi.gov/hate-crime/2018/tables/table-2.xls.

"A Brief History of Civil Rights in the United States: The Jim Crow Time Period." Georgetown Law. Accessed September 14, 2020. https://guides.ll.georgetown.edu/c.php?g=592919&p=4172697.

"A History of Craniology in Race Science and Physical Anthropology." Penn Museum online. Accessed October 5, 2020. https://www.penn.museum/sites/morton/craniology.php.

Abadi, Mark, Kevin Reilly, and Katie Nixdorf. "'Our society is evolving': What historians and activists are saying about the movement to remove statues." *Business Insider* online. July 1, 2020. https://www.businessinsider.com/confederate-statues-removal-slavery-protests-2020-6.

"About." Black Lives Matter.com. Accessed September 23, 2020. https://blacklivesmatter.com/about.

"About Race." United States Census Bureau. Accessed October 20, 2020. https://www.census.gov/topics/population/race/about.html.

Adams, Isaac. "Don't Be Color-Blind at Church." 9Marks.org. September 25, 2015. https://www.9marks.org/article/dont-be-color-blind-at-church.

AFP. "Tiny gene differences make us who we are." *ABC Local* online. February 4, 2008. https://www.abc.net.au/science/articles/2008/02/04/2153889. htm?site=tv&topic=latest.

Allen, Scott David. *Why Social Justice is Not Biblical Justice: An Urgent Appeal to Fellow Christians in a Time of Social Crisis.* Grand Rapids: Credo House Publishers, 2020.

"Allocution." In Bernard Pullman (ed. 1992). *The Emergence of Complexity in Mathematics, Physics, Chemistry and Biology: Proceedings of the Plenary Session of the Pontifical Academy of Sciences.* Vatican City: Pontificia Academia Scientarum, October 1992. 27-31. https://bertie.ccsu.edu/naturesci/cosmology/galileopope.html.

Anderson, Chris and Greg Habegger. "His Robes for Mine." Church Works Media. 2008. https://www.churchworksmedia.com/product/his-robes-for-mine-free.

Anderson, Jill. "Confronting Racism at an Early Age." Harvard Graduate School of Education online. August 28, 2017. https://www.gse.harvard.edu/news/uk/17/08/confronting-racism-early-age.

Andrews, Evan. "Was Jim Crow a real person?" History.com. August 31, 2018. https://www.history.com/news/was-jim-crow-a-real-person.

Angier, Natalie. "Do Races Differ? Not Really, Genes Show." *The New York Times* online. August 22, 2000. https://www.nytimes.com/2000/08/22/science/do-races-differ-not-really-genes-show.html.

Anyabwile, Thabiti. *Reviving the Black Church: A Call to Reclaim a Sacred Institution.* Nashville: B&H Publishing Group, 2015.

Arndt, William et al. *A Greek-English Lexicon of the New Testament and Other Early Christian Literature.* Chicago: University of Chicago Press, 2000.

Arora, Rav. "The fallacy of white privilege—and how it's corroding society." *New York Post* online. July 11, 2020. https://nypost.com/2020/07/11/the-fallacy-of-white-privilege-and-how-its-corroding-society.

Ash, Allison N. "White Fragility: Why this Book is Important for Evangelicals." *Christianity Today* online. August 4, 2020. https://www.christianitytoday.com/edstetzer/2020/august/white-fragility-why-this-book-is-important-for-evangelicals.html.

Augustine. *On the Free Choice of the Will, On Grace and Free Choice, and Other Writings*. ed. Peter King. New York: Cambridge University Press, 2010.

Azar, Beth. "IAT: Fad or Fabulous?" American Psychological Association online. August 2008. https://www.apa.org/monitor/2008/07-08/psychometric.

"Babel Reversed." Ligonier Ministries online. Accessed October 24, 2020. https://www.ligonier.org/learn/devotionals/babel-reversed.

Ball, Claude. "There Has to Be a Promised Land: Why Black Christians Should Leave White Evangelicalism." *The Witness* online. October 8, 2020. https://thewitnessbcc.com/there-has-to-be-a-promised-land-why-black-christians-should-leave-white-evangelicalism.

Barry, John D. et al. *The Lexham Bible Dictionary*. Bellingham, WA: Lexham Press, 2016.

Bailey, Sarah Pulliam and Michelle Boorstein. "Several Black pastors break with the Southern Baptist Convention over a statement on race." *The Washington Post* online. December 23, 2020. https://www.washingtonpost.com/religion/2020/12/23/black-pastors-break-southern-baptist-critical-race-theory.

Barthel, Margaret and Christian Zapata. "At Lincoln Park, Generations Disagree Over Statue Removal As Protests Enter Fifth Week." DCist.com. June 27, 2020. https://dcist.com/story/20/06/27/

at-lincoln-park-generations-disagree-over-statue-removal-as-protests-enter-fifth-week.

Baucham, Voddie. "Ethnic Gnosticism." Founders Ministries. March 28, 2019. YouTube video, 50:22. https://www.youtube.com/watch?v=Ip3nV6S_fYU&feature=emb_logo.

Be the Bridge. "Be the Bridge 101: Foundational Principles Every White Bridge-Builder Needs to Understand." Atlanta, GA: Be the Bridge, 2019. https://bethebridge.com/btb101.

Beebe, Ralph. "Voice of Calvary Has the Sound of a Friend." *Evangelical Friend*, 13, No. 3, November 1979. https://digitalcommons.georgefox.edu/cgi/viewcontent.cgi?referer=https://www.bing.com/&httpsredir=1&article=113 1&context=nwym_evangelical_friend.

Bhopal, Raj. "The beautiful skull and Blumenbach's errors: the birth of the scientific concept of race." *The BMJ*, 335 (December 2007): 1308-1309. https://www.bmj.com/content/335/7633/1308.

"Black Church and Orthodoxy, The." In *Keep Your Head Up: America's New Black Christian Leaders, Social Consciousness, and the Cosby Conversation*. Wheaton, IL: Crossway, 2012.

"Black Codes and Jim Crow Laws, The." *National Geographic* online. Accessed September 14, 2020. https://www.nationalgeographic.org/encyclopedia/black-codes-and-jim-crow-laws.

Black Lives Matter Philly's Facebook page. "April Open Meeting." Accessed August 15, 2020. https://www.facebook.com/events/248214382307156.

Blitz, Matt. "Once There Was a Segregation Wall in Arlington." *Arlington Magazine* online. June 1, 2020. https://www.arlingtonmagazine.com/once-there-was-a-segregation-wall-in-arlington.

Block, Elizabeth Sweeny. "White Privilege and the Erroneous Conscience: Rethinking Moral Culpability and Ignorance." *Journal of the Society of Christian Ethics* 39, no. 2 (2019): 370.

"Bob Jones University Apologizes for Its Racist Past." *The Journal of Blacks in Higher Education* online. Accessed October 20, 2020. https://www.jbhe.com/news_views/62_bobjones.html#:~:text=In%202000%20the%20university%20ended,the%20nation's%20other%20Bible%20colleges.

Borland, Elizabeth. *Britannica, s.v.* "Standpoint theory." Accessed August 15, 2020. https://www.britannica.com/topic/standpoint-theory.

Bradley, Anthony B. *Liberating Black Theology: The Bible and the Black Experience in America*. Wheaton, IL: Crossway, 2010.

Brooks, Christopher. "Historically speaking: Why we should discuss 'Black hurdle' instead of white privilege." *The Morning Call* online. August 22, 2020. https://www.mcall.com/opinion/mc-opi-historically-speaking-twelve-brooks-20200822-b5nwmoqj7fhmjpv3zngtrchgwe-story.html.

Brown, Francis, Samuel Rolles Driver, and Charles Augustus Briggs. *Enhanced Brown-Driver-Briggs Hebrew and English* Lexicon. Oxford: Clarendon Press, 1977.

Bull, Josiah. *But Now I See: The Life of John Newton*. Carlisle: The Banner of Truth Trust, 1998.

Burke, Daniel. "Why Black Christians Are Bracing for a 'Whitewash.'" *CNN* online. July 21, 2020. https://www.cnn.com/2020/07/10/us/white-black-christians-racism-burke/index.html.

Caldwell v. Texas, 137 U.S. 692 (1891). Justia US Supreme Court.

Calvin, John. *Institutes of the Christian Religion, Library of Christian Classics*. ed. John T. McNeill, trans. Ford Lewis Battles, 2 vols. Louisville, KY: Westminster/John Knox, 1960.

Carson, D. A. "Editorial." *Themelios* 34.1 (2009): 1-2.

Carter, Anthony J. *Black and Reformed: Seeing God's Sovereignty in the African-American Experience.* 2nd Ed. Phillipsburg, New Jersey: P&R Publishing Company, 2016.

Chambers, Robert. *Vestiges of the Natural History of Creation.* London: John Churchill, 1844.

Charles, H. B., et al. *A Biblical Answer for Racial Unity.* The Woodlands, Texas: Kress Biblical Resources, 2017.

Charles, H.B., Jr. "Biblical Principles for Ethnic Harmony." H. B. Charles, Jr.com. Accessed September 23, 2020. https://hbcharlesjr.com/resource-library/articles/biblical-principles-for-ethnic-harmony.

"Charleston church shooting: Nine die in South Carolina 'hate crime.'" *BBC News* online. June 18, 2015. https://www.bbc.com/news/world-us-canada-33179019.

Chuhan, Kuljit. "The development of racist theories and ideas." Revealing Histories.org. Accessed October 5, 2020. http://revealinghistories.org.uk/legacies-stereotypes-racism-and-the-civil-rights-movement/articles/the-development-of-racist-theories-and-ideas.html.

Cleveland, Christena. *Disunity in Christ: Uncovering the Hidden Forces That Keep Us Apart.* Downers Grove, IL: InterVarsity Press, 2013.

Clowney, Edmund P. "Kingdom Evangelism." In *The Pastor-Evangelist: Preacher, Model, and Mobilizer for Church Growth.* Roger S. Greenway, ed. Phillipsburg, NJ: Presbyterian & Reformed, 1987.

Coates, Ta-Nehisi. *Between the World and Me.* New York: One World, 2015.

Cone, James H. *A Black Theology of Liberation: Fortieth Anniversary Edition.* Maryknoll, New York: Orbis Books, 2020.

*Cross and the Lynching Tree, The.* Maryknoll, NY: Orbis Books, 2011.

"Critical Race Theory: Full Statement." Be the Bridge. Accessed August 29, 2020. https://bethebridge.com/wp-content/uploads/2020/08/Full-Statement-Aug-7.pdf.

Darwin, Charles. *On the Origin of Species by Means of Natural Selection, or The Preservation of Favoured Races in the Struggle for Life,* London: John Murray, 1859.

*Descent of Man, The.* Chicago, IL: William Benton in Great Books of the Western World, 1952.

Deggans, Eric. "'Me And White Supremacy' Helps You Do The Work Of Dismantling Racism." NPR.org. July 9, 2020. https://www.npr.org/2020/07/06/887646740/me-and-white-supremacy-helps-you-do-the-work-of-dismantling-racism.

Delgado, Richard and Jean Stefancic. *Critical Race Theory: An Introduction.* 3rd Ed. New York: New York University Press, 2017.

DeYoung, Kevin. "Thinking Biblically About Racial Tensions: Sin and Guilt." The Gospel Coalition.org. Accessed November 16, 2020. https://www.thegospelcoalition.org/blogs/kevin-deyoung/thinking-theologically-about-racial-tensions-sin-and-guilt.

DeYoung, Kevin and Greg Gilbert. *What Is the Mission of the Church: Making Sense of Social Justice, Shalom, and the Great Commission.* Wheaton, IL: Crossway, 2011.

DiAngelo, Robin. *White Fragility: Why It's So Hard for White People to Talk About Racism.* Boston: Beacon Press, 2018.

Dimmick, Iris. "Pastor Max Lucado asks forgiveness for Christian white supremacy." *San Antonio Report* online. August 9, 2020. https://sanantonioreport.org/pastor-max-lucado-asks-forgiveness-for-christian-white-supremacy.

Dionne, E.J., Jr. "Pope Apologizes to Africans for Slavery." *The New York Times* online. August 14, 1985. https://www.nytimes.com/1985/08/14/world/pope-apologizes-to-africans-for-slavery.html.

"Dividing Wall, The." Acts 242 Study. January 9, 2013. https://acts242study.com/the-dividing-wall.

Dixon, Mone. "The Influence of Slavery on the Black Body: Black Lives Matter's Intersectional Methodology and New Advancements." *CUNY Academic Works.* 2018. https://academicworks.cuny.edu/gc_etds/2658.

Du Bois, W. E. B. *The Souls of Black Folks: With "The Talented Tenth" and "The Souls of White Folk."* New York: Penguin Books, 2018.

Eberhardt, Jennifer L. *Biased: Uncovering the Hidden Prejudice That Shapes What We See, Think, and Do.* New York: Penguin Books, 2019.

Ellis, Bob and Rodney Fopp. "The Origins of Standpoint Epistemologies: Feminism, Marx and Lukacs." Lecture, TASA 2001 Conference. The University of Sydney (December 2001): 13-15.

Elwell, Walter A. and Barry J. Beitzel, eds. *Baker Encyclopedia of the Bible.* Grand Rapids, MI: Baker Book House, 1988.

Emerson, Michael O. and Christian Smith. *Divided by Faith: Evangelical Religion and the Problem of Race in America.* Oxford: Oxford University Press, 2000.

Equiano, Olaudah. *The Interesting Narrative of the Life of Olaudah Equiano or Gustavus Vassa, the African.* London: 1814.

*Faithful Preacher, The: Recapturing the Vision of Three Pioneering African-American Pastors*. Wheaton, IL: Crossway, 2007.

Flurry, Gerald. "Angela Merkel's Historic Holocaust Speech (But Does the Pope Agree?)." *The Trumpet* online. May 2008. https://www.thetrumpet.com/5027-angela-merkels-historic-holocaust-speech-but-does-the-pope-agree.

Fortin, Jacey. "Toppling Monuments, a Visual History." *The New York Times* online. August 17, 2017. https://www.nytimes.com/2017/08/17/world/controversial-statues-monuments-destroyed.html.

*Generous Justice: How God's Grace Makes Us Just*. New York: Penguin Books, 2010.

Glaze, Robert L. *Brittanica, s.v.* "Nathan Bedford Forrest." Accessed September 14, 2020. https://www.britannica.com/biography/Nathan-Bedford-Forrest.

Goldhill, Olivia. "The world is relying on a flawed psychological test to fight racism." *Quartz* online. December 3, 2017. https://qz.com/1144504/the-world-is-relying-on-a-flawed-psychological-test-to-fight-racism.

Gould, Stephen Jay. *Ontogeny and Phylogeny*. Cambridge, MA: The Belknap Press, 1977.

Gray, Arielle. "A Reading List On Race For Allies Who Want To Do Better." *The ARTery* online. June 17, 2020. https://www.wbur.org/artery/2020/06/17/reading-list-on-race-for-allies.

"Great Migration, 1910 to 1970, The." United States Census Bureau. September 13, 2012. https://www.census.gov/dataviz/visualizations/020.

Greenblatt, Alan. "This City Removed 2 Confederate Statues. Then the State Retaliated." Governing.com. July 25, 2018. https://www.governing.com/topics/politics/gov-shelby-tennessee-confederate-statue.html.

Guasco, Michael. "The Misguided Focus on 1619 as the Beginning of Slavery in the U.S. Damages Our Understanding of American History." *Smithsonian Magazine* online. September 13, 2017. https://www.smithsonianmag.com/history/misguided-focus-1619-beginning-slavery-us-damages-our-understanding-american-history-180964873.

Haeckel, Ernst. *The History of Creation: Vol II*. Translated by E. Ray Lancaster. London: Henry S. King & Co., 1876.

Ham, Ken and A. Charles Ware. *One Race, One Blood: The Biblical Answer to Racism*. Rev. Ed. Green Forest, AR: Master Books, 2010.

Hammerstein II, Oscar. "You've Got to Be Carefully Taught." *South Pacific*. https://rodgersandhammerstein.com/song/south-pacific/youve-got-to-be-carefully-taught.

Harris, Jon. *Social Justice Goes to Church: The New Left in Modern American Evangelicalism*. Greenville, SC: Ambassador International, 2020.

Harris, R. Laird, Gleason L. Archer Jr., and Bruce K. Waltke, eds. *Theological Wordbook of the Old Testament*. Chicago: Moody Press, 1999.

Haynes, Lemuel. "The Character and Work of a Spiritual Watchman Described." Accessed September 23, 2020. https://quod.lib.umich.edu/e/evans/N18083.0001.001/1:2?rgn=div1;view=fulltext.

Hiernaux, Jean and Michael Banton. *Four Statements on the Race Question*. Paris: UNESCO, 1969. https://unesdoc.unesco.org/ark:/48223/pf0000122962.

Hill, Daniel. *White Awake: An Honest Look at What It Means to Be White*. Downers Grove, IL: InterVarsity Press, 2017.

"History." Mount Olivet United Methodist Church. Accessed September 13, 2020. https://mountolivetumc.com/history.

Hitler, Adolf. *Mein Kampf.* Trans. by James Murphy. Camarillo, CA: Elite Minds Inc., 2010.

Holtz, Robert Lee. "Scientists Say Race Has No Biological Basis." *Los Angeles Times* online. February 20, 1995. https://www.latimes.com/archives/la-xpm-1995-02-20-mn-34098-story.html.

Huevel, Katrina vanden. "Opinion: How Can We Start Dismantling Systemic Racism." *The Washington Post* online. June 9, 2020. https://www.washingtonpost.com/opinions/2020/06/09/how-we-can-start-dismantling-systemic-racism.

Hunter, George William. *A Civic Biology Presented in Problems.* New York: American Book Company, 1914.

Ignatin, Noel and Ted Allen. "White Blindspot." Marxist.org. 1976. https://www.marxists.org/history/erol/ncm-1/whiteblindspot.pdf.

"Implicit Association Test." Project Implicit. Accessed November 7, 2020. https://implicit.harvard.edu/implicit/takeatest.html.

*It's Not Over in the South: School Desegregation in Forty-three Southern Cities Eighteen Years After Brown.* The Alabama Council on Human Relations. U.S. Department of Health, 1972.

Johnson, Jesse. "God's Compassion as a Mandate for Mercy: A Dispensationalist Perspective on Mercy Ministry." ThM thesis. The Master's Seminary. Los Angeles, 2010.

Jones, Robert P. *White Too Long: The Legacy of White Supremacy in American Christianity.* New York: Simon & Schuster, 2020.

Jones, Steve. *The Language of Genes: Solving the Mysteries of Our Genetic Past, Present, and Future.* New York: Anchor Books, 1993.

Josephus, Flavius and William Whiston. *The Works of Josephus: Complete and Unabridged*. Peabody: Hendrickson, 1987.

"Justice." Stanford Encyclopedia of Philosophy. June 26, 2017. https://plato.stanford.edu/entries/justice.

K., Marley. "Yes My Dear, All White People Are Racists." Medium.com. June 6, 2020. https://medium.com/age-of-awareness/yes-all-white-people-are-racist-eefa97cc5605.

Keller, Tim. "Cultural Renewal: The Role of the Intrapreneur and the Entrepreneur." Entrepreneurship Forum. March 25, 2006. MP3. https://web.archive.org/web/20060622051746/http://www.faithandwork.org/uploads/photos/461-1%20Cultural%20Renewal_%20The%20Role%20of%20th.mp3.

Kendi, Ibram X. *How to Be an Antiracist*. New York: One World, 2019.

Kidd, Thomas. "The Christianization of Slavery." The Gospel Coalition online. March 3, 2020. https://www.thegospelcoalition.org/blogs/evangelical-history/the-christianization-of-slavery.

King, Martin Luther, Jr. "MLK at Western." Speech. Western Michigan University. December 18, 1963. https://wmich.edu/sites/default/files/attachments/MLK.pdf.

Kinnaman, David. "Barna's Perspective on Race and the Church." Barna.com. June 17, 2020. https://www.barna.com/barnas-perspective-on-race-and-the-church.

Koch, Christof. "Does Brain Size Matter?" Scientific American.com. January 1, 2016. https://www.scientificamerican.com/article/does-brain-size-matter1/#:~:text=In%20healthy%20volunteers%2C%20total%20brain,overall%20variability%20in%20general%20intelligence.

KPRC 2 Click2Houston. "White people kneel, ask forgiveness from the black community in Third Ward." June 1, 2020. YouTube video. June 1, 2020, 0:30. https://www.youtube.com/watch?v=fdX6aVzPgHs&ab_channel=KPRC2Click2Houston.

Kruse, Kevin M. *White Flight: Atlanta and the Making of Modern Conservatism.* Princeton, NJ: Princeton University Press, 2005.

Kustura, Anthony. "Man known for booming 'Jesus saves' message doused with flour, glitter by protesters." WSOCTV9 online, August 28, 2020. https://www.wsoctv.com/news/local/protesters-throw-flour-glitter-man-sharing-his-own-message-during-demonstrations-uptown/7IZLKQUHYBDWDFPAS6I64NERF4.

*Lexico, s.v.* "Ethnicity." Accessed October 20, 2020. https://www.lexico.com/en/definition/ethnicity.

Leonard, William. "Check Your Race in the Box Below." *The American Biology Teacher,* 73, no. 7 (2011): 379.

Lincoln, Abraham. "Transcript of President Abraham Lincoln's Second Inaugural Address (1865)." OurDocuments.gov. Accessed November 12, 2020. https://www.ourdocuments.gov/doc.php?flash=false&doc=38&page=transcript.

Lynn, R. and G. Meisenberg. "Race Differences in Deaths from Coronavirus in England and Wales: Demographics, Poverty, Pre-existing Conditions, or Intelligence?" *Mankind Quarterly.* 60, no. 4 (2020): 511–524.

Mason, Betsy. "Making people aware of their implicit biases doesn't usually change minds. But here's what does work." *Knowable Magazine* online. June 10, 2020. https://www.pbs.org/newshour/nation/making-people-aware-of-their-implicit-biases-doesnt-usually-change-minds-but-heres-what-does-work.

Mason, Eric. *Woke Church: An Urgent Call for Christians in America to Confront Racism and Injustice.* Chicago: Moody Publishers, 2018.

McWhorter, John. *"Racist* Is a Tough Little Word." *The Atlantic* online. July 24, 2019. https://www.theatlantic.com/ideas/archive/2019/07/racism-concept-change/594526.

*Merriam Webster, s.v.* "racism." Accessed November 4, 2020. https://www.merriam-webster.com/dictionary/racism.

Miles, Vernon. "Storm Destroys Portion of Historic 'Segregation Wall' in Hall's Hill." ARLnow. July 8, 2019. https://www.arlnow.com/2019/07/08/storm-destroys-destroys-portion-of-historic-segregation-wall-in-halls-hill.

Milmo, Cahal. "Fury at DNA Pioneer's theory: Africans are less intelligent than Westerners." Independent.co. September 18, 2011. https://www.independent.co.uk/news/science/fury-at-dna-pioneers-theory-africans-are-less-intelligent-than-westerners-394898.html.

McCaulley, Esau. *Reading While Black: African American Biblical Interpretation as an Exercise in Hope.* Downers Grove, IL: IVP Academic, 2020.

McIntosh, Peggy. "White Privilege: Unpacking the Invisible Knapsack." Wellesly Centers for Women. Accessed November 16, 2020. https://nationalseedproject.org/images/documents/Knapsack_plus_Notes-Peggy_McIntosh.pdf.

Mohler, Albert. *The Briefing.* Podcast audio. Wednesday, June 24, 2020. https://albertmohler.com/2020/06/24/briefing-6-24-20.

Morrison, Latasha. *Be the Bridge: Pursuing God's Heart for Racial Reconciliation.* Colorado Springs: WaterBrook, 2019.

Morse, Greg. "Seeing the World in Black and White: How Much Do Assumptions Divide Us?" DesiringGod.org. July 8, 2020. https://www.desiringgod.org/articles/seeing-the-world-in-black-and-white.

"Mourners Pay Respect for Supreme Court Justice Ruth Bader Ginsburg." *UPI* online. September 21, 2020. https://www.upi.com/News_Photos/view/upi/65c1b31bcdb36663dc1cea15a0615fd6/Mourners-Pay-Respect-for-Supreme-Court-Justice-Ruth-Bader-Ginsburg.

Mouw, Richard. "Political Evangelism." *Sojourners* online. May 1, 1973. https://sojo.net/magazine/may-june-1973/political-evangelism.

Muller-Wille, Staffan. *Brittanica, s.v.* "Carolus Linnaeus." January 7, 2021. https://www.britannica.com/biography/Carolus-Linnaeus#ref273182.

"Murder of Emmett Till, The." In *The Civil Rights History Project.* Library of Congress. Accessed September 14, 2020. https://www.loc.gov/collections/civil-rights-history-project/articles-and-essays/murder-of-emmett-till.

Newbell, Trillia J. *United: Captured by God's Vision for Diversity.* Chicago: Moody Publishers, 2014.

Notton, David G. and Christopher Brian Stringer. "Who is the type of Homo sapiens?" International Commission on Zoological Nomenclature. Accessed October 5, 2020. https://www.researchgate.net/publication/260337719_Who_is_the_type_of_Homo_sapiens#:~:text=follow%20this%20example.-,...,class%20us%20primates%20%5B37%5D%20.

Orwell, George. *Animal Farm.* New York, Penguin Group, 1956.

"Our History." Mount Salvation Baptist Church. Accessed September 13, 2020. https://www.mtsalvationbaptistchurch.org/our-history.

Owen, John. *The Mortification of Sin.* Carlisle, PA: Banner of Truth Trust, 2004.

Patterson, Orlando. *The Ordeal of Integration: Progress and Resentment in America's "Racial" Crisis.* New York: Basic Civitas, 1997.

Paul II, John. "Address of the Holy Father to an International Symposium on John Hus." Lecture, The Vatican. December 17, 1999. http://www.vatican.va/content/john-paul-ii/en/speeches/1999/december/documents/hf_jp-ii_spe_17121999_jan-hus.html.

Perlstein, Rick. "Exclusive: Lee Atwater's Infamous 1981 Interview on the Southern Strategy." *The Nation* online. November 13, 2012. https://www.thenation.com/article/archive/exclusive-lee-atwaters-infamous-1981-interview-southern-strategy.

Perry, Jeffrey B. "The Growing Importance of Theodore W. Allen's Work On the Centrality of the Struggle Against White Supremacy." Democratic Left online. September 20, 2017. https://www.dsausa.org/democratic-left/the_growing_importance_of_theodore_w_allen_s_work-2.

Piper, John. *Bloodlines: Race, Cross, and the Christian.* Wheaton, IL: Crossway, 2011.

Pitner, Barrett Holmes. "Viewpoint: US must confront its Original Sin to move forward." *BBC News* online. June 3, 2020. https://www.bbc.com/news/world-us-canada-52912238.

"'Powerful moment': White parishioners kneel, ask for black community's forgiveness in George Floyd's hometown." *The Indian Express* online. June 2, 2020. https://indianexpress.com/article/trending/trending-globally/george-floyd-kneel-viral-video-6438938.

"Primary Resource: '20. and odd Negroes'; an excerpt from a letter from John Rolfe to Sir Edwin Sandys (1619/1620)." *Encyclopedia Virginia.* Last modified July 12, 2012. https://www.encyclopediavirginia.org/_20_and_odd_Negroes_an_excerpt_from_a_letter_from_John_Rolfe_to_Sir_Edwin_Sandys_1619_1620.

Quigley, Fran. "Liberation Theology Calls Together the Religious and the Political." Accessed August 8, 2020. https://sojo.net/articles/liberation-theology-calls-together-religious-and-political?fbclid=IwAR1xacA2zxny4T UVBC3yc-ZCFWV-h2f41FbEHu-q_DN5Q1BX5UjmeZp29ZI.

"Racial Justice: Introduction Letter: Minister for Racial Justice." The United Church of Christ. Accessed December 4, 2020. https://www.ucc.org/justice_racism.

"Racial Justice Response & Resources." National Association of Evangelicals. Accessed December 4, 2020. https://www.nae.net/racialjustice.

"Racism and Corporate Evil: A White Guy's Perspective." DesiringGod.org. Accessed November 16, 2020. https://www.desiringgod.org/messages/racism-and-corporate-evil.

Randall, Mitch. "Why Social Justice is a Vital Component of the Gospel." Good Faith Media.org. Accessed September 23, 2020. https://goodfaithmedia.org/why-social-justice-is-vital-component-of-the-gospel/.

"Racism definition: Merriam-Webster to make update after request." *BBC News* online. June 10, 2020. https://www.bbc.com/news/world-us-canada-52993306.

"Religious Congregations in 21st Century America." National Congregations Study, Duke University. Accessed September 13, 2020. https://sites.duke.edu/ncsweb/files/2019/02/NCSIII_report_final.pdf.

Rice, John R. *Dr. Rice, Here is My Question*. Murfreesboro, TN: Sword of the Lord Publishers, 1962.

"Robert Chambers." Harvard University online. Accessed October 5, 2020. https://early-evolution.oeb.harvard.edu/robert-chambers.

246 A HOUSE WITHOUT WALLS

Roberts, Dorothy. *Fatal Invention: How Science, Politics, and Big Business Re-Create Race in the Twenty-First Century*. New York: The New Press, 2011.

Roberts, J. Deotis. *Liberation and Reconciliation: A Black Theology*. 2nd Ed. Louisville, KY: Westminster John Knox Press, 2005.

Robertson, Campbell. "A Quiet Exodus: Why Black Worshipers Are Leaving White Evangelical Churches." *The New York Times* online, March 9, 2018. https://www.nytimes.com/2018/03/09/us/blacks-evangelical-churches.html.

Rubin, Erin. "Answering the Reparations Question." *NonProfit Quarterly* online. March 19, 2019. https://nonprofitquarterly.org/answering-the-reparations-question.

Rushton, J. Philippe and Arthur R. Jensen. "Thirty Years of Research on Race Differences in Cognitive Ability." *Psychology, Public Policy, and Law*. 11, no. 2 (2005): 235-294.

Rushton, J. Philippe and Elizabeth W. Rushton. "Brain Size, IQ, and racial-group differences: Evidence from musculoskeletal traits." *Science Direct*, 31, no. 2 (March-April 2003): 139-155.

Saini, Angela. *Superior: The Return of Race Science*. Boston: Beacon Press, 2019.

Sarah Blake Morgan's Facebook page. Accessed June 29, 2021. https://www.facebook.com/SarahBlakeMorgan/videos/1927834923928209.

Schildkrout, Enid. *Britannica, s.v.* "Anthropology: History of Anthropology." Accessed October 6, 2020. https://www.britannica.com/science/anthropology/History-of-anthropology#ref839878.

Schultz, Kyley. "DC Mayor on statues: 'We need to have a reasonable conversation . . . not have a mob decide that they want to pull it down.'" WUSA9 online. June 26, 2020. https://www.wusa9.com/article/news/local/dc/dc-mayor-bowser-statue-removals-dc/65-d241412b-08c9-40e8-a3dc-1c9b2517177c.

Sey, Samuel. "What Is Black Liberation Theology?" Ezra Institute.ca. Accessed September 23, 2020. https://www.ezrainstitute.ca/resource-library/articles/what-is-black-liberation-theology.

Sechrest, Love L., Johnny Ramirez-Johnson, and Amos Yong, eds. *Can "White" People Be Saved? Triangulating Race, Theology, and Mission*. Downers Grove, IL: IVP Academic, 2018.

Sider, Ronald J. ed. *The Chicago Declaration*. Eugene, OR: Wipf &Stock Publishers, 1974.

Sider, Ronald. "History Shows Us Why Being Evangelical Matters." *Christianity Today* online. November 26, 2016. https://www.christianitytoday.com/ct/2016/november-web-only/history-shows-us-why-being-evangelical-matters.html.

"Slavery by Another Name: Black Codes and Pig Laws." PBS online. Accessed September 14, 2020. https://www.pbs.org/tpt/slavery-by-another-name/themes/black-codes.

Stark, Rodney. *Wayward Shepherds: Prejudice and the Protestant Clergy*. New York: Harper and Row, 1971.

Stearns, Richard. *The Hole in Our Gospel*. Nashville: Nelson, 2009.

Stott, John R. W. *Christian Mission in the Modern World: What the Church Should Be Doing Now!* Downers Grove: IVP, 1975.

Sue, Derald Wing. "Racial Microaggressions in Everyday Life." *Psychology Today* online. October 5, 2010. https://www.psychologytoday.com/us/blog/microaggressions-in-everyday-life/201010/racial-microaggressions-in-everyday-life.

"Summa Theologiae: Question 58. Justice." New Advent. Accessed December 4, 2020. https://www.newadvent.org/summa/3058.htm#article1.

Swanson, David W. *Rediscipling the White Church: From Cheap Diversity to True Solidarity.* Downers Grove, IL: IVP, 2020.

Tatum, Beverly Daniel. *Why Are All the Black Kids Sitting Together in the Cafeteria?.* New York: Basic Books, 1997.

Taylor, Alan. "The Statues Brought Down Since the George Floyd Protests Began." TheAtlantic.com. July 2, 2020. https://www.theatlantic.com/photo/2020/07/photos-statues-removed-george-floyd-protests-began/613774.

*Theological Lexicon of the New Testament.* Peabody, MA: Hendrickson Publishers, 1994.

*Theological Lexicon of the Old Testament.* Peabody, MA: Hendrickson Publishers, 1997.

Tisby, Jemar. *The Color of Compromise: The Truth About the American Church's Complicity in Racism.* Grand Rapids: Zondervan, 2019.

*How to Fight Racism: Courageous Christianity and the Journey Toward Racial Justice.* Grand Rapids: Zondervan Reflective, 2021.

"United Methodists Stand Against Racism." The United Methodist Church. Accessed November 8, 2020. https://www.umc.org/en/how-we-serve/advocating-for-justice/racial-justice/united-against-racism.

VanDenburgh, Barbara. "Anti-racist book dethrones 'Hunger Games' prequel on best-seller list amid mass protests." *USA Today* online. June 10, 2020. https://www.usatoday.com/story/entertainment/books/2020/06/10/anti-racist-books-dominate-best-seller-list-white-fragility-how-to-be-an-antiracist-ta-nehisi-coates/5331188002.

Vestal, Christine. "Racism Is a Public Health Crisis, Say Cities and Counties." *PEW* online. June 15, 2020. https://www.pewtrusts.org/en/research-and-analysis/blogs/stateline/2020/06/15/racism-is-a-public-health-crisis-say-cities-and-counties.

Volou, Khalida. "21 protesters arrested near U.S. Supreme Court Building ahead of Judge Amy Barrett confirmation hearings." WUSA9 online. October 12, 2020. https://www.wusa9.com/article/news/local/protests/protesters-demonstrators-us-supreme-court-amy-coney-barrett/65-4a218782-9e82-4316-9132-ca27bedd1a49.

Vroegop, Mark. *Weep With Me: How Lament Opens a Door for Racial Reconciliation.* Wheaton, IL: Crossway, 2020.

Wallis, Jim. *America's Original Sin: Racism, White Privilege, and the Bridge to a New America.* Grand Rapids: Brazos Press, 2016.

Watkins, Loula V., compiler. "Report, Tulsa Race Riot Disaster Relief, American Red Cross." Tulsa, OK: Tulsa Historical Society & Museum, 1984.

Watson, Thomas. *A Body of Divinity.* Carlisle, PA: The Banner of Truth Trust, 2019.

"We won't stop until we dismantle the whole racist system." American Friends Service Committee. June 4, 2020. https://www.afsc.org/newsroom/we-wont-stop-until-we-dismantle-whole-racist-system.

Wester, Josh. "3 ways Christians should think about racial justice in America." Ethics and Religious Liberties Commission online. June 10, 2020. https://erlc.com/resource-library/articles/3-ways-christians-should-think-about-racial-justice-in-america.

Westminster Assembly, Douglas F. Kelly, Philip B. Rollinson, and Frederick T. Marsh, *The Westminster Shorter Catechism in Modern English.* Phillipsburg, N.J.: Presbyterian and Reformed Pub. Co, 1986.

Westminster Confession of Faith, The. 3rd ed. Lawrenceville, GA: Committee for Christian Education and Publications, 1990.

"What people have said about Linnaeus." Uppsala Universitet. May 3, 2011. https://web.archive.org/web/20110513033923/http://www.linnaeus.uu.se/online/life/8_3.html.

Wilkerson, Isabel. "The Long-Lasting Legacy of the Great Migration." *Smithsonian Magazine* online. September 2016. https://www.smithsonianmag.com/history/long-lasting-legacy-great-migration-180960118.

Williams, Derek. "The Weakness of Evangelical Ethics." *Third Way*, 1, no. 1 (January 13, 1977): 4-5.

Williams, Elliot C. "How The Lincoln Statue In Capitol Hill Became A Monument To Public Debate." NPR.org. July 3, 2020. https://www.npr.org/local/305/2020/07/03/887073442/how-the-lincoln-statue-in-capitol-hill-became-a-monument-to-public-debate.

Williams, Jarvis. "The Intersection of Race, Gospel, and Racial Reconciliation in Paul's Theology." Lecture. Southern Baptist Theological Seminary. Louisville, KY. Scribd.com. Accessed September 23, 2020. https://www.scribd.com/document/424625751/Williams-Class-Notes.

Williams, Thaddeus J., ed. *Confronting Injustice Without Compromising Truth: 12 Questions Christians Should Ask About Social Justice.* Grand Rapids: Zondervan Academic, 2020.

Williams, Yohuru. "Why Thomas Jefferson's Anti-Slavery Passage Was Removed from the Declaration of Independence." History.com, June 29, 2020, https://www.history.com/news/declaration-of-independence-deleted-anti-slavery-clause-jefferson.

Williamson, Marianne. "Prayer of Apology to African Americans." Marianne.com. Accessed on November 12, 2020. http://marianne.com/atonement.

Wilson-Hartgrove, Jonathan. *Reconstructing the Gospel: Finding Freedom from Slaveholder Religion*. Downers Grove, IL: InterVarsity Press, 2018.

Wong, Christy. "Exploring Race: Being Chinese-American." *Chicago Tribune Newsblogs*. June 25, 2008. https://newsblogs.chicagotribune.com/race/2008/06/being-chinese-a.html.

Yancey, George. *Beyond Racial Gridlock: Embracing Mutual Responsibility*. Downers Grove, IL: IVP Books, 2006.

York, Byron. "The National Museum of . . . " Twitter. July 15, 2020. https://twitter.com/ByronYork/status/1283372233730203651/photo/1.

# ENDNOTES

1. Claude Ball, "There Has to Be a Promised Land: Why Black Christians Should Leave White Evangelicalism," *The Witness* online, October 8, 2020, https://thewitnessbcc.com/there-has-to-be-a-promised-land-why-black-christians-should-leave-white-evangelicalism.

2. Daniel Burke, "Why Black Christians Are Bracing for a 'Whitewash,'" *CNN online*, July 21, 2020, https://www.cnn.com/2020/07/10/us/white-black-christians-racism-burke/index.html.

3. Sarah Pulliam Bailey and Michelle Boorstein, "Several Black pastors break with the Southern Baptist Convention over a statement on race," *The Washington Post* online, December 23, 2020, https://www.washingtonpost.com/religion/2020/12/23/black-pastors-break-southern-baptist-critical-race-theory.

4. Campbell Robertson, "A Quiet Exodus: Why Black Worshipers Are Leaving White Evangelical Churches," *The New York Times* online, March 9, 2018, https://www.nytimes.com/2018/03/09/us/blacks-evangelical-churches.html.

5. Walter A. Elwell and Barry J. Beitzel, "The Court of the Gentiles," in *Baker Encyclopedia of the Bible* (Grand Rapids, MI: Baker Book House, 1988), 856.

6. Jan H. Nylund, "Court of the Gentiles," ed. John D. Barry et al., in *The Lexham Bible Dictionary* (Bellingham, WA: Lexham Press, 2016).

7. "The Dividing Wall," Acts 242 Study, January 9, 2013, https://acts242study.com/the-dividing-wall.

8. Flavius Josephus and William Whiston, *The Works of Josephus: Complete and Unabridged* (Peabody: Hendrickson, 1987), 425.

9. Nylund, ibid.

10. William Arndt et al., *A Greek-English Lexicon of the New Testament and Other Early Christian Literature*, s.v. ἔθνος (Chicago: University of Chicago Press, 2000), 276.

11. John Piper, *Bloodlines: Race, Cross, and the Christian* (Wheaton, IL: Crossway, 2011), 19.

12. Vernon Miles, "Storm Destroys Portion of Historic 'Segregation Wall' in Hall's Hill," ARLnow, July 8, 2019, https://www.arlnow.com/2019/07/08/storm-destroys-destroys-portion-of-historic-segregation-wall-in-halls-hill.

13. Matt Blitz, "Once There Was a Segregation Wall in Arlington," *Arlington Magazine* online, June 1, 2020, https://www.arlingtonmagazine.com/once-there-was-a-segregation-wall-in-arlington.

14. "Our History," Mount Salvation Baptist Church, accessed September 13, 2020, https://www.mtsalvationbaptistchurch.org/our-history.

15. "History," Mount Olivet United Methodist Church, accessed September 13, 2020, https://mountolivetumc.com/history.

16. Ibid.

17. "Religious Congregations in 21st Century America," National Congregations Study, Duke University, accessed September 13, 2020, https://sites.duke.edu/ncsweb/files/2019/02/NCSIII_report_final.pdf.

18. "Primary Resource: '20. and odd Negroes'; an excerpt from a letter from John Rolfe to Sir Edwin Sandys (1619/1620)," *Encyclopedia Virginia*, last modified July 12, 2012, https://www.encyclopediavirginia.org/_20_and_odd_Negroes_an_excerpt_from_a_letter_from_John_Rolfe_to_Sir_Edwin_Sandys_1619_1620.

19. Michael Guasco, "The Misguided Focus on 1619 as the Beginning of Slavery in the U.S. Damages Our Understanding of American History," *Smithsonian Magazine* online, September 13, 2017, https://www.smithsonianmag.com/history/misguided-focus-1619-beginning-slavery-us-damages-our-understanding-american-history-180964873.

20. Jemar Tisby, *The Color of Compromise: The Truth About the American Church's Complicity in Racism* (Grand Rapids: Zondervan Reflective, 2019), 29.

21. Thomas Kidd, "The Christianization of Slavery," The Gospel Coalition online, March 3, 2020, https://www.thegospelcoalition.org/blogs/evangelical-history/the-christianization-of-slavery.

22. Olaudah Equiano, *The Interesting Narrative of the Life of Olaudah Equiano or Gustavus Vassa, the African* (London: 1814), 63-66.

23. Anthony Carter, *Black and Reformed: Seeing God's Sovereignty in the African-American Christian Experience*, 2nd ed. (Philipsburg, NJ: P&R Publishing, 2016), 72-77.

24. Ibid, 77-78.

25. "The Black Codes and Jim Crow Laws," *National Geographic* online, accessed September 14, 2020, https://www.nationalgeographic.org/encyclopedia/black-codes-and-jim-crow-laws.

26. "Slavery by Another Name: Black Codes and Pig Laws," PBS online, accessed September 14, 2020, https://www.pbs.org/tpt/slavery-by-another-name/themes/black-codes.

27. "A Brief History of Civil Rights in the United States: The Jim Crow Time Period," Georgetown Law, accessed September 14, 2020, https://guides.ll.georgetown.edu/c.php?g=592919&p=4172697.

28. Robert P. Jones, *White Too Long: The Legacy of White Supremacy in American Christianity* (New York: Simon & Schuster, 2020), 34-38.

29. Robert L. Glaze, Brittanica, s.v. "Nathan Bedford Forrest," accessed September 14, 2020, https://www.britannica.com/biography/Nathan-Bedford-Forrest.

30. Jones, 28-31.

31. Tisby, 118.

32. Loula V. Watkins, compiler, "Report, Tulsa Race Riot Disaster Relief, American Red Cross," (Tulsa, OK: Tulsa Historical Society & Museum, 1984), 10-43.

33. "The Great Migration, 1910 to 1970," United States Census Bureau, September 13, 2012, https://www.census.gov/dataviz/visualizations/020.

34. Isabel Wilkerson, "The Long-Lasting Legacy of the Great Migration," *Smithsonian Magazine* online, September 2016, https://www.smithsonianmag.com/history/long-lasting-legacy-great-migration-180960118.

35. "The Murder of Emmett Till," in *The Civil Rights History Project*, Library of Congress, accessed September 14, 2020, https://www.loc.gov/collections/civil-rights-history-project/articles-and-essays/murder-of-emmett-till.

36. *It's Not Over in the South: School Desegregation in Forty-three Southern Cities Eighteen Years After Brown*, The Alabama Council on Human Relations (U.S. Department of Health, 1972), 1-9.

37. Kevin M. Kruse, *White Flight: Atlanta and the Making of Modern Conservatism* (Princeton, NJ: Princeton University Press, 2005), 92.

38. Rick Perlstein, "Exclusive: Lee Atwater's Infamous 1981 Interview on the Southern Strategy," *The Nation* online, November 13, 2012, https://www.thenation.com/article/archive/exclusive-lee-atwaters-infamous-1981-interview-southern-strategy.

39. "Charleston church shooting: Nine die in South Carolina 'hate crime,'" *BBC News* online, June 18, 2015, https://www.bbc.com/news/world-us-canada-33179019.

40. "2018 Hate Crime Statistics," FBI: UCR, accessed September 14, 2020, https://ucr.fbi.gov/hate-crime/2018/tables/table-2.xls.

41. Carter, 66.

42. Thabiti M. Anyabwile, *The Faithful Preacher: Recapturing the Vision of Three Pioneering African-American Pastors* (Wheaton, IL: Crossway. 2007), 16-19.

43. Lemuel Haynes, "The Character and Work of a Spiritual Watchman Described," accessed September 23, 2020, https://quod.lib.umich.edu/e/evans/N18083.0001.001/1:2?rgn=div1;view=fulltext.

44. Josiah Bull, *But Now I See: The Life of John Newton* (Carlisle: The Banner of Truth Trust, 1998), 246.

45. Rodney Stark, *Wayward Shepherds: Prejudice and the Protestant Clergy* (New York: Harper and Row, 1971), 102-103.

46. Thabiti Anyabwile, *Reviving the Black Church: A Call to Reclaim a Sacred Institution* (Nashville: B&H Publishing Group, 2015), 81.

47. William Arndt, et al., *A Greek-English Lexicon of the New Testament and Other Early Christian Literature*, s.v. "σῴζω" (Chicago: University of Chicago Press, 2000), 982.

48. Ceslas Spicq and James D. Ernest, *Theological Lexicon of the New Testament*, s.v. "σῴζω, σωτήρ, σωτηρία, σωτήριος," (Peabody, MA: Hendrickson Publishers, 1994), 345.

49. John E. Hartley, *Theological Wordbook of the Old Testament*, s.v. "יָשַׁע," ed. R. Laird Harris, Gleason L. Archer Jr., and Bruce K. Waltke (Chicago: Moody Press, 1999), 414.

50. Ernst Jenni and Claus Westermann, *Theological Lexicon of the Old Testament*, s.v. "טלף" (Peabody, MA: Hendrickson Publishers, 1997), 987.

51. Ceslas Spicq and James D. Ernest, *Theological Lexicon of the New Testament*, s.v. "σῴζω, σωτήρ, σωτηρία, σωτήριος" (Peabody, MA: Hendrickson Publishers, 1994), 344.

52. William Arndt et al., *A Greek-English Lexicon of the New Testament and Other Early Christian Literature*, s.v. "σῴζω" (Chicago: University of Chicago Press, 2000), 982.

53. Richard Delgado and Jean Stefancic, *Critical Race Theory: An Introduction*, 3rd ed. (New York: New York University Press, 2017).

54. James Cone, *A Black Theology of Liberation: Fortieth Anniversary Edition* (Maryknoll, NY: Orbis Books, 2020), 69.

55. Ibid, 114.

56. Ibid, 16.

57. Ibid, 16.

58. Ibid, 7.

59. James Cone, *The Cross and the Lynching Tree* (Maryknoll, NY: Orbis Books, 2011), 158.

60. Cone, 128.

61. Deotis Roberts, *A Black Political Theology* (Louisville, KY: Westminster Press, 1974), 139.

62. Fran Quigley, "Liberation Theology Calls Together the Religious and the Political," accessed August 8, 2020, https://sojo.net/articles/liberation-theology-calls-together-religious-and-political?fbclid=IwAR1xacA2zxn y4TUVBC3yc-ZCFWV-h2f41FbEHu-q_DN5Q1BX5UjmeZp29ZI.

63. Jonathan Wilson-Hartgrove, *Reconstructing the Gospel: Finding Freedom from Slaveholder Religion* (Downers Grove, IL: InterVarsity Press, 2018), 3.

64. Ibid, 132.

65. Ibid, 102.

66. "About," Black Lives Matter.com, accessed September 23, 2020, https://blacklivesmatter.com/about.

67. Wilson-Hartgrove, 40.

68. Daniel Hill, *White Awake: An Honest Look at What It Means to Be White* (Downers Grove, IL: InterVarsity Press, 2017), 143.

69. Jarvis Williams, "The Intersection of Race, Gospel, and Racial Reconciliation in Paul's Theology," (Lecture, Southern Baptist Theological Seminary, Louisville, KY) Scribd.com, accessed September 23, 2020, https://www.scribd.com/document/424625751/Williams-Class-Notes."

70. Anthony Carter, "The Black Church and Orthodoxy," in *Keep Your Head Up: America's New Black Christian Leaders, Social Consciousness, and the Cosby Conversation* (Wheaton, IL: Crossway, 2012), 160.

71. Samuel Sey, "What Is Black Liberation Theology?" Ezra Institute. ca accessed September 23, 2020, https://www.ezrainstitute.ca/resource-library/articles/what-is-black-liberation-theology.

72. Anyabwile, *Reviving the Black Church*, 79.

73. D. A. Carson, "Editorial" Themelios 34.1 (2009): 1-2. https://s3.amazonaws.com/tgc-documents/journal-issues/34.1/Themelios_34.1.pdf.

74. Mitch Randall, "Why Social Justice is a Vital Component of the Gospel," Good Faith Media.org,, accessed September 23, 2020, https://goodfaithmedia.org/why-social-justice-is-vital-component-of-the-gospel.

75. Piper, 84-85.

76. H.B. Charles, Jr., "Biblical Principles for Ethnic Harmony," H. B. Charles, Jr.com, accessed September 23, 2020, https://hbcharlesjr.com/resource-library/articles/biblical-principles-for-ethnic-harmony.

77. Hill, 22.

78. Robin Di'Angelo, *White Fragility: Why It's So Hard for White People to Talk About Racism* (Boston: Beacon Press, 2018), 129.

79. Be the Bridge, "Be the Bridge 101: Foundational Principles Every White Bridge-Builder Needs to Understand," (Atlanta, GA: Be the Bridge, 2019), 19, https://bethebridge.com/BTB101.

80. David Kinnaman, "Barna's Perspective on Race and the Church," Barna.com, June 17, 2020, https://www.barna.com/barnas-perspective-on-race-and-the-church.

81. Bob Ellis and Rodney Fopp, "The Origins of Standpoint Epistemologies: Feminism, Marx and Lukacs," (Lecture, TASA 2001 Conference, The University of Sydney, December 2001): 13-15.

82. Elizabeth Borland, *Britannica, s.v.* "standpoint theory," accessed August 15, 2020, https://www.britannica.com/topic/standpoint-theory.

83. Voddie Bacham, "Ethnic Gnosticism," Founders Ministries, March 28, 2019, YouTube video, 50:22, https://www.youtube.com/watch?v=Ip3nV6S_fYU&feature=emb_logo.

84. Barbara VanDenburgh, "Anti-racist book dethrones 'Hunger Games' prequel on best-seller list amid mass protests," *USA Today* online, June 10, 2020, https://www.usatoday.com/story/entertainment/books/2020/06/10/anti-racist-books-dominate-best-seller-list-white-fragility-how-to-be-an-antiracist-ta-nehisi-coates/5331188002.

85. Black Lives Matter Philly's Facebook page, "April Open Meeting," accessed August 15, 2020, https://www.facebook.com/events/248214382307156.

86. Mark Vreogop, *Weep With Me: How Lament Opens a Door for Racial Reconciliation* (Wheaton, IL: Crossway, 2020), 48.

87. George Orwell, *Animal Farm* (New York, Penguin Group, 1956), 39.

88. Richard Delgado and Jean Stefancic, *Critical Race Theory: An Introduction*, 3rd ed. (New York, New York University Press, 2017), 11.

89. Di'Angelo, 9.

90. William Arndt et al., *A Greek-English Lexicon of the New Testament and Other Early Christian Literature, s.v.* "δέχομαι," (Chicago: University of Chicago Press, 2000), 221.

91. "Critical Race Theory: Full Statement," Be the Bridge, accessed August 29, 2020, https://bethebridge.com/wp-content/uploads/2020/08/Full-Statement-Aug-7.pdf.

92. Allison N. Ash, "White Fragility: Why this Book is Important for Evangelicals," *Christianity Today* online, August 4, 2020, https://www.christianitytoday.com/edstetzer/2020/august/white-fragility-why-this-book-is-important-for-evangelicals.html.

93. Richard Caldwell, "The Sufficient Word on Racial Unity," in *A Biblical Answer for Racial Unity* (Woodlands, TX: Kress Biblical Resources, 2017), 11-12.

94. The Westminster Confession of Faith, 3rd ed. (Lawrenceville, GA: Committee for Christian Education and Publications, 1990), 1.6.

95. Arielle Gray, "A Reading List On Race For Allies Who Want To Do Better," *The ARTery* online, June 17, 2020, https://www.wbur.org/artery/2020/06/17/reading-list-on-race-for-allies.

96. "What people have said about Linnaeus," Uppsala Universitet, May 3, 2011, https://web.archive.org/web/20110513033923/http://www.linnaeus.uu.se/online/life/8_3.html.

97. Staffan Muller-Wille, *Brittanica, s.v.* ""Carolus Linnaeus," January 7, 2021, https://www.britannica.com/biography/Carolus-Linnaeus#ref273182.

98. David G. Notton and Christopher Brian Stringer, "Who is the type of Homo sapiens?," International Commission on

Zoological Nomenclature, accessed October 5, 2020, https://www.
researchgate.net/publication/260337719_Who_is_the_type_of_
Homo_sapiens#:~:text=follow%20this%20example.-,...,class%20
us%20primates%20%5B37%5D%20.

99. Kuljit Chuhan, "The development of racist theories and ideas,"
    Revealing Histories.org, accessed October 5, 2020, http://
    revealinghistories.org.uk/legacies-stereotypes-racism-and-the-
    civil-rights-movement/articles/the-development-of-racist-
    theories-and-ideas.html.

100. Dorothy Roberts, *Fatal Invention: How Science, Politics, and Big
     Business Re-Create Race in the Twenty-First Century* (New York: The
     New Press, 2011), 26-54.

101. Raj Bhopal, "The beautiful skull and Blumenbach's errors: the birth
     of the scientific concept of race," *The BMJ*, 335 (December 2007):
     1308-1309, https://www.bmj.com/content/335/7633/1308.

102. "A History of Craniology in Race Science and Physical Anthropology,"
     Penn Museum online, accessed October 5, 2020, https://www.penn.
     museum/sites/morton/craniology.php.

103. "Robert Chambers," Harvard University online, accessed October 5,
     2020, https://early-evolution.oeb.harvard.edu/robert-chambers.

104. Robert Chambers, *Vestiges of the Natural History of Creation* (London:
     John Churchill, 1844), 307.

105. Charles Darwin, *On the Origin of Species by Means of Natural Selection,
     or The Preservation of Favoured Races in the Struggle for Life* (London:
     John Murray, 1859), 1-234.

106. Darwin, 451.

107. Enid Schildkrout, *Britannica, s.v.* "Anthropology: History of Anthropology," accessed October 6, 2020, https://www.britannica.com/science/anthropology/History-of-anthropology#ref839878.

108. Charles Darwin, *The Descent of Man* (Chicago, IL: William Benton in Great Books of the Western World, 1952), 336.

109. Ibid, 404-405.

110. Ta-Nehisi Coates, *Between the World and Me* (New York: One World, 2015), 7.

111. Stephen Jay Gould, *Ontogeny and Phylogeny* (Cambridge, MA: The Belknap Press, 1977), 127.

112. Steve Jones, *The Language of Genes: Solving the Mysteries of Our Genetic Past, Present and Future* (New York: Anchor Books, 1993), 13-16.

113. Jones, 19.

114. Ernst Haeckel, *The History of Creation: Vol II,* translated by E. Ray Lancaster (London: Henry S. King & Co., 1876), 365-366.

115. Adolf Hitler, *Mein Kampf,* trans. by James Murphy (Camarillo, CA: Elite Minds Inc., 2010), 333.

116. Jones, 20.

117. Ken Ham and Charles Ware, *One Race, One Blood: The Biblical Answer to Racism,* 7th ed. (Green Forest, AR: Master Books, 2019), 14-17.

118. George William Hunter, *A Civic Biology Presented in Problems* (New York: American Book Company, 1914), 196.

119. John R. Rice, *Dr. Rice, Here is My Question* (Murfreesboro, TN: Sword of the Lord Publishers, 1962), 240.

120. "Bob Jones University Apologizes for Its Racist Past," *The Journal of Blacks in Higher Education* online, accessed October 20, 2020, https://www.jbhe.com/news_views/62_bobjones.html#:~:text=In%20 2000%20the%20university%20ended,the%20nation's%20other%20 Bible%20colleges.

121. Tisby, 163-164.

122. Ibid, 83.

123. Jean Hiernaux and Michael Banton, *Four Statements on the Race Question* (Paris: UNESCO, 1969), https://unesdoc.unesco.org/ ark:/48223/pf0000122962.

124. Natalie Angier, "Do Races Differ? Not Really, Genes Show," *The New York Times* online, August 22, 2000, https://www.nytimes. com/2000/08/22/science/do-races-differ-not-really-genes-show. html.

125. AFP, "Tiny gene differences make us who we are," ABC Local online, February 4, 2008, https://www.abc.net.au/science/ articles/2008/02/04/2153889.htm?site=tv&topic=latest.

126. William Leonard, "Check Your Race in the Box Below," in *The American Biology Teacher*, 73, no. 7 (2011): 379.

127. Ibid.

128. Angela Saini, *Superior: The Return of Race Science* (Boston: Beacon Press, 2019), 117-119.

129. "About Race," United States Census Bureau, accessed October 20, 2020, https://www.census.gov/topics/population/race/about.html.

130. Saini, ibid.

131. Robert Lee Holtz, "Scientists Say Race Has No Biological Basis," *Los Angeles Times* online, February 20, 1995, https://www.latimes.com/archives/la-xpm-1995-02-20-mn-34098-story.html.

132. Jones, 206.

133. Ibid, 199.

134. *Lexico, s.v.* "Ethnicity," accessed October 20, 2020, https://www.lexico.com/en/definition/ethnicity.

135. *Ibid.*

136. R. Laird Harris, Gleason L. Archer Jr., and Bruce K. Waltke, eds., *Theological Wordbook of the Old Testament*, s.v. "מֶלֶךְ" (Chicago: Moody Press, 1999), 767.

137. Walter A. Elwell and Barry J. Beitzel, *Baker Encyclopedia of the Bible,* s.v. "Pentecost" (Grand Rapids, MI: Baker Book House, 1988), 1639.

138. "Babel Reversed," Ligonier Ministries online, accessed October 24, 2020, https://www.ligonier.org/learn/devotionals/babel-reversed.

139. H. B. Charles, Jr., "Biblical Principles for Ethnic Harmony," H. B. Charles Jr.com, March 11, 2019, https://hbcharlesjr.com/resource-library/articles/biblical-principles-for-ethnic-harmony.

140. Isaac Adams, "Don't Be Color-Blind at Church," 9Marks.org, September 25, 2015, https://www.9marks.org/article/dont-be-color-blind-at-church.

141. H. B. Charles Jr., "The Peaceful Solution to Racial Unity," *A Biblical Answer for Racial Unity* (The Woodlands, TX: Kress Biblical Resources, 2017), 39.

142. J. Philippe Rushton and Elizabeth W. Rushton, "Brain Size, IQ, and racial-group differences: Evidence from musculoskeletal traits," *Science Direct*, 31, no. 2 (March-April 2003): 139-155.

143. J. Philippe Rushton and Arthur R. Jensen, "Thirty Years of Research on Race Differences in Cognitive Ability," *Psychology, Public Policy, and Law*, 11, no. 2 (2005): 235-294.

144. Christof Koch, "Does Brain Size Matter?," Scientific American.com, January 1, 2016, https://www.scientificamerican.com/article/does-brain-size-matter1/#:~:text=In%20healthy%20volunteers%2C%20total%20brain,overall%20variability%20in%20general%20intelligence.

145. R. Lynn and G. Meisenberg, "Race Differences in Deaths from Coronavirus in England and Wales: Demographics, Poverty, Pre-existing Conditions, or Intelligence?," *Mankind Quarterly*, 60, no. 4 (2020): 511–524.

146. Cahal Milmo, "Fury at DNA Pioneer's theory: Africans are less intelligent than Westerners," Independent.co, September 18, 2011, https://www.independent.co.uk/news/science/fury-at-dna-pioneers-theory-africans-are-less-intelligent-than-westerners-394898.html.

147. Trillia Newbell, *United: Captured by God's Vision for Diversity* (Chicago: Moody Publishers, 2014), 97.

148. Carter, 85.

149. Elliot C. Williams, "How The Lincoln Statue In Capitol Hill Became A Monument To Public Debate," NPR.org, July 3, 2020, https://www.npr.org/local/305/2020/07/03/887073442/how-the-lincoln-statue-in-capitol-hill-became-a-monument-to-public-debate.

150. Margaret Barthel and Christian Zapata, "At Lincoln Park, Generations Disagree Over Statue Removal As Protests Enter Fifth Week," DCist.com, June 27, 2020, https://dcist.com/story/20/06/27/at-lincoln-park-generations-disagree-over-statue-removal-as-protests-enter-fifth-week.

151. Alan Taylor, "The Statues Brought Down Since the George Floyd Protests Began," The Atlantic.com, July 2, 2020, https://www.theatlantic.com/photo/2020/07/photos-statues-removed-george-floyd-protests-began/613774.

152. Jacey Fortin, "Toppling Monuments, a Visual History," *The New York Times* online, August 17, 2017, https://www.nytimes.com/2017/08/17/world/controversial-statues-monuments-destroyed.html..

153. Mark Abadi, Kevin Reilly, and Katie Nixdorf, "'Our society is evolving': What historians and activists are saying about the movement to remove statues," *Business Insider* online, July 1, 2020, https://www.businessinsider.com/confederate-statues-removal-slavery-protests-2020-6.

154. Alan Greenblatt, "This City Removed 2 Confederate Statues. Then the State Retaliated," Governing.com, July 25, 2018, https://www.governing.com/topics/politics/gov-shelby-tennessee-confederate-statue.html.

155. Kyley Schultz, "DC Mayor on statues: 'We need to have a reasonable conversation... not have a mob decide that they want to pull it down,'" WUSA9 online, June 26, 2020, https://www.wusa9.com/article/news/local/dc/dc-mayor-bowser-statue-removals-dc/65-d241412b-08c9-40e8-a3dc-1c9b2517177c.

156. Christine Vestal, "Racism Is a Public Health Crisis, Say Cities and Counties," *PEW* online, June 15, 2020, https://www.pewtrusts.org/en/research-and-analysis/blogs/stateline/2020/06/15/racism-is-a-public-health-crisis-say-cities-and-counties.

157. Jill Anderson, "Confronting Racism at an Early Age," Harvard Graduate School of Education online, August 28, 2017, https://www.gse.harvard.edu/news/uk/17/08/confronting-racism-early-age.

158. "We won't stop until we dismantle the whole racist system," American Friends Service Committee, June 4, 2020, https://www.afsc.org/newsroom/we-wont-stop-until-we-dismantle-whole-racist-system.

159. Eric Deggans, "'Me And White Supremacy' Helps You Do The Work Of Dismantling Racism," NPR.org, July 9, 2020, https://www.npr.org/2020/07/06/887646740/me-and-white-supremacy-helps-you-do-the-work-of-dismantling-racism.

160. Katrina vanden Huevel, "Opinion: How Can We Start Dismantling Systemic Racism," *The Washington Post* online, June 9, 2020, https://www.washingtonpost.com/opinions/2020/06/09/how-we-can-start-dismantling-systemic-racism.

161. John McWhorter, "Racist Is a Tough Little Word," *The Atlantic* online, July 24, 2019, https://www.theatlantic.com/ideas/archive/2019/07/racism-concept-change/594526.

162. Tisby, 16.

163. Beverly Daniel Tatum, *Why Are All the Black Kids Sitting Together in the Cafeteria?*, (New York: Basic Books, 1997), 45.

164. Di'Angelo, 21.

165. Be the Bridge, 5.

166. "Racism definition: Merriam-Webster to make update after request," *BBC News* online, June 10, 2020, https://www.bbc.com/news/world-us-canada-52993306.

167. *Merriam Webster, s.v.* "racism," accessed November 4, 2020, https:// www.merriam-webster.com/dictionary/racism.

168. Ibram Kendi, *How to Be an Antiracist* (New York: One World, 2019), 8.

169. Ibid, 13.

170. Ibid, 18.

171. Ibid, 19.

172. Ibid.

173. Ibid, 17.

174. Ibid.

175. Evan Andrews, "Was Jim Crow a real person?," History.com, August 31, 2018, https://www.history.com/news/was-jim-crow-a-real-person.

176. Albert Mohler, *The Briefing*, Podcast audio, Wednesday, June 24, 2020, https://albertmohler.com/2020/06/24/briefing-6-24-20.

177. Piper, 85.

178. Barrett Holmes Pitner, "Viewpoint: US must confront its Original Sin to move forward," *BBC News* online, June 3, 2020, https://www. bbc.com/news/world-us-canada-52912238.

179. Yohuru Williams, "Why Thomas Jefferson's Anti-Slavery Passage Was Removed from the Declaration of Independence," History. com, June 29, 2020, https://www.history.com/news/declaration-of-independence-deleted-anti-slavery-clause-jefferson.

180. John Calvin, *Institutes of the Christian Religion*, Library of Christian Classics, ed. John T. McNeill, trans. Ford Lewis Battles, 2 vols. (Louisville, KY: Westminster/John Knox, 1960), 2:23:8.

181. Augustine, *On the Free Choice of the Will, On Grace and Free Choice, and Other Writings*, ed. Peter King (New York: Cambridge University Press, 2010), 3.

182. Marley K., "Yes My Dear, All White People Are Racists," Medium. com, June 6, 2020, https://medium.com/age-of-awareness/yes-all-white-people-are-racist-eefa97cc5605.

183. Delgado and Stefancic, 91.

184. Byron York, "The National Museum of..." Twitter, July 15, 2020, https://twitter.com/ByronYork/status/1283372233730203651/photo/1.

185. Francis Brown, Samuel Rolles Driver, and Charles Augustus Briggs, *Enhanced Brown-Driver-Briggs Hebrew and English Lexicon, s.v. "אָטָה"* (Oxford: Clarendon Press, 1977), 306.

186. Westminster Assembly, Douglas F. Kelly, Philip B. Rollinson, and Frederick T. Marsh, *The Westminster Shorter Catechism in Modern English* (Phillipsburg, N.J.: Presbyterian and Reformed Pub. Co, 1986), Q14.

187. G. Herbert Livingston, and Bruce K. Waltke, *Theological Wordbook of the Old Testament, s.v. "638 אָטָה,"* ed. R. Laird Harris, Gleason L. Archer Jr. (Chicago: Moody Press, 1999), 277.

188. Martin Luther King, Jr., "MLK at Western," Speech, Western Michigan University, December 18, 1963, https://wmich.edu/sites/default/files/attachments/MLK.pdf.

189. Virgil Walker in discussion with the author, October 29, 2020.

190. Vroegop, 158.

191. Jennifer L. Eberhardt, *Biased: Uncovering the Hidden Prejudice That Shapes What We See, Think, and Do* (New York: Penguin Books, 2019), 48.

192. Delgado and Stefancic, 143.

193. Di'Angelo, 69.

194. Eberhardt, 6.

195. "Implicit Association Test," Project Implicit, accessed November 7, 2020, https://implicit.harvard.edu/implicit/takeatest.html.

196. Olivia Goldhill, "The world is relying on a flawed psychological test to fight racism," *Quartz* online, December 3, 2017, https://qz.com/1144504/the-world-is-relying-on-a-flawed-psychological-test-to-fight-racism.

197. Betsy Mason, "Making people aware of their implicit biases doesn't usually change minds. But here's what does work," *Knowable Magazine* online, June 10, 2020, https://www.pbs.org/newshour/nation/making-people-aware-of-their-implicit-biases-doesnt-usually-change-minds-but-heres-what-does-work.

198. Elizabeth Sweeny Block, "White Privilege and the Erroneous Conscience: Rethinking Moral Culpability and Ignorance," *Journal of the Society of Christian Ethics*, 39, no. 2 (2019): 370.

199. Beth Azar, "IAT: Fad or Fabulous?," American Psychological Association online, August 2008, https://www.apa.org/monitor/2008/07-08/psychometric.

200. Mason, ibid.

201. John Owen, *The Mortification of Sin* (Carlisle, PA: Banner of Truth Trust, 2004), 46.

202. Piper, 223.

203. Kendi, 46.

204. Derald Wing Sue, "Racial Microaggressions in Everyday Life," *Psychology Today* online, October 5, 2010, https://www. psychologytoday.com/us/blog/microaggressions-in-everyday-life/201010/*racial-microaggressions*-in-everyday-life.

205. Christy Wong, "Exploring Race: Being Chinese-American," *Chicago Tribune* Newsblogs, June 25, 2008, https://newsblogs.chicagotribune. com/race/2008/06/being-chinese-a.html.

206. Greg Morse, "Seeing the World in Black and White: How Much Do Assumptions Divide Us?," DesiringGod.org, July 8, 2020, https:// www.desiringgod.org/articles/seeing-the-world-in-black-and-white.

207. Newbell, 63.

208. E.J. Dionne, Jr., "Pope Apologizes to Africans for Slavery," *The New York Times* online, August 14, 1985, https://www.nytimes.com/1985/08/14/ world/pope-apologizes-to-africans-for-slavery.html.

209. Pope John Paul II, "Allocution", in Bernard Pullman (ed. 1992), *The Emergence of Complexity in Mathematics, Physics, Chemistry and Biology: Proceedings of the Plenary Session of the Pontifical Academy of Sciences*, (Vatican City: Pontificia Academia Scientarum, October 1992), 27-31, https://bertie.ccsu.edu/naturesci/cosmology/galileopope.html.

210. John Paul II, "Address of the Holy Father to an International Symposium on John Hus," (lecture, The Vatican, December 17, 1999),

http://www.vatican.va/content/john-paul-ii/en/speeches/1999/
december/documents/hf_jp-ii_spe_17121999_jan-hus.html.

211. Jones, 232.

212. Vroegop, *Weep With Me*, 120-121.

213. Michael O. Emerson and Christian Smith, *Divided by Faith: Evangelical Religion and the Problem of Race in America* (Oxford: Oxford University Press, 2000), 171-175.

214. KPRC 2 Click2Houston, "White people kneel, ask forgiveness from the black community in Third Ward," June 1, 2020, YouTube video, June 1, 2020, 0:30, https://www.youtube.com/watch?v=fdX6aVzPgHs&ab_channel=KPRC2Click2Houston.

215. Mone Dixon, "The Influence of Slavery on the Black Body: Black Lives Matter's Intersectional Methodology and New Advancements," *CUNY Academic Works*, 2018, https://academicworks.cuny.edu/gc_etds/2658.

216. Jim Wallis, *America's Original Sin: Racism, White Privilege, and the Bridge to a New America* (Grand Rapids: Brazos Press, 2016), xvii.

217. "United Methodists Stand Against Racism," The United Methodist Church, accessed November 8, 2020, https://www.umc.org/en/how-we-serve/advocating-for-justice/racial-justice/united-against-racism.

218. Morrison, 150-166.

219. Iris Dimmick, "Pastor Max Lucado asks forgiveness for Christian white supremacy," *San Antonio Report* online, August 9, 2020, https://sanantonioreport.org/pastor-max-lucado-asks-forgiveness-for-christian-white-supremacy.

220. "'Powerful moment': White parishioners kneel, ask for black community's forgiveness in George Floyd's hometown," *The Indian Express* online, June 2, 2020, https://indianexpress.com/article/trending/trending-globally/george-floyd-kneel-viral-video-6438938.

221. Marianne Williamson, "Prayer of Apology to African Americans," Marianne.com, accessed on November 12, 2020, http://marianne.com/atonement.

222. Ernst Jenni and Claus Westermann, *Theological Lexicon of the Old Testament, s.v.* "מָשָׁא" (Peabody, MA: Hendrickson Publishers, 1997), 194.

223. G. Herbert Livingston, *Theological Wordbook of the Old Testament, s.v.* "180 מָשָׁא," ed. R. Laird Harris, Gleason L. Archer Jr., and Bruce K. Waltke (Chicago: Moody Press, 1999), 79.

224. *Britannica, s.v.,* "Talion," accessed November 12, 2020, https://www.britannica.com/topic/talion.

225. Ludwig Koehler, Walter Baumgartner, et al., *The Hebrew and Aramaic Lexicon of the Old Testament, s.v.* "שְׁאָר" (Leiden: E.J. Brill, 1994–2000), 1167.

226. William Arndt, Frederick W. Danker, et al., A Greek-English Lexicon of the New Testament and Other Early Christian Literature, s.v. "αἴτιος" (Chicago: University of Chicago Press, 2000), 31.

227. Abraham Lincoln, "Transcript of President Abraham Lincoln's Second Inaugural Address (1865)," OurDocuments.gov, accessed November 12, 2020, https://www.ourdocuments.gov/doc.php?flash=false&doc=38&page=transcript.

228. Gerald Flurry, "Angela Merkel's Historic Holocaust Speech (But Does the Pope Agree?)," *The Trumpet* online, May 2008, https://www.thetrumpet.com/5027-angela-merkels-historic-holocaust-speech-but-does-the-pope-agree.

229. Erin Rubin, "Answering the Reparations Question," Erin Rubin, *NonProfit Quarterly* online, March 19, 2019, https://nonprofitquarterly.org/answering-the-reparations-question.

230. Tim Keller, "Racism and Corporate Evil: A White Guy's Perspective," DesiringGod.org, accessed November 16, 2020, https://www.desiringgod.org/messages/racism-and-corporate-evil.

231. Tisby, 199.

232. Vroegop, 113.

233. Morrison, 68-69.

234. Kevin DeYoung, "Thinking Biblically About Racial Tensions: Sin and Guilt," The Gospel Coalition.org, accessed November 16, 2020, https://www.thegospelcoalition.org/blogs/kevin-deyoung/thinking-theologically-about-racial-tensions-sin-and-guilt.

235. Ibid.

236. Oscar Hammerstein II, "You've Got to Be Carefully Taught," *South Pacific*, Goodard Liebersen, 1958, https://rodgersandhammerstein.com/song/south-pacific/youve-got-to-be-carefully-taught.

237. W.E.B. Du Bois, *The Souls of Black Folk with "The Talented Tenth" and "The Souls of White Folk"* (New York: Penguin Books, 2018), 229.

238. Noel Ignatin and Ted Allen, "White Blindspot," Marxists.org, 1976, https://www.marxists.org/history/erol/ncm-1/whiteblindspot.pdf

239. Jeffrey B. Perry, "The Growing Importance of Theodore W. Allen's Work On the Centrality of the Struggle Against White Supremacy," Democratic Left online, September 20, 2017, https://www.dsausa.

org/democratic-left/the_growing_importance_of_theodore_w_allen_s_work-2.

240. Peggy McIntosh, "White Privilege: Unpacking the Invisible Knapsack," Wellesly Centers for Women, accessed November 16, 2020, https://nationalseedproject.org/images/documents/Knapsack_plus_Notes-Peggy_McIntosh.pdf.

241. Derek Williams, "The Weakness of Evangelical Ethics," *Third Way*, 1, no. 1 (January 13, 1977): 4-5.

242. George Yancey, *Beyond Racial Gridlock: Embracing Mutual Responsibility* (Downers Grove, IL: InterVarsity Press, 2006), 89.

243. Rav Arora, "The fallacy of white privilege—and how it's corroding society," *New York Post* online, July 11, 2020, https://nypost.com/2020/07/11/the-fallacy-of-white-privilege-and-how-its-corroding-society.

244. Christopher Brooks, "Historically speaking: Why we should discuss 'Black hurdle' instead of white privilege," *The Morning Call* online, August 22, 2020, https://www.mcall.com/opinion/mc-opi-historically-speaking-twelve-brooks-20200822-b5nwmo-qj7fhmjpv3zngtrchgwe-story.html.

245. McIntosh, ibid.

246. Yancey, 95.

247. Chris Anderson and Greg Habegger, "His Robes for Mine," Church Works Media, 2008, https://www.churchworksmedia.com/product/his-robes-for-mine-free.

248. Khalida Volou, "21 protesters arrested near U.S. Supreme Court Building ahead of Judge Amy Barrett confirmation hearings,"

WUSA9 online, October 12, 2020, https://www.wusa9.com/article/ news/local/protests/protesters-demonstrators-us-supreme-court- amy-coney-barrett/65-4a218782-9e82-4316-9132-ca27bedd1a49.

249. "Mourners Pay Respect for Supreme Court Justice Ruth Bader Gins- burg," *UPI* online, September 21, 2020, https://www.upi.com/News_ Photos/view/upi/65c1b31bcdb36663dc1cea15a0615fd6/Mourners-Pay- Respect-for-Supreme-Court-Justice-Ruth-Bader-Ginsburg.

250. Anthony Kustura, "Man known for booming 'Jesus saves' message doused with flour, glitter by protesters," WSOCTV9 online, August 28, 2020, https://www.wsoctv.com/news/local/protesters- throw-flour-glitter-man-sharing-his-own-message-during- demonstrations-uptown/7IZLKQUHYBDWDFPAS6I64NERF4.

251. Sarah Blake Morgan's Facebook page, accessed June 29, 2021, https:// www.facebook.com/SarahBlakeMorgan/videos/1927834923928209.

252. Kevin DeYoung and Greg Gilbert, *What Is the Mission of the Church?: Making Sense of Social Justice, Shalom, and the Great Commission* (Wheaton, IL: Crossway, 2011), 26.

253. "Racial Justice: Introduction Letter: Minister for Racial Justice," The United Church of Christ, accessed December 4, 2020, https://www. ucc.org/justice_racism.

254. "Racial Justice Response & Resources," National Association of Evangelicals, accessed December 4, 2020, https://www.nae.net/racialjustice.

255. Josh Wester, "3 ways Christians should think about racial justice in America," Ethics and Religious Liberties Commission online, June 10, 2020, https://erlc.com/resource-library/articles/3-ways- christians-should-think-about-racial-justice-in-america.

256. Tisby, 194.

257. Ibid, 195-97.

258. Ibid, 200-12.

259. Ibid, 193.

260. Robert D. Culver, *Theological Wordbook of the Old Testament, s.v.* "2443 שָׁפַט," ed. R. Laird Harris, Gleason L. Archer Jr., and Bruce K. Waltke (Chicago: Moody Press, 1999), 947-49.

261. Thomas Watson, *A Body of Divinity*, (Carlisle, PA: The Banner of Truth Trust, 2019), 87.

262. Tim Keller, *Generous Justice: How God's Grace Make's Us Just*, (New York: Penguin Books, 2010), 4.

263. "Justice," Stanford Encyclopedia of Philosophy, June 26, 2017, https://plato.stanford.edu/entries/justice.

264. "Summa Theologiae: Question 58. Justice," New Advent, accessed December 4, 2020, https://www.newadvent.org/summa/3058.htm#article1.

265. Keller, 10.

266. Scott David Allen, *Why Social Justice Is Not Biblical Justice: An Urgent Appeal to Fellow Christians in a Time of Social Crisis* (Grand Rapids: Credo House Publishers, 2020), 22-23.

267. Watson, 88.

268. Robert D. Culver, *Theological Wordbook of the Old Testament, s.v.* "2443 שָׁפַט," ed. R. Laird Harris, Gleason L. Archer Jr., and Bruce K. Waltke, (Chicago: Moody Press, 1999), 947.

269. Caldwell v. Texas, 137 U.S. 692 (1891), Justia US Supreme Court.

270. DeYoung and Gilbert, 161.

271. Jesse Johnson, "God's Compassion as a Mandate for Mercy: A Dispensationalist Perspective on Mercy Ministry," ThM thesis, The Master's Seminary, Los Angeles, 2010, 90.

272. Ronald J. Sider, ed., *The Chicago Declaration* (Eugene, OR: Wipf &Stock Publishers, 1974), 30.

273. Ronald Sider, "History Shows Us Why Being Evangelical Matters," *Christianity Today* online, November 26, 2016, https://www.christianitytoday.com/ct/2016/november-web-only/history-shows-us-why-being-evangelical-matters.html.

274. John R. W. Stott, *Christian Mission in the Modern World: What the Church Should Be Doing Now!* (Downers Grove: IVP, 1975), 27.

275. Ralph Beebe, "Voice of Calvary Has the Sound of a Friend," Ralph Beebe, *Evangelical Friend*, 13, No. 3, November 1979, https://digitalcommons.georgefox.edu/cgi/viewcontent.cgi?referer=https://www.bing.com/&httpsredir=1&article=1131&context=nwym_evangelical_friend.

276. Richard Stearns, *The Hole in Our Gospel* (Nashville: Nelson, 2009), 123.

277. Keller, 127.

278. Ibid, 140.

279. Ibid, 142.

280. DeYoung and Gilbert, 162-65.

281. The Westminster Confession of Faith, 3rd ed. (Lawrenceville, GA: Committee for Christian Education and Publications, 1990), 26.2.

282. "Critical Race Theory: Full Statement," Be the Bridge, accessed August 29, 2020, https://bethebridge.com/wp-content/uploads/2020/08/Full-Statement-Aug-7.pdf.

283. Jon Harris, *Social Justice Goes To Church: The New Left in Modern American Evangelicalism* (Greenville, SC: Ambassador International, 2020), 21.

284. DeYoung and Gilbert, 194.

285. Edmund P. Clowney, "Kingdom Evangelism," in *The Pastor-Evangelist: Preacher, Model, and Mobilizer for Church Growth*, Roger S. Greenway, ed. (Phillipsburg, NJ: Presbyterian & Reformed, 1987), 22.

286. Richard Mouw, "Political Evangelism," *Sojourners* online, May 1, 1973, https://sojo.net/magazine/may-june-1973/political-evangelism.

287. Tim Keller, "Cultural Renewal: The Role of the Intrapreneur and the Entrepreneur," Entrepreneurship Forum, March 25, 2006, MP3, https://web.archive.org/web/20060622051746/http://www.faithandwork.org/uploads/photos/461-1%20Cultural%20Renewal_%20The%20Role%20of%20th.mp3.

288. Johnson, 8.

289. Charles, ibid.

For more information about

# Dan Crabtree
and
## *A House Without Walls*
please visit:

www.dancrabtree.com

Ambassador International's mission is to magnify the Lord Jesus Christ and promote His gospel through the written word.

We believe through the publication of Christian literature, Jesus Christ and His Word will be exalted, believers will be strengthened in their walk with Him, and the lost will be directed to Jesus Christ as the only way of salvation.

For more information about
AMBASSADOR INTERNATIONAL
please visit:

www.ambassador-international.com

*Thank you for reading this book. Please consider leaving us a review on your social media, favorite retailer's website, Goodreads or Bookbub, or our website.*

# More from Ambassador International

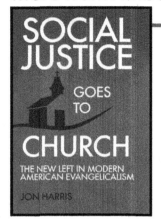

*Social Justice Goes to Church: The New Left in Modern American Evangelicalism* answers, from a historical perspective, the vital question, "Why are American evangelicals moving Left?"

Author Douglas Kruger traces the unfolding ideology from its dark genesis (the French Revolution and subsequent terror) through its various incarnations— Marxism, relativism, post-modernism, and all the way to today's identity-politics. He points out the flaws, fallacies, and in many cases, the body-counts these ideologies have wracked up. Become a master at identifying, debunking, and dismantling dangerous ideas.

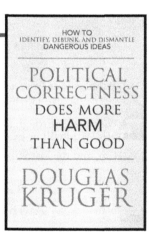

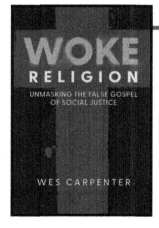

Has "woke" become simply another religion, another ploy of Satan's to shred the fabric of Christianity? As woke critical theory seeps through the teachings of the Church, many Christians are being misled by their own spiritual leaders to take part in the newest attempt for their souls.

In *Woke Religion: Unmasking the False Gospel of Social Justice*, Wes Carpenter unashamedly addresses these heretical teachings, calling on those in spiritual authority to deny woke philosophies and cling to the teachings of Scripture.